Reinhold Wandel · Laraine MacDevitt ·
Helene Decke-Cornill · Viola Beyer-Kessling

Fundgrube Englisch
handlungsorientiert

 **Kostenloses Zusatzangebot
für die Käufer der Fundgrube:
Kopiervorlagen und Materialien im Internet**

Kopiervorlagen und Materialien dieser Fundgrube bieten wir Ihnen als kostenloses Zusatzangebot auch online an.

Sie können diese Materialien und Kopiervorlagen verändern und Ihren Bedürfnissen anpassen, da diese im Word-Format angelegt sind.

Als Bonus stehen Ihnen online weitere ausgewählte Cornelsen-Materialien für Ihre Unterrichtsvorbereitung kostenfrei zur Verfügung.

Wie finden Sie diese editierbaren Versionen der Kopiervorlagen? Rufen Sie einfach die Internetseite www.cornelsen.de/fundgruben auf und geben Sie dort Ihren unten genannten Webcode ein. Sie werden dann unmittelbar zu den Materialien weitergeleitet.

   http://www.cornelsen.de/fundgruben

Ihr Webcode für den Zugriff auf das Material: FGHE221844

Reinhold Wandel ist Hochschuldozent für englische Fachdidaktik an der Otto-von-Guericke-Universität in Magdeburg.

Laraine MacDevitt hat lange Jahre Berufserfahrung als Lehrerin für Englisch und Französisch an einem Gymnasium.

Helene Decke-Cornill ist Professorin der Erziehungswissenschaft/Didaktik der englischen Sprache und Literatur an der Universität Hamburg.

Viola Beyer-Kessling ist in der Lehrerfortbildung und Lehrerausbildung tätig. Sie ist Autorin zahlreicher Fachartikel und Unterrichtsmaterialien.

Reinhold Wandel · Laraine MacDevitt ·
Helene Decke-Cornill · Viola Beyer-Kessling

Fundgrube
Englisch
handlungsorientiert

Nicht in allen Fällen war es uns möglich, den Rechteinhaber ausfindig zu machen. Berechtigte Ansprüche werden selbstverständlich im Rahmen der üblichen Vereinbarungen abgegolten. Wir bitten um Verständnis.

Die in diesem Werk angegebenen Internetadressen haben wir überprüft (Redaktionsschluss Dezember 2006). Dennoch können wir nicht ausschließen, dass unter einer solchen Adresse inzwischen ein ganz anderer Inhalt angeboten wird. Deshalb empfehlen wir Ihnen dringend, die Adressen vor der Nutzung im Unterricht selbst noch einmal zu überprüfen.

 http://www.cornelsen.de

Bibliografische Information: Die Deutsche Bibliothek verzeichnet diese Publikation in der Deutschen Nationalbibliografie; detaillierte bibliografische Daten sind im Internet über http://dnb.ddb.de abrufbar.

Dieser Band folgt den Regeln der deutschen Rechtschreibung, die seit August 2006 gelten.

5.	4.	3.	2.	1.	Die letzten Ziffern bezeichnen
11	10	09	08	07	Zahl und Jahr der Auflage.

© 2007 Cornelsen Verlag Scriptor GmbH & Co. KG, Berlin
Das Werk und seine Teile sind urheberrechtlich geschützt. Jede Nutzung in anderen als den gesetzlich zugelassenen Fällen bedarf deshalb der vorherigen schriftlichen Einwilligung des Verlags.
Hinweis zu § 52a UrhG: Weder das Werk noch seine Teile dürfen ohne eine solche Einwilligung eingescannt und in ein Netzwerk eingestellt werden. Dies gilt auch für Intranets von Schulen und sonstigen Bildungseinrichtungen.

Redaktion: Daniela Brunner
Herstellung: Brigitte Bredow, Berlin
Umschlagentwurf: Simone Büchner, Berlin,
unter Verwendung einer Zeichnung von Klaus Puth, Mühlheim
Layout und Satz: FROMM MediaDesign, Selters/Ts.
Druck und Bindearbeiten: Clausen & Bosse, Leck
Printed in Germany
ISBN 978-3-589-22184-4

 Gedruckt auf säurefreiem Papier, umweltschonend hergestellt aus chlorfrei gebleichten Faserstoffen.

Inhalt

Vorwort		9
1	**Who's that, then?**	11
	Finding Partners	11
	Cuddly Toys	13
	Identity Parade	15
	Eavesdropping	16
	Matchmaking	16
	Family Life	17
	How Well Do You Know Your Classmates?	20
2	**Words, Words, Words**	22
	Vocabulary Game	22
	All About Travelling	23
	Words Beginning With "P"	25
	Dead Metaphors – Reanimated	26
	Ideogrammes	29
3	**Games**	30
	Making a Memory Game	30
	Playing Taboo	31
	Making Taboo Cards	35
	Making Board Games	36
	Finding Families	38
4	**Sketches, Role-Plays, Simulations**	40
	Right and Wrong: Contradicting Each Other	40
	Market-Place	42
	"The Cold" – A Sketch	44
	Making up Dialogues	49
	"An Accident" – An Improvised Radio Play	50
	"Welsh Werewolf" – A Panel of Experts	53
	This Is Your Life	57

	The Case of Little Red Ridinghood	59
	Schooltown	64
5	**Dabbling in Poetry**	**70**
	Put It in a Picture	70
	Edward Lear "The Owl and the Pussy-Cat"	71
	"The Rainbow Fairies"	75
	Relativity	76
	Imitating Jabberwocky	78
	Christopher Marlowe "The Passionate Shepherd to His Love"	83
	Robert Browning "Home Thoughts, from Abroad"	86
	Percy Bysshe Shelley "Ozymandias"	89
	Poemtelling	93
	William Carlos Williams "The Artist"	95
	Zig-Zag-Translations	98
6	**Once there was ...**	**100**
	The Gunpowder Plot	100
	A Modern Myth in Halves	103
	From Word to Story	105
	Suniti Namjoshi "Bird Woman"	107
7	**Getting into Fiction and Getting on with It**	**112**
	O. Henry "By Courier"	112
	Puzzling W. Somerset Maugham's "The Outstation"	117
	Ray Bradbury "The Veldt"	127
	Oscar Wilde "The Nightingale and the Rose"	141
	Carson McCullers "The Member of the Wedding"	150
8	**Use your Eyes!**	**154**
	Discovery Trip	154
	Up My Street	156
	Biography	156
	Picture Gallery	157
	What's My Line?	158
	Fantasy Flight	159
	Still Life	160
	Sticky Situations	161
	Inside a Picture	165
	From Picture to Text	166

9 The Sound of Music — 168
Making up a Song — 168
There Was a Man and His Dog — 169
Play Me a Picture — 172
Penny Lane, a Liverpool Street — 173
There Is Music in the Air — 175
You're so vain — 176
Dance me to the End of Love — 178

10 Write it down — 180
The Starters — 180
Poetry Corner — 182
I Am a J — 185
Full Stop and Comma — 187
Collage — 188
A Mere Scrap of Poetry — 189
One, Two, Buckle My Shoe — 191
Living on an Island — 194
Hilaire Belloc "A Conversation with a Cat" — 196
Rewriting Schoolbook Texts — 202

11 The Joy of Grammar — 204
Pep it up a bit! — 204
What will be, will be! — 205
The Girl Was Waiting — 209
What Have You Been Doing? — 210
Questions and Answers — 212

12 Intercultural Learning — 214
Normality — 214
Birthday — 216
Visitors from Funnia — 219
Balan and Bungan: A Borneo Tale — 221
The Simpsons discover Tokyo (von Annett Prietzsch) — 228
Barnga – A Simulation on Cultural Communication (von Anne Wiegand) — 235
Means of Communication among the Naeporue (von Gordon Motschenbach) — 245

13 Working with Film — 251
Cinema Experiences — 251

Thinking about film 252
Storyboarding 254
Film Beginnings 256
A Scene of their Choice 260
A Film of their Choice 261
A Taste of Terminology 262
A Film in 45 Minutes 266
Tackling a full-length film 268

14 Projects 271
Class Library 271
Extra-terrestrials 274
AUSTRALIA 278
Students as Storytellers 283

Register 286

Vorwort

Vor Ihnen liegt die zweite, neu bearbeitete „Fundgrube Englisch handlungsorientiert". Die Reihe der Fundgruben ist längst ein Begriff geworden, der für praktische und gut umsetzbare Vorschläge für den Schulalltag steht. Wie der Vorgängerband so ist auch dieses Buch ganz an der Praxis orientiert und für sie gedacht, dabei aber durchaus theoriegeleitet. Dass wir „handlungsorientiert" im Titel führen, verrät die didaktische Schule, der wir uns verpflichtet fühlen. Das ist wahrlich kein ganz neuer Begriff; im Gegenteil, er scheint eher in Gefahr, zur wohlfeilen Leerformel zu gerinnen. Vorschnell und zu Unrecht, wie wir meinen.

Mittel- und Ausgangspunkt unseres Konzepts sind die Lernenden und ihr Handeln, bei dem die Unterrichtenden unterstützend mitwirken. Die Aktivitäten zielen nicht auf Einlösung vorgefertigter Lernprogramme mit vorhersehbaren Ergebnissen, sondern bieten den Schülerinnen und Schülern Gelegenheit, sich auf vielfältige, offene Weise mit der Welt der Sprache, aber auch mit sich selbst und anderen auseinanderzusetzen. Sie erweitern dabei nicht nur ihre kognitiv-begrifflichen Kompetenzen, sondern vor allem auch ihre darstellerischen, argumentativen, forschenden und sozialen Kräfte. Grammatik muss sich in diesem Konzept auf eine dienende Rolle beschränken. Dagegen betonen wir freie Äußerungsmöglichkeiten, spielerische Textproduktion und interaktive Sinnstiftungsprozesse, die geeignet sind, die rezeptiven und produktiven Sprachkompetenzen effizienter, autonomer und langfristiger zu fördern als metasprachliches Wissen. Am Ende einer Unterrichtseinheit stehen häufig Produkte wie eine Ausstellung, ein Reader oder eine Aufführung. Gesammelt in Ordnern können sie Bestandteil der Klassenbibliothek werden.

Den eher skeptischen Kolleginnen und Kollegen raten wir, sich auf diese Form von Unterricht – zumindest im Sinne einer Repertoire-Erweiterung – einfach einmal einzulassen. Handlungsorientierter Unterricht ist nicht nur für die Lernenden interessanter, sondern auch für die Lehrenden.

Für die Überarbeitung dieser „handlungsorientierten" Fundgrube wurden alle Kapitel neu bearbeitet. In jedem Kapitel finden sich neue Texte und Aktivitäten. Die Bereiche „Interkulturelles Lernen" und „Working with

Film" (Kapitel 12 und 13) waren vorher nicht berücksichtigt. Ihre Aufnahme in diesen Band trägt der zunehmenden unterrichtlichen Relevanz dieser Themen Rechnung.

Zum Schluss einige Hinweise für die Nutzung des Bandes:

- Viele unserer Vorschläge lassen sich unmittelbar umsetzen, andere benötigen Vorbereitungszeit und manche die Herstellung bzw. Beschaffung von Materialien. Aber: einmal zusammengestellte Sammlungen von impulsgebenden Bildern, Fotos, Ansichts- und Aufgabenkarten lassen sich immer wieder verwenden.
- Allen Vorschlägen sind zur ersten Orientierung Angaben über die vorausgesetzten Lernstufen, den inhaltlichen, methodischen oder sprachlichen Kontext, die vermutliche Dauer und das notwendige Material vorangestellt, die jeweils im Einzelfall modifiziert werden müssen.
- Die 14 Kapitel sind in sich nach Lernstufen – beginnend mit den Anfängen – geordnet.
- Fast alle Unterrichtsvorschläge stammen von uns, bei den übrigen haben wir unsere Quellen genannt. Möglicherweise sind wir aber auch durch eine weit zurückliegende Begegnung, ein Flurgespräch, eine längst vergessene Lektüre zu einem Vorschlag inspiriert worden.
- Alle für Unterrichtszwecke angebotenen Materialien sind für das Fotokopieren freigegeben.
- Auf die unschöne Koppelung der männlichen und weiblichen Schreibweise haben wir verzichtet, stattdessen wechseln wir die Formen.

Ihnen und Ihren Klassen wünschen wir viel Spaß und Erfolg mit den Anregungen der Fundgrube!

1 Who's that, then?

Finding Partners

Lernstufe: Beginners
Kontext: Wortschatzwiederholung, einfache Strukturen, sich selbst vorstellen, mit anderen Kontakt aufnehmen, Dialoge
Material: für jeden Schüler eine Rollenkarte
Dauer: 20 Minuten und mehr

What to do

1. Role-cards are handed out to the pupils. On these cards some information (about a man or a woman, a girl or a boy) is given: Christian name, surname, age, home town, profession, hobby, favourite colour. (More items may, of course, be added – depending on the language level of the group.)
   It is essential that the same information is found on a second, third etc. card so that the students are able to find one or more partners. But there might also be instances when no partner can be found.
2. Now the students are asked to find one or more partners by walking around, saying aloud or whispering the information given on their cards. For this activity it is useful to introduce the phrase "I beg your pardon", so that the students know what to say – in case they have not understood the information given to them.
   a) The teacher may ask the pupils to find somebody
   who shares the same surname • Christian name • age • home town • hobby • favourite colour.
   b) The students may be asked to form a line
   starting with the oldest person present • according to the initial of their surname • according to the initial of their first name.
   c) The teacher asks the pupils to form two groups
   Americans and British • those over 40, those under 40 • male and female.

3. For groups that have a more advanced command of the language (after two or three years of learning English) additional tasks can be provided.

Examples of role-cards: (for groups of 12, of 20 and of 28 students)

1.	William Black, 52, Cardiff, greengrocer, jazz, blue	2.	Jim Taylor, 29, Bristol, taxi-driver, jazz, white
3.	Jim Miller, 41, New York, tourist guide, pottery, green	4.	William Jones, 9, Liverpool, schoolboy, roller-blading, red
5.	Kevin Pearson, 60, Liverpool, teacher, tap-dancing, blue	6.	Susan Hill, 22, New York, shop assistant, tap-dancing, white
7.	Paul Taylor, 19, San Francisco, tennis player, roller skating, black	8.	John Thomas, 41, London, taxidriver, bird watching, black
9.	Dorothy Thomas, 52, Leeds, teacher, tennis, black	10.	Susan Miller, 9, San Francisco, schoolgirl, tennis, pink
11.	Barbara Thomas, 22, Cardiff, greengrocer, pottery, red	12.	Barbara Black, 29, London, tourist guide, bird watching, pink
13.	Emily Jones, 32, New York, shop assistant, collecting stamps, orange	14.	Kevin Hill, 22, Chicago, tennis player, collecting stamps, green
15.	Herbert Pearson, 12, Chicago, schoolboy, watching movies, red	16.	Herbert Smith, 12, Liverpool, schoolboy, rowing, orange
17.	Sarah Smith, 22, Cardiff, policewoman, tap-dancing, black	18.	Sarah Jones, 67, Denver, tourist guide, rowing, yellow
19.	Hilary White, 92, Denver, teacher, watching movies, pink	20.	Hilary Miller, 47, London, policewoman, motor cars, yellow
21.	George Newman, 51, Manchester, mechanic, table tennis, red	22.	Emily Newman, 35, Boston, actress, sailing, white
23.	Peter Fisher, 51, Boston, policeman, motor cars, green	24.	Linda Clark, 15, Manchester, schoolgirl, football, white
25.	Peter Clark, 22, Sydney, student, gardening, violet	26.	Linda Wilson, 47, Sydney, mechanic, sailing, yellow
27.	Jane Fisher, 15, Bristol, schoolgirl, sailing, violet	28.	Jane Wilson, 35, Bristol, actress, gardening, yellow

© Cornelsen Verlag Scriptor, Berlin • Fundgrube Englisch handlungsorientiert

Some examples:
The people who have got the same job must talk about their job. • Those who come from the same town must present their town/city – e.g. in a way that the rest of the class has to guess the name of the town/city. • Those who share a hobby must talk about their hobby. • Two "partners" with different jobs, hometowns etc. present a dialogue/role-play, in which they ask questions about their different "backgrounds" and talk about their jobs or countries. • All students make up the life story of their "roles". • Each person present can be interviewed by the rest of the class. • Two partners have fallen in love with each other and talk about that. • Two partners are breaking up a relationship/are getting divorced and tell the class why they can't stand the partner any more. • Two partners engage in a bitter argument or fight.

Bemerkung
In dieser Aktivität lernen die Schüler, sich (als eine imaginäre Person) vorzustellen; sie müssen Partner finden und – in fortgeschritteneren Lerngruppen – mit diesen ins Gespräch kommen. Da viel Platz benötigt wird, sollten Tische und Stühle eventuell an die Seite gerückt werden.

Cuddly Toys

Lernstufe: Beginners
Kontext: einfacher Wortschatz, leichte Dialoge, leichte Szenen/Rollenspiele spielen
Material: Kuscheltiere (cuddly toys, soft toys), natürlich auch Puppen, Plastiktiere oder Science-Fiction-Figuren
Dauer: 1–2 Stunden (und/oder mehr)

What to do

1. Ask your students to bring along a cuddly toy or a puppet or a doll. (Or hand out a cuddly toy or puppet to each student, if you should have that many ...)
   If the group is fairly big, pair the pupils, and each pair should have one cuddly toy/puppet. It is advisable that there are not only bears and cats

and dogs present in the classroom. From our experience we have learnt that for some productive and interactive communication it is essential to have some "animals" with a negative connotation in the classroom, e.g. a rat, a spider, a snake, a fly, a witch etc. We usually also include a very small elephant (who suffers from his smallness), a robot and an alien that looks rather strange.
2. Make each student introduce her cuddly toy or puppet. Name, age, favourite food, drinks and colours, friends, family, home town, favourite subjects at school, hobbies etc. should be mentioned and explained. If need be, give the students some minutes and let them make notes to prepare this presentation before they actually begin to speak. You may also prepare a worksheet on which the various items can be noted.
3. In a kind of press conference each cuddly toy or puppet is asked questions by the rest of the class.
4. Each "toy" has to find one or two partners, and the two or three of them prepare and act out/role-play a scene either according to their own choice or as told by the teacher. Possible suggestions for such role-plays could include: an argument – who is the prettiest, the most powerful, the most intelligent etc.; a love scene; a family scene; a scene on the way home from school, a party scene etc.
5. **a)** If you should like to extend this activity, you may ask "naughty" provocative questions in order to start some interaction between at least two or even more of the toys. This should be done before **4**.
Examples: Dog, why did you bite the cat last week, when it was peacefully sleeping in front of the fireside? • Cat, why did you eat the mouse, although your family loved the mouse? • Snake, why did you attack the fox last night? • Koala Bear, tell me: Why are you always so terribly sleepy? • Robot, we'll have to arrest you, we don't allow non-humans to be here. • Chinese doll, why don't you stop crying? • Lion, aren't you sad that you can't go hunting here? • Tiger, why did you injure the innocent young sheep? • Witch, come on, show us some of your magic powers. • Spider, explain to us how you hunt flies and other animals.
b) You may also divide the class into groups of five "toys", the students are then asked to prepare a (further) role-play in which the five animals/puppets take part.

Examples of tasks: Produce a fairy-tale • a tragic story • a music videoclip • an advertisement • a TV-show or a school lesson in which all the "toys" in your group participate. (Produce it in front of the class).
6. Make the class evaluate the interaction – both from the point of view of language and of the quality of the acting. Discuss some grammatical or semantical mistakes that have appeared frequently in the presentations. A video recording of the role-plays is a great help for the evaluation.

Bemerkung
Mit Hilfe von Kuscheltieren wird freie, informelle Kommunikation und Interaktion geübt.

Identity Parade

Lernstufe: Beginners/Lower Intermediate
Kontext: Interview, Fragepronomen, sprechen
Topic: Personenbeschreibung, Charakterisierungen
Material: Bilder aus Illustrierten, die Menschen zeigen
Dauer: 1 Stunde

What to do
1. Ask the students to form groups of 4–5. One member of each group chooses one of the pictures (without showing it to anyone) and takes it out of the room, where she assumes the identity which she thinks would suit this person. The pupils in this group should be advised to help each other. Each "character" should have a fairly extensive history and a definite personality when they come back into the room.
2. In the meantime, the other students should prepare questions within their group which they would like to ask an interesting stranger. Circulate while they are doing this and give help if necessary.
3. After 4–5 minutes, bring in the "new identities" and let the class fire questions at them. Each group takes it in turns to ask a question. You may have to give the "new identities" a prompt now and again, if they get stuck. Once the exercise gets going, students are usually willing to repeat it with other pictures.

Eavesdropping

Lernstufe: Intermediate
Kontext: kreatives Schreiben, sprechen
Material: 6 bis 10 Bilder, auf denen sich zwei Personen unterhalten. Es ist wünschenswert, dass die Bilder eine gewisse Originalität haben, damit die Fantasie angeregt wird.
Dauer: 1 Stunde

What to do

1. Ask the students to work in pairs.
2. Pin the pictures up and ask the pairs of students to look at them closely and choose one picture, without telling anyone else which one it is.
3. They should then prepare a short dialogue which they think goes well with their picture.
4. Each pair speaks the dialogue and the rest of the class must guess what picture they have used.

Matchmaking

Lernstufe: Intermediate
Kontext: begründen, erklären, Argumente abwägen, Fragen stellen
Material: eine große Auswahl von Bildern aus Zeitschriften. Die Auswahl der Bilder könnte sich nach Themen des Lehrbuches oder nach dem Wortschatz richten, der geübt werden soll.
Dauer: 1 Stunde

What to do

1. Form groups of 3–4.
2. Give each group an envelope containing several pictures.
3. Ask the students to select pictures which they think go well together. They must have at least 3 pairs or groups of pictures.
   They should agree in their groups on reasons for their choice. They may make notes if they wish and should decide on the picture combination that all of them like best.

4. Each group presents their picture combinations, explaining why they have chosen it.

Variation

5. Jede Gruppe zeigt der Klasse ihre Bildkombination. Die anderen stellen Fragen, um die Gründe für ihre Auswahl herauszufinden.

Mögliche Fragen:
- Hat die Auswahl etwas mit den Menschen zu tun, die auf den Bildern zu sehen sind?
- Hat der Hintergrund oder das Hauptmotiv den Ausschlag für die Auswahl gegeben?
- Kann die Gruppe eine Kategorie *benennen*, der sie die Bilder zuordnen würde?
- Ist es naheliegender, Bilder nach inhaltlichen (Stadt, Land, Werbung ...) oder nach äußeren (schwarzweiß, bunt, hell, dunkel) Gesichtspunkten zu ordnen?

Family Life

Lernstufe: Upper Intermediate
Kontext: Charakterisierung von Personen und Beziehungen
Material: Farbfolie eines Familiengemäldes, Fotoapparat (noch besser: Sofortbildkamera), Wörterbücher, vorbereitete Karteikarten mit Aufgaben
Dauer: mindestens 4 Stunden

Bemerkung

In dieser Einheit geht es um Beziehungen von Menschen zueinander, und zwar in dem komplizierten Zusammenhang „Familie". Die Schüler haben dabei Gelegenheit, einerseits ihr lebensweltliches Wissen und Empfinden sowie ihre Familienerfahrungen, andererseits ihre sprachlichen Fähigkeiten ins Spiel zu bringen. Die Einheit gliedert sich in vier Hauptabschnitte:
- Im ersten nähern sich die Schüler über ein Bild an die Thematik an.
- Im zweiten erfinden sie in Gruppen je eine Familienkonstellation, charakterisieren sie und stellen sie dar. Ihr szenisches Familienarrangement wird von dem Lehrer fotografiert.

- Im dritten bilden diese Fotos den Ausgangspunkt. Jede Gruppe erhält das Familienfoto einer anderen Gruppe. Die darin „kodierte" Familienstruktur muss jetzt – wie im ersten Schritt geübt – verbal dekodiert werden.
- Im vierten Unterrichtsabschnitt findet ein Vergleich statt, bei dem die visuelle Familienkonstellation mit der verbal rekonstruierten verglichen wird.

Es ist sinnvoll, eine Arbeitsmappe für diese Einheit anzulegen, in der die Ergebnisse gesammelt werden.

What to do

1. Suchen Sie ein (möglichst altes) Gemälde von einer Familie aus einem Kunstband aus oder ein altes Familienfoto aus dem eigenen Album oder ein Bild aus der Werbung oder eine Kinderzeichnung. Je vieldeutiger die Familienbeziehungen darauf erscheinen, desto besser. Insofern eignen sich auch Bilder aus anderen Kulturkreisen. Das Bild soll zum Nachdenken über Familienverbände und Familienverhältnisse anregen. Zeitliche bzw. kulturelle Distanz fordern zu Spekulationen heraus und aktivieren dadurch das Vorwissen und die Vorurteile der Schüler, zwingen aber zugleich dazu, diese zu relativieren.

   Fertigen Sie eine Farb-OH-Folie von Ihrem gewählten Gemälde an.

   Projizieren Sie das Bild, und fordern Sie die Klasse zum Beschreiben und Kommentieren auf ("What kind of a family is this?"). Notieren Sie die Überschrift "A Family" an der Tafel und sammeln Sie darunter die Äußerungen der Schüler in Stichpunkten, sodass ein Grundstock an Wörtern und Formulierungen zur Beschreibung und Deutung von Familienbeziehungen entsteht.

2. Informieren Sie die Klasse über ihre folgende Aufgabe: "You will now work in groups. Each group is a family. You can create your family as you like: a single father family with four children and a grandmother; or a childless couple with a dog and a cat; or a 'standard family' with parents and two children; or two women or two men living together with or without children; a poor family; a rich family; a pleasant one or an unpleasant one; any sort of family that you can think of."

   Bilden Sie Gruppen von etwa vier bis sechs Schülern. Geben Sie jeder Gruppe eine Karteikarte mit den folgenden Aufgaben:

> Read through all the tasks carefully before beginning to work on them.
> 1. Discuss what type of family you would like to enact in your group.
> 2. Distribute the roles necessary and find names for each member of your family.
> 3. Write down characteristic features of your family and of each of its members and describe the relationship between everybody.
> 4. Invent a short scene out of the life of your family and write the dialogue.
> 5. Prepare a still, i.e. a characteristic frozen moment from this scene, for a photo session. When you are ready with your preparations ask your teacher to take a picture.
>
> **Warning:** Do not reveal anything about your family to the other groups. Keep your family top secret for a while.

3. Lassen Sie den Film gleich entwickeln, jede Aufnahme möglichst vergrößern und zweimal abziehen. Ein Abzug bleibt unverändert, der andere wird im Laufe der folgenden Aufgabenbearbeitung mit Denk- und Sprechblasen versehen werden. Bitten Sie die Schüler, wieder in der gleichen Gruppenkonstellation zusammenzukommen.

Geben Sie jeder Gruppe ihr Foto, und lassen Sie den Schülern Zeit, ihre Neugier zu stillen und sich in Ruhe zu studieren, damit sie bereit sind für die kommenden Aufgaben.

Jede Gruppe reicht nun ihr Foto einer anderen Gruppe weiter.

In dieser Phase wird das im zweiten Schritt angewandte Verfahren umgekehrt: Während die Schüler zunächst eine Familie ersannen und dann visuell gestalteten, sollen sie jetzt aus der visuellen Gestaltung auf eine zugrunde liegende Familienstruktur schließen, die im Gespräch entstandene visuelle Gestaltung also wieder versprachlichen. Auch hier ist es sinnvoll, jeder Gruppe die Liste der Aufgaben auf gleich lautenden Karteikarten zu geben.

> Take notes while you work on the following tasks so that you can present your group results later on to the whole class. Organize your presentation so that everyone is included.
>
> Here are your tasks:
> 1. Describe the scene. What went on before the picture was taken? What happened just after the snapshot?
> 2. Characterize the family and its members and describe the relationships between all of them.
> 3. Give names to the people in the picture.
> 4. Put the photograph on a larger piece of paper, draw thought or speech bubbles and fill them with the people's thoughts and utterances.

4. In dieser abschließenden Phase sollten alle Schüler im Halbkreis um die Tafel zusammenkommen. Jede Gruppe heftet nun das Foto an die Tafel, das sie gedeutet hat, und präsentiert die Ergebnisse ihrer Gruppe. Die Gruppe, in der das Foto entstanden ist, nimmt dann aus ihrer Sicht Stellung zu dieser Deutung und vergleicht sie mit ihrem Entwurf. Entsprechen Konzeption und Deutung einander? Warum? Warum nicht? Danach wird das Plenum einbezogen.

Bevor die Arbeitsergebnisse nach Durchsicht und Korrektur in die Arbeitsmappe geheftet werden, sollten die Fotos ohne und mit Denk-/Sprechblasen im Klassenraum bzw. Flur ausgestellt werden.

How Well Do You Know Your Classmates?

Lernstufe: Intermediate
Kontext: sich gegenseitig austauschen und kennenlernen, sprechen
Material: Arbeitsbogen für alle Schüler (S. 21)
Dauer: 1/2 – 2 Stunden

What to do

1. Hand out the worksheet and ask the students to mark (**r** or **w**) whether the given statements are right or wrong. In statement 25 you have to fill in the title of a movie which is currently very popular or of a classic.
2. Take a vote on the various statements. Discuss the issues raised here. Mind! Statistics are not important here. The statements should, must be used as opportunities for the pupils to get into contact with, to learn about their classmates. It is vital that the students start talking to each other and about each other, that they exchange their views and experiences.

Bemerkung

Dieser Arbeitsbogen kann als Kennenlern-Aktivität benutzt werden; er ist auch für Vertretungsstunden gut einsetzbar, und die Klasse erkennt damit vielleicht, dass sie sich gar nicht kennt!

How well Do You Know Your Classmates?

	What do you think about your classmates? Are these statements **right** or **wrong**?	right (r)	wrong (w)
1.	Most people in the class do some sport; the most popular sport is football.		
2.	Most people do not own a bicycle.		
3.	Most people (in the class) prefer cats to dogs.		
4.	Most people have more than one brother or sister.		
5.	Most people like strawberry-flavoured icecreams.		
6.	Most people play a musical instrument.		
7.	Most people have visited at least two foreign countries.		
8.	No one in the class has ever broken their leg.		
9.	Most male people are interested in football.		
10.	Most people in this class smoke.		
11.	No one here has ever written a letter to a newspaper.		
12.	Most people like horror movies.		
13.	Most people used to have a teddy bear.		
14.	Most male students in this class drink beer.		
15.	Most people have ridden a horse.		
16.	Most people dream of driving a Porsche or a Ferrari.		
17.	Most people in this class believe that learning Latin is useless.		
18.	Most people watch more than ten hours of TV a week.		
19.	Most people have more than one Christian name.		
20.	Most female students would like to go dancing more often.		
21.	Most people in this class think that there are too many foreigners in Germany.		
22.	There is someone in the class who almost always gets up at half past five.		
23.	Most people feel that men and women should have equal responsibility in child care.		
24.	Not more than three people have a laptop.		
25.	At least half the class has seen _____ .		
26.	At least half the class enjoys going to school.		

© Cornelsen Verlag Scriptor, Berlin • Fundgrube Englisch handlungsorientiert

2 Words, Words, Words

Vocabulary Game

Lernstufe: Beginners
Kontext: Wortschatzwiederholung, -übung (Wörterabfragen)
Material: –
Dauer: 5–15 Minuten

What to do

1. Divide the class into two teams and number off the students.
2. Ask the students to stand in two lines facing each other – at a distance of approximately one or two yards. It is essential that the two lines of students are placed at an equal distance (about 5, 6 yards) from the side-lines (in the schoolyard) or from the walls (inside the building).
3. Now ask student 1 from team A about the meaning of a word or an expression. If she gives the correct answer, her whole team can progress one step. At the same time team B has to retreat a step. Then ask student 1 from team B. Again, if she answers correctly team B can walk one step forward, while team A has to reverse one step. Go on like that giving each student her turn. Make sure that the ways of answering have been agreed upon, before the activity commences. For example: Is it OK if a student simply translates the word into German? Or does she need to explain it in English?
4. During the course of the game the two teams may for some time have to move forward and backward. If one team, however, is not able to answer three or four times, their opposing team will have the chance of advancing fast. The game is over when one team has progressed so far that their opponents are "pushed" towards the wall or over the sideline.

Variation

The two teams may ask each other questions about the meaning of words or expressions: Student 1 from team A asks student 1 from B who will ask student 2 from team A. She will, in turn, ask student 2 from team B etc. Of course, this activity can be used for any kind of quiz (on *Landeskunde topics* etc.).

Bemerkung
Dies ist eine Variation des „Wörterabfragens", für die allerdings genügend Platz zur Verfügung stehen sollte. Geeignet dafür ist der Schulhof, der Pausenhof, ein breiter Gang oder ein Klassenraum, in dem die Möbel zur Seite gerückt sind.

All About Travelling

Lernstufe: Beginners
Kontext: Wortschatzarbeit, Dialoge entwickeln, kreatives Schreiben
Material: Vorlage als Arbeitsblatt oder Overheadfolie, Overheadprojektor
Dauer: 1–2 Stunden

What to do

1. Tell your students that the parts of words (see page 24) have got to do with travelling. Ask them to put them together and to write them down in the left column.
2. When they have finished the students compare the results either with a partner or in groups.
3. Should they have any difficulties they can come to the teacher's desk to have a look at the correct answers in the teacher's key.
4. Ask your students to add verbs and adjectives to their list which they think match the words they have found. Once again they talk to each other about the words they have chosen. They may even swap words they like particularly well. Encourage them to use a dictionary or to leaf through their textbook to find a greater number of words if they feel like it.
5. Then the students talk to a partner and tell them what made them choose these words.

24 Words, Words, Words

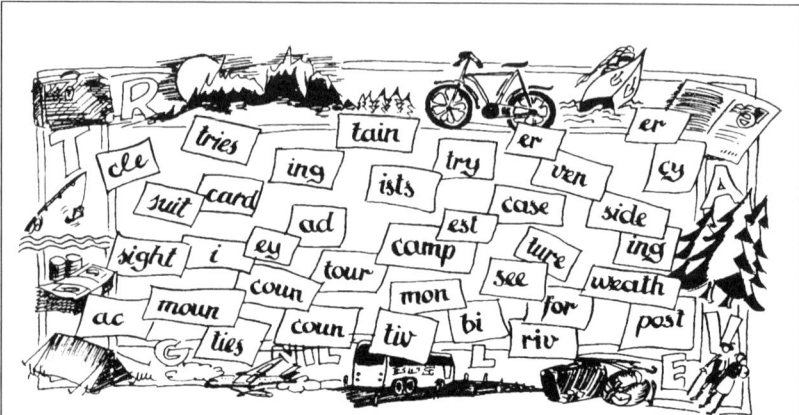

aus: Fremdsprachenunterricht 3/94. Päd. Zeitschriftenverlag

words you have found	verbs	adjectives
1.		
2.		
3.		
4.		
6.		
7.		
8.		
9.		
10.		
11.		
12.		
13.		
14.		
15.		

© Cornelsen Verlag Scriptor, Berlin • Fundgrube Englisch handlungsorientiert

6. Your students will certainly have lots of ideas and feelings about travelling. Ask them to write a text using their collected words. It could be about a real situation or a fantasy journey.
They may write any sort of text they like, e.g. a poem, a mini-saga, a dialogue, an advertisement, etc.
Teacher's key: activities • adventure • bicycle • camping • countries • countryside • forest • money • mountain • postcard • river • sightseeing • suitcase • tourists • weather

Bemerkung
Dieser Aufgabentyp fordert die Schüler dazu heraus, den ihnen schon bekannten Wortschatz zu wiederholen und ihn gleichzeitig innerhalb eigener Konzepte zu erweitern. Da sie am Ende außerdem noch die Wörter in einem Text verarbeiten, entsteht die Möglichkeit, den Wortschatz im Abrufgedächtnis zu verankern.
Dieser Aufgabentyp eignet sich für jedes Thema und kann bei einiger Übung bald von den Schülern selbst erstellt werden. Als sehr effektiv hat sich erwiesen, wenn sie (in Partnerarbeit) die Aufgaben formulieren und untereinander austauschen.

Words Beginning With "P"

Lernstufe: Intermediate
Kontext: erzählen, improvisieren, Wortschatzarbeit
Material: folgendes Bild als Overheadfolie (wahlweise Einwickelpapier o. Ä.)
Dauer: 30–45 Minuten

What to do
1. Show your students the picture and ask them what they associate with it using the letter P. They must explain why they think their word is suitable and should gradually try to develop a story for the picture.
2. Our picture would lend itself to speculation on what the man and woman will find in the castle, what kind of relationship they have, what sort of people they are, what the situation is all about, description of their clothes, scenery, weather, mood, etc.

Bemerkung
Diese Aufgabe kann natürlich jederzeit auch mit anderen Buchstaben gelöst werden, je nach Themenfeld oder Wortfeldern.

© Cornelsen Verlag Scriptor, Berlin • Fundgrube Englisch handlungsorientiert

Dead Metaphors – Reanimated

Lernstufe: Upper Intermediate/Advanced
Kontext: working with words, language awareness, creative writing
Material: evtl. OH-Folie mit der Zeichnung eines Bücherwurms; OH-Folie mit dem Gedicht; OH-Folien, Folienstifte; Wörterbücher
Dauer: 2 Stunden

What to do

1. Instead of telling the class what the lesson is going to be about, draw a picture of a book with a worm eating its way through it on the board and make the class guess the topic of the lesson. If you can't do the drawing, enlarge the picture on the right, copy it onto a transparency and show it via the overhead projector.

2. Announce the poem as written a thousand years ago by an anonymous writer.
3. Read the poem to the class. Read it again, this time accompanied by the text on transparency.

> **Bookworm**
>
> A worm ate words. I thought that wonderfully
> Strange – a miracle – when they told me a crawling
> Insect had swallowed noble songs,
> A night-time thief had stolen writing
> So famous, so weighty. But the bug was foolish
> Still, though its belly was full of thought.
>
> (Old English, 10th century, anonymous, translated by Michael Alexander)

4. Give room for a brief exchange of thoughts about the poem: Do you like it? What do you find strange or interesting about it? Do you have any fantasy about the writer of the poem? Who is he? Who is he talking to? Can a bookworm be foolish?
5. Ask the class to think of words like "bookworm" in English and in their own language, German or otherwise. Collect all the words on the blackboard with a literal and a metaphorical explanation, i.e. *Leseratte* (= a reading rat; someone who loves to read and devours books like a bookworm) or *Löwenzahn* etc. Ask the speakers of other languages to write words in their languages on the board, teach their pronunciation to the class, translate them literally and explain them.
6. Now focus on English metaphors and ask the class to collect as many as they can think of.
7. Distribute the letter next page and ask them to find the seven words hidden in it. Compare the results.

The hidden words are: flowerbed, butterfly, playboy, seahorse, wallflower, bodybuilding, honeymoon.

8. Pair the students (or let them work individually) and ask them to write a little poem – in free verse or rhyming or rhythmical, as they choose –

in which a metaphor is taken literally. They can use the above poem as a model. Give hints and corrections if necessary.
9. Have them read out their poems.
10. Tell them to give their poems an attractive form and layout and to illustrate them. This can be done at home, too.
11. Collect all the final versions in a folder entitled *Bookworm* with a book-eating worm munching its way through the book from back cover to front cover. Add the book to the class library.

Bemerkung
Die Beschäftigung mit Metaphern ist ein spannender Weg, Erfahrungen mit Sprache und ihren Möglichkeiten zu machen. Bei häufigem Alltagsgebrauch aber schwindet unser Bewusstsein von der Bildhaftigkeit und Anschaulichkeit von Metaphern und stumpft so ab, dass wir sie nicht mehr wirklich sehen. Sie sind verschüttet. Diese Übung ist ein Versuch der Wiederbelebung.

I	Y	N	R	P	H	C	E	O	N	G	B	U	Y
A	G	Z	X	F	L	O	W	E	R	B	E	D	R
B	C	D	P	Z	G	I	N	O	S	Z	E	G	A
U	O	D	L	G	I	G	S	E	C	M	P	S	T
T	D	D	A	P	U	N	E	J	Y	C	Y	L	V
T	F	X	Y	A	U	L	H	G	J	M	F	E	J
E	W	C	B	B	R	K	G	P	R	Y	O	H	U
R	P	S	O	I	U	A	N	T	B	E	H	O	V
F	G	M	Y	N	K	I	Y	W	I	P	L	T	N
L	J	Z	O	W	A	L	L	F	L	O	W	E	R
Y	O	P	M	V	L	D	O	D	V	U	Q	D	A
K	Q	U	V	F	B	Y	Q	Q	I	P	F	W	H
S	E	A	H	O	R	S	E	D	L	N	W	B	C
O	F	I	H	N	G	P	I	O	R	I	G	T	U

Ideogrammes

Lernstufe: Intermediate
Kontext: Wortschatz, kreatives Schreiben, language awareness
Material: Papier, Schreibgerät, Overheadfolie, Overheadprojektor
Dauer: beliebig

What to do

1. Make a transparency of the following ideogrammes and show it to your students.
2. Talk to your students about the effects the ideogrammes have on them and try to get them to explain how they work.
   They could say, for example, that the letters O, flying away, symbolize round balloons floating away in the air. This is, of course, the first association most people have with the word balloon.

3. Now ask all your students, working alone or in groups, to think up different ideogrammes for the same word.

   As an example you could give the word (hole) like this:

   or like this

   The following words lead themselves to this activity:
   giraffe   **skyscraper**   **words**
4. Now your students should be able to choose their own words and make ideogrammes for them.

3 Games

Making a Memory Game

Lernstufe: Beginners
Kontext: einfacher Wortschatz
Material: genügend kartoniertes Papier, Scheren, alte Bilder aus Illustrierten, Prospekten usw. zum Ausschneiden, Malstifte
Dauer: 1–2 Stunden

What to do

1. Ask the students to bring along old magazines, brochures etc. with pictures that can be cut out.
2. Explain to the class that they have to make a memory game. In this memory game a picture and the English word for the object or the person in this picture must match. (Give an example: car, shoe, book …)
3. Pair the students and tell the class to cut out same-sized square cards. Make sure the cards are of the same size and of the same colour. The pupils have to find suitable pictures with objects, animals or people. On one card they have to glue this picture, on the other card they have to write down the English word for it. Instead of using pictures from magazines etc., the pupils may also draw pictures themselves. If the students have problems finding suitable words (and pictures), they can use the word lists in their English textbook. The teacher may even organize this activity in such a way that each pair of students is given the vocabulary from a certain unit (or half a unit) to use for the production of cards. (In this way a thorough revision of the vocabulary that has already been learnt can be brought about.)
4. Check the cards and let the pupils play the game. They should not use their own cards, rather those made by their classmates.

Bemerkung

Die Karten können auch in Freiarbeitsphasen verwendet werden.

Playing Taboo

Lernstufe: Beginners to Advanced
Kontext: Wortschatzarbeit, vor allem Wortschatzwiederholung; Umschreibungen, sprechen, Definitionen, Relativsätze
Material: Taboo cards; Sanduhr/Eieruhr/Uhr mit Sekundenzeiger
Dauer: 1/2–1 Stunde

What to do

1. Have a fair amount of taboo cards ready.
2. Divide the class in groups of 6 to 8 pupils. The game should be played in these groups.
3. Divide the players into two teams (Team A and Team B) and hand out the pile of clue-cards to the player who is the first to give clues.
   Play according to the following instructions:
a) Team A chooses one of their players to be the first clue-giver. He takes the pile of taboo cards. The other members in his team sit opposite and are not allowed to see the cards. Team B sits beside or behind Team A's clue-giver so that they can read the cards as he draws them. They must see the "taboo words", since they have to control the clue-giver.
b) Team B has control over the "timer" – either an hour-glass, an egg-timer or a watch. If a watch is used, a time limit – e.g. 45 seconds – for a team to play should be agreed upon before the game begins.
c) The clue-giver draws a card. He must communicate the "Guess Word" to his team without using any of the taboo words listed on the card. The clues given may consist of detailed sentences, phrases or single word units.
d) In "traditional taboo" no gestures, miming, sound effects or noises may be made to explain the "Guess Word". For beginners, however, this rule need not apply.
e) As the clue-giver gives clues, his team-mates shout out words which they think might be the "Guess Word". There is no penalty for wrong guesses.
f) When a team-mate shouts out the correct "Guess Word", the clue-giver's team scores a point. If the clue-giver uses a taboo word, the opposing team signals that the card is dead, and the clue-giver has to choose the next card.

g) The clue-giver's turn continues until the time is up. Then the teams reverse their roles (i.e. team B takes over as the clue-giving and guessing team). Players in each team take turns as the clue-giver!

h) When the time allotted – let's say 15 to 20 minutes – is up, the team that has scored most points is the winner. Another way of choosing a winner: The teams agree on a total score to be reached – e.g. 20 or 25 points – and the first team to reach this score wins the game.

Note: It is essential that – either in class or in the group – the rules must be discussed and agreed upon before the game is played. If there should be disagreement on certain rules, these different opinions provide a good chance of negotiating meaning or agreement in English! Of course, the rules can be changed.

Liste von (einfachen) Begriffen und ihren „Tabus" für 60 Tabukarten

school	– teacher, pupil, to learn
apple	– red, fruit, to eat
chair	– furniture, to sit, leg
house	– home, building, garden, flat
to write	– paper, book, pen, pencil, exercise
money	– bank, to pay, shop, to buy
picture	– to paint, colour, paper, wall
dog	– cat, animal, mouse, stick
uncle	– mother, aunt, father, son, daughter
to repair	– bike, car, mechanic
blue	– sky, colour, yellow, green, red, sea
hour	– day, minute, time, clock
north	– south, east, west, opposite, polar bear
department store	– cheap, expensive, shop, to buy
sponge	– classroom, blackboard, clean, to wash
pen	– pencil, to write, biro
sugar	– sweet, milk, coffee, tea
to throw	– stick, fetch, ball, catch
desk	– table, chair, school
afternoon	– morning, lunch, evening, night

Playing Taboo

cup	– kitchen, tea, coffee, to drink
game	– to play, computer, taboo, tennis
to bark	– dog, animal, noise, loud
animal	– zoo, budgie, dog, cat, fish, pet
brother	– family, sister, son, mother, father
building	– house, big, architect
police	– safe, gangster, cop, to arrest
castle	– tower, knight, wall, high
book	– to read, paper, page
warm	– hot, cold, fire, home
girl	– boy, woman, young, daughter
kitchen	– cup, fridge, room, to cook
road	– street, car, traffic, city
sentence	– word, letter, book, to speak
present	– birthday, party, surprise
class	– school, teacher, pupil, room
job	– industry, work, money, office
nice	– bad, sweet, fine, beautiful
car	– to drive, street, road, dangerous
queen	– king, England, woman, famous, Elizabeth
bottle	– to drink, thirsty, milk, water, glass
town	– city, village, car, people
radio	– news, music, to listen, car
short	– long, small, distance
ruler	– long, number, maths
to watch	– TV, cinema, to look, film
to talk	– to speak, to tell, debate, mouth
station	– train, railway, ticket-office
new	– old, to buy, clean, modern
garden	– house, tree, flower, green, grass
exercise	– school, lesson, teacher, book
ghost	– castle, night, to be afraid, legend, past
shop assistant	– to sell, to help, work, supermarket
hungry	– to eat, thirsty, bread, food
journey	– to travel, plane, car, bus
quiet	– loud, mouth, noisy, to shout
music	– radio, jazz, instrument, concert
English	– language, country, queen, island, German
window	– wall, glass, to look, room
stamp	– post-office, card, letter, to collect

Redemittel, die (beim Wettspiel) vorgegeben werden können
- We need two teams./Form two groups./Sort yourselves out into two teams./Split up in two teams.
- Whose go/turn is it?
- Who goes first?/Who starts?
- OK, go./Ready, steady, go.
- We've scored a point./Add a point to the score./What's the score?
- That was our point.
- That's not allowed./That's not fair./That's cheating.
- We've won/lost.
- We are five points ahead./We are leading.
- Don't look at the card before you are told.
- Which are your taboo words?
- You must guess the 'guess word' at the top of the card.
- No taboo word written on the card may be given as a clue.
- You may decide whether gestures/noises are allowed or not.
- The team that shouts out the correct word scores a point.

Structures:
- relative clause/contact clause
- It's a thing that/which
- He/She is a person who/that
- You go there to .... e.g. study
- You use it to/for .... e.g. cook/ing

Bemerkung

Vermutlich dürfte „Taboo" vielen Schülern als Gesellschaftsspiel bekannt sein. Es geht dabei darum, dass ein Begriff erklärt werden muss, wobei bestimmte Wörter, die normalerweise bei dieser Erklärung benutzt würden, nicht verwendet werden dürfen, also „tabu" sind. Das im Handel erhältliche Tabu-Spiel mit englischen Ausdrücken ist für Anfangsklassen zu schwierig. So müssen eigene Tabukarten entwickelt und hergestellt werden, die dem Sprachniveau der jeweiligen Lerngruppe entsprechen. Diese Tabukarten können entweder von der Lehrkraft oder – und das ist natürlich vorzuziehen – von der Klasse (in Gruppen) hergestellt werden. (Vgl. den Unterrichtsvorschlag „Making Taboo Cards", S. 35 f.)

Beispiele: present: Taboo words: birthday, party, surprise, buy
information: Taboo words: tourist, ask, airport, time-table

black: Taboo words: white, colour, dirty, dark
(to) miss: Taboo words: love, look, search, find

Auf jeder Tabukarte steht also oben der zu ratende Begriff; darunter sind 3–5 Tabuwörter aufgelistet. Im Anfangsunterricht genügen durchaus drei Tabuwörter. Insgesamt ist das Tabu-Spiel eine motivierende Methode zur Vokabelübung und -wiederholung, die auch innerhalb von Freiarbeit eingesetzt werden kann. Das „Taboo-Spiel" mag etwas kompliziert wirken, ist aber in der Praxis sehr leicht einzusetzen.

Making Taboo Cards

Lernstufe: Beginners (plus)
Kontext: Wortschatzarbeit
Material: Karteikarten oder festes Papier zum Herstellen der Tabu-Karten, evtl. Scheren, evtl. ein- oder zweisprachige Wörterbücher
Dauer: 2–3 Stunden

What to do

1. Divide the class into groups of 2–4 students and provide the groups with file cards or paper and scissors. Tell them that it is their task to make taboo cards. Explain the layout of a taboo card.
2. (For beginners) The teacher and the students check the vocabulary lists of each unit of the text-book or the alphabetical word list at the end of the book to find words that are suitable for Taboo. Give each group about 10 (or more) words to make cards that can be used for Taboo.
   An alternative way: The students are given the homework to find appropriate taboo words for at least ten words chosen by the teacher. The homework should be discussed in class, before the actual cards are produced. It may be difficult for younger pupils to find abstract terms etc. (For advanced classes) Each group is allocated one unit of the text-book. The students must select words from this unit that are suitable for Taboo and make taboo cards.
3. The groups produce their clue-cards (without letting the other groups know about their choices). In order to find taboo words they may consult the text-books, dictionaries, the teacher.

4. In the end they hand in their cards to the teacher, and in the next lesson taboo can be played.

Bemerkung

Das Herstellen von Tabu-Karten und das Spielen mit diesen Karten eignet sich vor allem als Vokabelwiederholung (anhand eines Lehrbuchs) nach einem halben Jahr oder nach einem Schuljahr. Es empfiehlt sich jedoch, ein Tabuspiel erst dann selbstständig herstellen zu lassen, wenn die Schüler – zumindest in Ansätzen – mit dem Spiel vertraut sind.

Making Board Games

Lernstufe: Lower Intermediate
Kontext: Anwendung der bislang erworbenen Kenntnisse, Ausdrücke des Spielens
Material: gebrauchte Brettspiele, Bilder usw., Schere, Kleber
Dauer: 2–4 Stunden

What to do

1. Preparation: Ask your class and your colleagues to bring along old (used) board games and some old magazines (to cut out pictures and photos). The pupils should also have scissors and glue.
2. Tell the class that they are going to make new (English) board games using the old playing-boards. Explain to them the general set-up and procedures of making such a game. They should use the background of the old boards (castle, forest, city etc.), but a number of new items or pictures or drawings should be added.
   The pupils are to make up a way (or use the old route on the board) that has to be followed and have to think of and write down the rules of the game. Some squares/points should have numbers and when a player lands there, she has to do what is stated in the rules. It is essential that the tasks include both a number of oral (language) activities and the ordinary board game rules such as missing a turn, moving forward, having to go back, taking the wrong way, starting again from the beginning etc. It might be advisable to use activity cards for the language tasks.

Making Board Games 37

3. Split the class into groups of three to five students and set the groups to work. The groups should hand in their sets of rules so that the language can be corrected.
4. When the groups have finished their new board game, they may, of course, play it. And in due course they can also play the other groups' games.

Bemerkung
Dies ist eine Anregung zur Wiederverwendung gebrauchter Brettspiele. Die Schüler stellen ihre eigenen Brettspiele her, die dann z.B. in Freiarbeitsphasen gespielt werden können.

Some useful expressions
- the dice, the counter, the board, the playing-board
- rules of play, rules of the game
- to throw the dice
- to throw a six, a one (to start)
- If you throw a six, you can take another turn.
- The player with the highest throw starts the game.
- You can throw (the dice) again.
- to go/move on to ...
- to move the counter forward
- If another player already has a counter on that number, she/he must remove it/go back to ...
- to miss a turn/two turns
- to go back to (the start)
- the counter lands on a black/white/red square/at 10
- to stick to the rules
- to break the rules
- The game is up/over.

Some ideas for oral tasks or activities
- Sing an English/American song. Tell a joke in English. Recite a nursery rhyme/a short poem.
- Talk about your pet/favourite animal/favourite pop group/favourite sport/favourite teacher/a subject at school etc.
- Advertise a product (some drink/fast food/sweet/detergent etc.)
- How do you get to school?
- What did you do yesterday/last Saturday?
- What did you do during your last holidays?
- Introduce a film/a book that you have seen/read.
- Tell some lies about yourself/about some classmate.
- Describe a friend/classmate/teacher (who must be guessed by the other players).

- Walk up to the teacher and ask an embarassing/impolite question.
- Imitate/Impersonate a teacher/classmate. (He must be guessed by the rest of the group.)
- Ask some questions that have to/cannot be answered by the rest of the group.
- Talk about TV habits. (Which TV programmes do you like/dislike/watch? How many hours a day/a week do you watch TV?)
- Tell a story about .... Story-telling cards could be produced, too. There is just one word on a card, e.g. castle. The pupil then must tell a story about a castle. Or the pupil who has to tell the story must draw three or four cards and must invent a story using all the words on his cards.

Finding Families

Lernstufe: Beginners
Kontext: einfache Wortschatzarbeit
Material: Wörter, auf Zettel geschrieben
Dauer: 10–15 Minuten

What to do

1. Prepare the slips of paper (see "Examples of 'families'" and "Rhyming 'families'"). For each "round" each pupil will need one word.
2. Explain to the class what's going to happen. They will each be given a word (on a slip of paper) and must find matching partners ("they have something in common, they form a family") by walking around and speaking out or whispering their word. The pupils do not know whether they will find one or more partners.
3. Have the class stand in a circle. Hand out the slips of paper. The slips may not be shown to other students.
4. The students are asked to find their families/matching partners.
5. The families should read out their words and find their generic (general) term.
6. Repeat the same procedure. This time the students must find "rhyming partners", i.e. the family members' "rhyme".

Finding Families 39

Bemerkung
Für diese Aktivität, bei der Partner bzw. Familien gefunden werden müssen, wird Platz benötigt. Tische und Bänke evtl. zur Seite räumen. Achtung: Es kann etwas laut werden.

Examples of "families"

family:	– grandmother, brother, sister, daughter, son, uncle, aunt, nephew
vehicles:	– car, train, lorry, bike, moped, motor-bike
colours:	– red, green, yellow, black, white, pink, orange
furniture:	– bed, chair, table, wardrobe
rooms:	– kitchen, bedroom, living-room, dining-room, bathroom, toilet
animals:	– horse, cat, dog, hamster, guinea-pig, mouse, elephant, bird
countries:	– Britain, Germany, USA, France, Switzerland, Austria, Australia
people:	– girl, boy, man, woman
sports:	– football, basketball, tennis, swimming, hockey, judo
fruits:	– banana, apple, orange, cherry, strawberry, pear
jobs/professions:	– teacher, baker, shop assistant, taxi-driver
food:	– bread, cheese, sandwich, potatoes, sausages, eggs
clothes:	– trousers, shirt, skirt, pullover, suit, jacket, socks, blouse, dress, sweater

Rhyming "families"

- two, shoe, who, you, blue, zoo, do, through
- eye, try, my, fly, die
- year, here, beer, near, hear
- three, tea, me, he, she, we
- white, night, right, write
- throw, blow, go, no, know
- town, brown, down, clown
- meet, sweet, meat, seat, street
- tall, all, wall, small

4 Sketches, Role-Plays, Simulations

Right and Wrong: Contradicting Each Other

Lernstufe: Beginners/Lower Intermediate
Kontext: In einem Rollenspiel/Sketch werden die Redemittel des „Widersprechens" verwendet.
Material: ausgearbeitete Szenenbeschreibungen; falls vorhanden: Videokamera
Dauer: 1–2 Stunden

What to do

1. Walk around the classroom. At random, take a student's book, pen, case etc. away and claim that it is yours. Make sure that the students react and try to get their property back – by using the proper words and expressions in which somebody is contradicted. In this way of presenting a situation, the following expressions should be made known to the pupils:

That's my book etc. It is not your book ... Yes, it is. No, it isn't. It's mine/ours. It's not yours. Sorry, it's mine ... I am right, and you are wrong. I haven't got it. You've got it. Yes, you have. No, I haven't. I'm always right. No, you aren't, you are wrong. I'm a teacher, and a teacher is always right.

You can introduce *"It's his/hers/theirs."* by addressing a student's neighbour or the rest of the class and seeking confirmation from them that the book, pen etc. belongs to you and does not belong to the student ... It is essential that emphasis and proper intonation, supported by mime and gestures, are applied. It is important, too, that this is done

in a funny way so that the students can easily and joyfully imitate and repeat the usage of the notional category "contradicting".
2. Pair the students and make them practise the scene (taking away of things), using the words and expressions of contradicting each other. Don't overdo it. 5 minutes will be enough.
3. Divide the class into groups of three students and hand out one "scene description" to each group. If there are more than four groups, hand out the same description to two or more groups. Tell the students that they have to make up a sketch using the given scene.

The task must include (either orally or in written form):

Make up a sketch.
Remember the phrases that you can use when you contradict a person.
Try to find an amusing ending.

4. The students prepare the sketches.
5. Make the students role-play the sketches in front of the class and, if available, record the presentations using a video camera.
6. (Next lesson) Present the recordings to the class and evaluate the use of the language of contradiction.

Scene descriptions
I
CHARACTERS: Mike, Susan, woman at the door of the cinema
PLACE: You are in front of the cinema.
SITUATION: At five o'clock Susan and Mike buy tickets for a film. The film begins at six o'clock, and so they go for a walk. When they come back to the cinema at six, the woman at the door asks them for their tickets. They can't find them. Susan says that Mike has got them, and Mike says that Susan has got them and the woman at the door says she has not seen them before.

II
CHARACTERS: Ann, Rose, Fiona
PLACE: You are in a hospital.
SITUATION: Ann is in hospital. Her friends Rose and Fiona go and see her. On the way to the hospital they buy some sweets for Ann. But when they come into Ann's room, they can't find the sweets. Rose says that Fiona has got them, and Fiona says that Rose has got them ...

III
CHARACTERS: Louise, Peter, waiter
PLACE: You are in a café.
SITUATION: Louise and Peter are in a café. They have an icecream or a cup of coffee. Now they want to pay, but they can't find their money. Louise thinks that Peter has got it, and Peter thinks that Louise has got it ...

IV
CHARACTERS: Jane, Tim (her brother), shop-assistant
PLACE: You are in a bookshop.
SITUATION: Jane and Tim are in a bookshop. Tomorrow is their mother's birthday, and they want to buy a book for her. When they want to pay, they can't find their money. Jane says that Tim has got it, and Tim says that Jane has got it ...

Bemerkung
Für das Thema „Widersprechen" sind die Sketche „Right and Wrong" und „Asking the Way" aus dem von Leslie Dunkling verfassten Heftchen *Seven Sketches,* erschienen im Longman-Verlag, gut geeignet und schon nach einem Jahr Englischunterricht einsetzbar.

Market-Place

Lernstufe: Beginners/Lower Intermediate
Kontext: Wortschatz "Shopping"
Material: Tische als Marktstände, evtl. „Waren", Einkaufszettel; (Spiel-)Geld
Dauer: 1 Stunde Vorbereitung, 1 Stunde Durchführung

What to do

1. Inform the student about the next lesson's activity: *We want to role-play scenes in a market-place.* Choose one or two pupils for each stall to take over the roles of stall owners: greengrocer's, toy stall, stationer's (Mrs White's stall), clothes stall, Mr Black's supermarket, butcher, baker. Of course, you may do with only four or five different stalls. Divide the rest of the class into teams of three or four pupils. They are to act as families

who will go shopping. Discuss with the class which or what kind of goods can be bought at each shop. If necessary, use the blackboard and draw up lists of things for each shop (see page 44). Organise with the class that for each shop (at least some) goods should be brought to school the next day. If toy money or real British or Americans coins – and notes – should be available, use it/them.
2. Either at school or for homework: a) Tell the shopkeepers to paint signs and price-lists for their stalls. b) Tell the "families" to make up shopping-lists – either one long list for the whole family or different lists for each family (group) member.
3. At the beginning of the next lesson: Arrange a market-place by using the desks as market stalls and by putting them on the four sides of the class-room. The stallkeepers put their signs and prices up and display their goods. They have pens and pencils and some sheets of paper at hand.
4. Tell the stallkeepers to be ready at their stalls and then let the families start shopping. The family members should move from stall to stall and buy all the items mentioned on their shopping-lists. If the stallkeepers don't have the "real" thing, they may note down what has been asked for and hand out this slip of paper to the customers. The teacher can take over the role of a policeman in order not to lose track of what is going on. In the end the families hand in their purchases to the teacher – together with their shopping-list so that he can check if the family have had successful "shopping trips". If time allows, the families can be sent on another shopping round – with a different group's shopping list. Or you may also swap around the shopkeepers and the customers so that the pupils have to take over different roles.

Bemerkung
Diese Aktivität eignet sich zur Durchführung, nachdem eine Unterrichtseinheit zum Thema „Einkaufen" oder „Geschäfte" behandelt wurde und die Redemittel des Kaufens, Verkaufens, Nach-dem-Preis-Fragens usw. bekannt sind. Sicherlich geht es bei dieser Inszenierung eines Marktplatzes authentischer zu, wenn tatsächlich Waren vorhanden sind und angeboten werden.

Lists of shopping items (suggestions)

Greengrocer's
(tin of) pineapples, pound(s) of strawberries, bananas, apples, oranges, lemons, grapefruits, pears, peaches, cherries, carrots, tomatoes, potatoes, onions, broccoli, cabbage, cauliflower, cucumber

Toys stall
teddy bear, water-pistol, toy car, model railway, model plane, cuddly toy (dog), watch, football, cassettes, records, in-line-skates, kite

Stationer's (Mrs White's stall)
biro, a green, red, blue... felt-tip, comic, newspaper, magazine, pencil, rubber, ruler, exercise-book, pen, pencil-case, schoolbag, book, map, birthday card, poster, calculator

Clothes stall
pullover, dress, shirt, pair of socks, pair of trousers, pair of jeans, pair of shorts, coat, raincoat, jacket, T-shirt, sweater, scarf, pair of gloves, bathing suit (swimsuit)

Mr Black's supermarket
cornflakes, bar of chocolate, bottle of lemonade/tonic water/milk/orange-juice, cheese, ice-cream, tomato ketchup, packet of crisps, eggs, tea, coffee, sugar, salt, butter, oil, yoghurt, matches, toilet paper, beefburgers, fishfingers

Butcher
pound of sausages, chicken, beef, pork, minced meat, bacon

Baker
loaf of bread (white/brown/French), rolls, slices of toast bread, piece of cake, packet of biscuits, pizza

"The Cold" – A Sketch

Lernstufe: Lower Intermediate
Kontext: sprechen, Aussprache
Material: Text des Sketches, evtl. Kostüme
Dauer: 1 Stunde oder mehr

Anmerkung: Dieser (übertriebene, leicht absurde) Sketch eignet sich z.B. auch für Vertretungsstunden oder für eine Aufführung beim Elternabend oder Ähnliches.

"The Cold" – A Sketch   45

What to do

1. If need be, introduce some of the words that might be new to the class.
2. Let the students read out the text in roles (once or twice).
3. Talk about the text briefly (by asking questions about the content) to make sure everyone has understood it.
4. Practise the pronunciation, get the students to identify with their roles, to articulate properly.
5. Divide the class and let the students practise simultaneously in groups. You have to proceed from group to group, advising and correcting.
6. Make the students, who will now take over the roles, sit in "the train compartment" (in front of the class or in the middle of the classroom) facing each other. The following arrangement is advised:

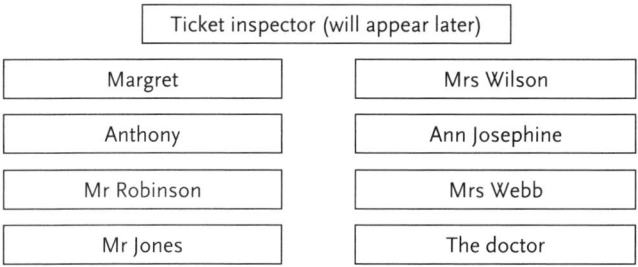

7. The students should now act out the sketch.
8. If necessary, rehearse with the students. Don't forget about the costumes!
9. Produce the play at a parents' evening, for example, or at a school festival.

The Cold

Mr Jones has a terrible cold and sneezes and sneezes.
Mr Robinson is reading a newspaper.
Anthony loves Margaret.
The Ticket Inspector checks the tickets.
Margaret loves Anthony.
Mrs Webb is in the wrong train.
Mrs Wilson is very strict with her daughter.
Ann Josephine, Mrs Wilson's daughter, is seven years old.
Doctor
Place: In a train compartment

JONES:	SNEEZE
ALL:	Bless you!
JONES:	Thank you. SNEEZE
ALL:	Bless you!
ROBINSON:	Terrible weather today, isn't it?
WEBB:	Yes, it is. It's really bad today.
WILSON:	It's raining cats and dogs.
ROBINSON:	Terrible.
JONES:	SNEEZE I'm sorry.
WEBB:	You've got a terrible cold.
JONES:	Yes, I know.
WEBB:	You must take an aspirin. That'll help, I'm sure.
JONES:	Yes, thank you. SNEEZE
ANTHONY:	I love you, Margaret.
MARGARET:	And I love you, Anthony.
ANTHONY:	Darling.
MARGARET:	Darling!
ANN J.:	I must go to the toilet, Mummy!
WILSON:	Please don't speak so loud.
ANN J.:	But I must go, Mummy, I really must go.
WILSON:	Be quiet.
ANN J.:	I can't hold on any longer.
WILSON:	OK, go, hurry up. She goes to the toilet every five minutes.
WEBB:	She is still young. She will learn.
JONES:	SNEEZE
ROBINSON:	Terrible weather today.
WEBB:	Dreadful.
WILSON:	Awful.
ANTHONY:	You are wonderful, darling. I love you.
MARGARET:	I love to hold your hand, darling.
ANTHONY:	I would like to kiss you, darling.
MARGARET:	But not here, darling. There are so many people in the train.
JONES:	SNEEZE
ROBINSON:	Here. It is in the newspaper: When you have a cold, you must stay in bed for a week. Stay in bed, they say here.
JONES:	Yes, I ... SNEEZE
ROBINSON *(to doctor):*	I see you're reading a book.
DOCTOR:	Yes, I am.
ROBINSON:	I am reading my newspaper. It is very interesting.
DOCTOR:	Yes ...
ANN J.:	I am back from the toilet, Mummy.
WILSON:	Be quiet and sit down, Ann Josephine.
JONES:	SNEEZE

"The Cold" – A Sketch

WILSON:	You should wrap up. Here, look at me. One, two, three, four pullovers, a coat, one scarf, two scarves, a pair of gloves. That'll keep you warm.
JONES:	Yes, I know, I ... SNEEZE
ROBINSON:	And don't forget an umbrella.
JONES:	Yes, I've got one, I ... SNEEZE
ANN J.:	Mummy, that man keeps on sneezing.
WILSON:	Yes, we know, my child.
ANN J.:	But why is he sneezing?
WILSON:	Well ...
JONES:	SNEEZE
ANN J.:	Have a sweet. That'll help.
JONES:	Yes, thank you ...
MARGARET:	I love you, Anthony. I love you so much.
ANTHONY:	I love you, too. Margaret. You are so beautiful. Your hair is beautiful, your eyes are beautiful, your nose is beautiful.
JONES:	SNEEZE
ANTHONY:	Your nose doesn't sneeze, Margaret.
MARGARET:	No, Anthony, it doesn't.
ANTHONY (to Jones):	You should try a hot water bottle.
JONES:	Yes, I ...
TICKET INSPECTOR:	Tickets, please.
ROBINSON:	Where is my ticket?
TICKET INSPECTOR:	Well, you must look for it.
ROBINSON:	Oh, here it is. I always keep it in my shoe.
WEBB:	When will the train arrive in Liverpool?
TICKET INSPECTOR:	This is not the Liverpool train, it's the London train.
WEBB:	London?! But I don't want to go to London. I want to go to Liverpool. What can I do?
JONES:	SNEEZE Sorry.
WEBB:	Help! What can I do? Help. I want to go to Liverpool.
ROBINSON:	I think she's had a shock.
ANN J.:	What's the matter? What's the matter?
WILSON:	You shut up, Ann Josephine.
ANTHONY:	Here, conductor. Here are our tickets.
MARGARET:	Yes, here are our tickets.
TICKET INSPECTOR:	Thank you.
JONES:	SNEEZE
WEBB:	I don't want to go to London. I want to go to Liverpool.
ROBINSON:	You'll have to take a train back from London.
WEBB:	Yes? From London?
TICKET INSPECTOR:	That's a very good idea. Take a train from London to Liverpool. There is a train at ten tomorrow morning.

WEBB:	Tomorrow morning? I can't wait until tomorrow. That's terrible!
TICKET INSPECTOR:	There are trains today, too.
WEBB:	Oh!
JONES:	SNEEZE
TICKET INSPECTOR:	You've got a cold. You should drink whisky. It keeps out the cold.
JONES:	Yes, good idea. Thank you. I'll drink whisky.
TICKET INSPECTOR:	Good bye then.
ALL:	Good bye.
ANN J.:	I must go to the toilet, Mummy.
WILSON:	You can't go now.
JONES:	SNEEZE
WILSON:	We will be in London soon. In just a minute.
ANN J.:	But I must go, Mummy, I really must go.
WILSON:	You wait, Ann Jospehine, or I will tell Daddy.
ANN J.:	Oh, please don't tell Daddy!
JONES:	SNEEZE
MARGARET:	Oh, you've got a terrible cold.
JONES:	Yes ...
ANTHONY:	Margaret!
MARGARET:	Yes, darling?
ANTHONY:	Sometimes I get a cold, too.
MARGARET:	Oh, do you? I love men with colds.
JONES:	SNEEZE
MARGARET:	You should see a doctor. See a doctor.
ANTHONY:	Margaret!
MARGARET:	Yes, darling?
ANTHONY:	We're in London.
MARGARET:	Oh, are we? That's wonderful, darling.
WILSON:	Get up, Ann Josephine, we're in London.
JONES:	Well, we ... SNEEZE
ROBINSON:	Here. They write: Hundreds of people have got colds. Terrible.
WEBB:	Where is my train to Liverpool? My train to Liverpool!
WILSON:	Goodbye, and don't forget. Wrap up.
ANN J.:	And have a sweet.
ROBINSON:	Stay in bed for a week.
WEBB:	Take an aspirin. I must go to Liverpool.
JONES:	Yes ... SNEEZE
ANTHONY:	Try a hot water bottle. That'll help.
MARGARET:	Goodbye, and don't forget. You should see a doctor.

JONES: Yes, thank you, I ... SNEEZE Well, *(to doctor)* everyone's telling me what I should do. Why don't you say anything? What do you think?
DOCTOR: Oh, well, you see, I am a doctor, and I really cannot tell you what you can do about a cold.

Making up Dialogues

Lernstufe: Lower Intermediate
Kontext: Dialoge, Rollenspiel, freies Schreiben und Sprechen
Material: für jeweils zwei Schüler einen Satz/eine Frage auf einer Karte
Dauer: 1–2 Stunden

What to do

1. Pair the students. Each pair is handed out the first sentence of a possible dialogue/scene/discussion/argument etc.
2. The students are asked to make up a dialogue/scene/argument starting with the given sentence. The length of the dialogue must be decided by the teacher – according to the time available and to the language level. The students should write down their dialogue, they may write down the text in detail or just jot down some notes. Then they role-play the situation in front of the class.
3. If you want to develop this kind of making up dialogues, just give each pair another "starter" and have the students role-play this scene spontaneously, i.e. without allowing time for preparation.
4. You may also give each pair/group three of these sentences and get the students to integrate them in a dialogue. Or the same "starter" can be given to a number of pairs in class so that the different solutions can be compared later on.

Note: The students should be encouraged to use funny, comic, absurd, or highly dramatic and even tragic elements and sequences to develop their scenes. If their dialogues are made up in a matter-of-fact way, the role-play will be boring and the fun will be lost. In the course of the role-play the background of the "starter" should be revealed. Otherwise the dialogues will hardly convey any meaning.

Suggestions for "starters"

- Aren't you listening?
- What was that?
- What did you do that for?
- Get out of here.
- I can't believe it.
- No, I won't, and that's final.
- I'm sorry, darling, I didn't mean to ...
- Did you find it?
- What the hell has happened?
- When did he die?
- I didn't do it.
- I'm sorry, I'm really sorry.
- Why are you late?
- I would never have thought that you could do something like that.
- How on earth did he do it?
- I can't swim.
- I can't stand it any longer.
- Well, that's terrible.
- Oh no. That can't be true.
- Welcome to the party.
- It's great to see you again.
- I always felt it would end like that.
- Does he know about it?
- We had a great time.
- You would, wouldn't you?

"An Accident" – An Improvised Radio Play

Lernstufe: Lower Intermediate
Kontext: freies Sprechen, spontane Kommunikation, Wortschatz zum Thema "Accident"
Material: Tafel, Aufnahmegerät mit Mikrofon
Dauer: 1 Stunde

What to do

1. Construct the map of a town centre with a traffic junction by drawing it on the blackboard; make the students participate in this construction. They may use the names of all kinds of buildings that are supposed to be in a town. It is of no importance at all where which building is situated. There are just some essentials: There are traffic-lights at the crossroads; the school is not far from there, and outside the school there is a zebra-crossing. Draw a lorry in the sketch. It is stopping in front of the zebra-crossing, just outside the school. Draw a car, too. It is behind the lorry and is now overtaking it.

A possible sketch may look like this:

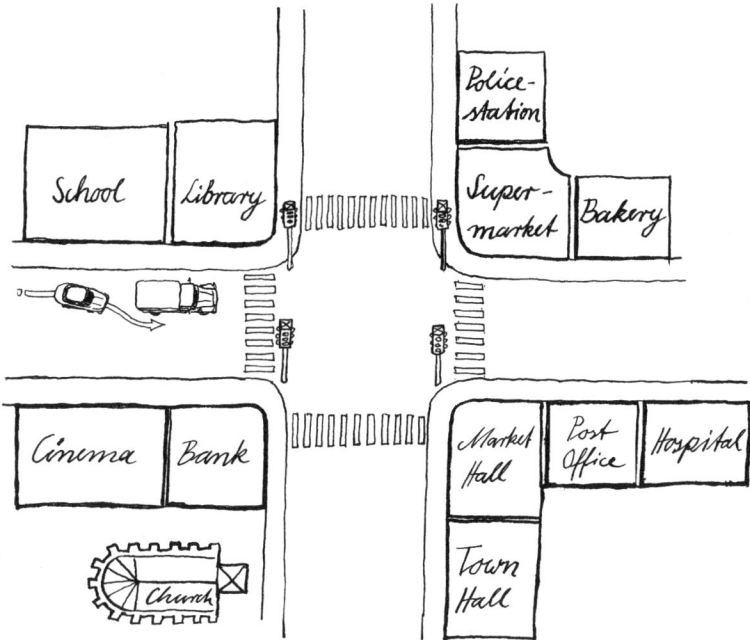

2. Now take up the role of a reporter and develop a story by asking the pupils (spontaneously) about what happened. Use the microphone and record the proceedings without interruption. When addressing a pupil you must name the role he or she is to take so that they can react according to the role. Make sure that all pupils can participate in the play. (For a list of roles, see page 53; it is also advisable to have role-cards ready – to be placed in front of the students so that the teacher knows who is who.) In order to keep the whole group active, you can have them help you create a "traffic atmosphere" or an "accident atmosphere".

The plot is developed along the lines of the answers given by the pupils (who play the roles of people involved in the events). A general narrative outline could be as follows: *While the car is overtaking the lorry, some pupils come rushing out of the school and are crossing the street at the zebra-crossing. The driver of the car doesn't see them in time to stop. Thus at least one pupil is injured (or killed?). The ambulance and the police arrive, look after the injured and interrogate the witnesses. The teachers, classmates, parents of the injured pupil(s) are shocked.*

A possible beginning of this radio play could sound like that:
R (= Reporter): Well, ladies and gentlemen, it is a beautiful day today. The sky is blue, the birds are singing.
C (= Class): *imitate the singing of the birds ...*
R: The dogs are barking.
C: *bark*
R: But we are in the centre of the town, and the traffic here is really heavy.
C: *traffic noises*
R: Well, you are a policeman in this town. *(turns to student 1)* What do you think about the traffic?
S (= Student) 1: It is very bad.
R: Have you got many traffic problems here?
S 1: Yes, many.
R: And you are the headmistress of this school here. *(turning to student 2)* Could you tell us something about the school?
S 2: Ah ... it is a very good school.
R: How many pupils have you got?
S 2: 300.
R: And how many teachers?
S 2: 25.
R: Well, the school is very close to a traffic junction. Do your pupils know how to behave with all this traffic about.
S 2: Yes, they are very good pupils, and they know the traffic very well.
R: Thank you. *(turning to student 3)* You have been standing at these crossroads for quite some time. May I ask what you are doing here.
S 3: I am waiting for a friend.
R: For a boyfriend?
S 3: No, no, for a friend.
R: OK, well, *(turning to student 4)* here we've got the lorry driver. Excuse me, why are you stopping here – right in front of the zebra crossing.
S 4: I'm not from this town. I don't know my way. And people are crossing.
R: Don't you think it's dangerous to stop here?
S 4: No.
R: And now three girls are leaving the school-building. They are really in a hurry, and now they are crossing the street. Excuse me *(turning to students 5,6,7)*, why are you in such a hurry? ...

List of 20 roles

1. policeman/-woman 1
2. headmistress
3. person waiting for a friend at the crossrads, witness of the accident
4. lorry-driver
5. pupil crossing the street
6. pupil crossing the street (getting injured?)
7. pupil crossing the street and getting injured (or killed?)
8. teacher standing outside the school gate, witness of the accident
9. driver of the car
10. friend of injured pupil
11. friend of injured pupil
12. ambulance driver
13. doctor
14. nurse
15. policeman/-woman 2
16. father of the injured pupil
17. mother of the injured pupil
18. form teacher of the injured pupil
19. bank clerk, witness of the accident
20. lady who goes shopping and hasn't seen the accident

3. After having finished reporting, play your recordings to the students so that they can enjoy their production and listen to their improvised "radio play". You may take up some mistakes regarding pronunciation or sentence structure and discuss these with the students.

"Welsh Werewolf" – A Panel of Experts

Lernstufe: Upper Intermediate
Kontext: Horror, Wales, Human Interest Story, Simulation, freies Sprechen
Material: Text, Rollenkarten
Dauer: mindestens 1 Stunde, besser 2 und mehr

What to do

Pre-reading
1. Ask the students if they know what a werewolf is and if they know any story featuring a werewolf.

2. Write the following words on the blackboard and make sure the students know them. Brainstorm what connection they could have with werewolves.

words:
line 2: creature – think of German 'Kreatur'
line 6: violent – gewalttätig (violence)
line 9: stagecoach – Postkutsche
line 13: dusk – Sonnenuntergang
line 17: to tremble – zittern
line 18: dotted with – übersät mit
line 32: to spot – sehen

While-reading
3. Ask the students to read the first part of the text that deals with incidents in the 18th century. They should mime or act out the scene in which the farmer is attacked by the beast and hides in his house. Let them check the place-names (Denbigh, Wrexham, Ruthin) on a map of Wales.
4. Ask the students to read the second part of the story set at the end of the 20th century. Again, check the place-names (Wrexham, Mold).
5. Apparently the end of the story has been left open. Well, it is up to the students to make up an ending. What happened when Matthew saw the beast? They should write down their version and/or act it out in a role-play.

Post-reading
6. Ask the students if they think that these stories about werewolves or beasts are true? Discuss in class. (This may be a very brief step, if there is no disagreement among the students.)
7. A meeting of many people concerned with werewolves and strange beasts is held in the classroom. Hand out role-cards to the students and allow them to have some time to prepare their roles. If possible, all students should participate. (If there are more than 25 pupils in the class, add additional roles. The roles, of course, are meant to be funny, and the whole procedure shouldn't be taken too seriously, but should have an ironical, funny tone.)

The teacher acts as a journalist. He/she chairs the meeting or 'round of experts', asks questions, invites the participants to comment and tries to get a lively, controversial and amusing discussion going. Everybody present is asked about his experience with the 'beast', how they feel about it, and what has been seen and/or experienced. The students have to keep to the general outline as given in the text, but within their roles they can improvise, define their character along their own ideas, comment and get involved in arguments. The interviewer must ask provocative questions so that these terrible events really are invoked again. Funny and comic aspects should be emphasized, though.

8. If you would like to continue this activitiy, ask the students to write a eport about their encounters with werewolves – from the point of view of their characters.

List of role-cards:

1. Mr Miller, who was in the stagecoach in 1790
2. Mrs Miller, who also was in the stagecoach in 1790
3. Daisy Miller, 15 (in the stagecoach in 1790)
4. James Miller, 17 (in the stagecoach in 1790)
5. A coachhorse (in 1790) that managed to gallop away
6. The farmer of Ruthin
7. The farmer's friend who found the Ruthin farmer hiding in his house
8. The farmer's dog, killed by the beast
9. The wooden door (of the farmer of Ruthin)
10. The farmer in 1992, whose lambs were killed
11. Matthew, the schoolboy
12. Emma, Matthew's girlfriend
13. Ms Temple, Matthew's biology teacher
14. Ms Jones, a newspaper reporter from Wrexham
15. Mr Smith, a BBC reporter from London
16. Mr Baker, who believes that all these werewolf stories are nonsense
17. Ms Williams, a true Christian who believes that the beast is the devil
18. Mr Thomas, a policeman who wants to kill the beast
19. A lamb that is very much afraid of the beast
20. Dr Frankenstein, who wants to hunt down the beast
21. Mr King, a writer who wants to write about the werewolf
22. Mr Blair, the Prime Minister (or another famous British politician)
23. Prince Charles
24. Ms Merkel from Germany (or another famous German politician)

The Welsh Werewolf

As most horror film fans know, a werewolf is a person who changes into a wolf-like creature when the moon is full. A real werewolf, some people say, is a large wolf which has no tail and is usually quite long; often more than seven feet in length, and the animal usually hunts at night when the moon is full. But some of these strange creatures go on the prowl most nights – whether the moon is full or not – and they may even kill people. One of the most violent night creatures is known as the Welsh Werewolf.

The stories and legends about an enormous wolf-like animal in North Wales date back to 1790, when a stagecoach travelling between Denbigh and Wrexham was attacked and overturned by an enormous black beast almost as long as a horse. This terrible animal attacked one of the horses and killed it, while the other horses escaped and galloped off into the night. The attack took place just after dusk, with a full moon on the horizon.

In the winter of 1791 a farmer went into his snow-covered fields just seven miles east of Ruthin, and he saw enormous tracks that looked like those belonging to a huge wolf. He followed the tracks for two miles and they led to a scene of terrible violence which made the villagers in the area tremble with fear: One snow-covered field was a lake of blood dotted with dead sheep, cattle and even the farmer's dog. A huge beast, standing there and howling in the winter night, went for the farmer, but he managed to run into the farmhouse in time. He bolted the heavy wooden door and hid under a table in the kitchen. The farmer said the wolf threw itself against the heavy door, almost breaking it down. The animal then stood on two legs like a human being and looked in through the windows of the farmhouse. Its eyes were blue and seemed intelligent and almost human-like.

The farmer was found locked in his house in a terrible state. He wasn't injured, but he was terrified and for some months did not leave his home. The church organised patrols in search of this beast or werewolf, and bands of villagers tried to hunt down the animal, but only found its tracks.

The attacks by the large black wolf gradually stopped; but two centuries later they were reported again.

In February 1992 a newspaper wrote that a strange bear-like animal had been seen in Wales. In the north of the country, a farmer had spotted the animal on the night of a full moon and afterwards found that two of his lambs had been killed. The latest report was given by sixth-form pupil Matthew from Wrexham, who was working on a biology project at Alex's Pool near Mold, when he saw what he describes as a 'beast': It was black and had a tail about one metre long, and the body was even bigger. I heard something moving in the bushes and when I looked around, there it was ...

(www.bbc.co.uk/wales/northeast/guides/weird/mythsandlegends/pages/werewolf.shtml)

This Is Your Life

Lernstufe: Advanced
Kontext: freies Sprechen, Rollenspiel
Material: Role-cards
Dauer: 1–2 Stunden

What to do

1. Refer to the British TV show and explain to the students what's going to happen during the lesson: "We are going to role-play a TV show in which the life history of a person is presented to the audience. The VIP sits in the studio and is interviewed about his life and career by the host of the show. Suddenly and unexpectedly friends or relatives of this person turn up in the studio, telling anecdotes, remembering the 'old times'. In 'our' show some embarassing incidents and details in the VIP's life should be revealed." Each student is to take a role.
2. Distribute the role-cards, explain to the students that for their roles they have to make up more details themselves. Allow them five minutes to prepare.
3. Start the show. You (the teacher) act as the host and you start talking to the VIP about his life. One by one, friends and relatives are introduced who contribute incidents and events, likes and dislikes in the VIP's life. All the "guests" should first be made welcome by the host and the VIP (the actor John Harrison). But when they start revealing the truth about John's life, the situation gets embarrassing …

We feel that the fun in this activity might even be increased, if some female students take male roles and vice versa. Just distribute the role-cards – and see who is who. Don't let the students exchange the cards – because of reasons of gender.

If you wish to include more students, they can act as further members of the audience who should be allowed to ask questions, to comment, to appear on stage (e.g. because one of John's "friends" is an old pal of yours, too.)

Role-cards

1. You are John Harrison, a movie star: good-looking, arrogant, totally convinced of yourself. Born in 1957, you had quite a number of jobs before you made your way to Hollywood. First films about 1980, breakthrough with "The Hungry Lover" in 1984. You got an Oscar for best actor in 1987; you are married to Helen MacDevitt, an NBC newscaster.

2. You are Mrs Mountwell, John's mother. You have been married four times. You didn't really care about your son who was a notorious liar. You don't think much of him.

3. Mr Strong, John's headmaster. John was an ill-disciplined boy with hardly any academic merits. After beating up some classmates he was expelled from school.

4. Bob Fisher, John's classmate. You remember being beaten up by John over and over again. John was a bully; he even mugged you once to get two dollars.

5. Molly Brown (now about 65), John's beloved auntie, who seduced John when he was fifteen. "He was dashing and good-looking!" She owns a night-club.

6. Mr Ford, for whom John worked as a gardener after he left school. John was unreliable, tended to be late and was rather aggressive when he was told that his work attitude was bad. You sacked him after half a year.

7. Mary White, John's girlfriend, when they were eighteen. John left you after some months: he disappeared suddenly, although he knew you were pregnant. You look worn-out and appear to be older than you actually are (about 40).

8. Jean White, Mary's and John's daughter (about 20 years old). John didn't know you existed. On the one hand, you are quite intrigued by being the daughter of such a famous movie star; on the other hand, you've got one aim: to make money from this embarrassing situation. You are not really clever.

9. Jim Miller, Hollywood producer, who gave John his first minor role in a movie. You are a shrewd businessman. When being interviewed, you should at one point make it clear that you gave John the role, because you were blackmailed by him. John had seen you with a prostitute and he was going to talk to your wife ...

10. Alan Little, one of John's neighbours. You say you are a close friend of his, but apparently you hardly know him. You just wanted to get on the "show". In the course of the interview you should, involuntarily, reveal that you have earned (at least part of) your money by drug trafficking.

11. Helen Lively (25). You are a stupid starlet and had a minor role in a film with John. You are an ex-lover and still love him in a way.

12. Agatha March. You are in charge of managing John's household. He is chaotic and dirty. Without you John's everyday life would fall to pieces.
13. Barbara Dickson. You are a famous movie star and were John's partner in "The Hungry Lover". You remember John needing a "hell of a lot" of coaching to master his role. Many scenes had to be shot over and over again, because John didn't act in the way he was supposed to. Sometimes he turned up drunk in the studio. As for the love scenes, they were a nightmare for you. You despise John and you never were nor would be in a film with him again.
14. Dr. Lewinson, John's psychoanalyst. You see John as a victim of his "fatherless" youth. He was unloved, lonely. He never managed to mature. But you keep defending John and apologizing for his misconduct. (Well, you are paid by him.) You should not forget to mention that John has got problems with alcohol.
15. Helen MacDevitt, John's wife, an NBC newscaster and a "career woman". You only married John to gain popularity: "It was positive – for my career." You talk about your married life with John. He is selfish, unreliable, like a child ... Half a year ago you moved out of your common house. In the end of the interview you tell John (and the audience) that you are suing him for divorce.
16. Tony Spencer, a member of the audience. When Alan Little is interviewed, you recognize him: He used to be a drug dealer. You make this known to the host of the show and to the audience.

© Cornelsen Verlag Scriptor, Berlin • Fundgrube Englisch handlungsorientiert

Bemerkung
Diese Aktivität lehnt sich an die britische Fernsehsendung „This is your life" an. Ein Prominenter wird im Studio vorgestellt, und nach und nach tauchen dort (überraschend) Freunde und Bekannte auf, die den Lebensweg dieser Person begleitet haben. So wird im Fernsehen mosaikartig und meist äußerst schönfärberisch die Vita nachgestellt. Im Unterrichtsraum hingegen sollen eher Peinlichkeiten und „Fettnäpfchen" im Vordergrund stehen.

The Case of Little Red Ridinghood

Lernstufe: Advanced
Kontext: freies Sprechen, debattieren, argumentieren, simulating a court-case
Material: Role-cards, evtl. Liste mit Wortschatz zur Rechtsprechung
Dauer: 1–2 Stunden

What to do

1. Tell the students that they are going to be involved in a court-case. If necessary, make them familiar with the vocabulary needed to understand the court proceedings and to take up their roles at court. (List of words: see page 63.)
2. Hand out the role-cards – either arbitrarily or according to the students' ability. Allow the students some preparation time to get acquainted with their roles. Arrange the seating plan: the accused must sit next to his lawyer, the prosecutor must face them, the jury box is facing the judge, the witness box is on the right and Mrs and Miss Wolf, of course, should sit together (and so do Grandmother and Little Red Ridinghood), the policeman has to stand in the back so that he can observe the scene etc.
3. We advise the teacher to act as judge in order to organize and structure the court proceedings. At the beginning the judge (= the teacher) should give an outline of the case and explain the different views. In the "case" of Little Red Ridinghood the judge ought to tell the fairy tale, emphasizing the fact that the wolf (Mr Wolf) was killed by the hunter. The hunter (Mr Hunter) is accused of killing Mr Wolf. He has to defend himself.
4. The prosecutor and the barrister are given the opportunity to state their views in opening statements.
5. Witnesses (Little Red Ridinghood, the grandmother, Mrs and Miss Wolf, some woodcutters, the police inspector, the doctor etc.) are interrogated. The knife should be interrogated, too.
6. The defendant (the hunter) may state his point of view.
7. At any time members of the jury may ask questions.
8. The prosecutor and the barrister sum up their opinion and plead guilty or not guilty.
9. The jury decides upon the case.
10. The judge gives his judgement and passes the sentence (or releases the accused hunter).
11. A reporter interviews the people involved in the case.
12. If you want to continue the trial, make the students write down their reports (as witnesses) or the summing up of the case (by the prosecutor or the barrister) or the last statement of the accused or a newspaper report (for a serious paper or for the tabloid press) about the case.

Bemerkung

Eine Gerichtsverhandlung als Rollenspiel bzw. Simulation kann stets dann erfolgreich und motivierend als Sprechanlass eingesetzt werden, wenn alle Schüler mit dem Fall vertraut sind. Entweder handelt es sich um eine bekannte Handlung wie etwa ein Märchen (im vorliegenden Fall um „Rotkäppchen"), oder aber *„the case"* wurde vorher (in einem Text) behandelt (z.B. Tankerunglück, Verkehrsunfall usw.) oder die Gerichtsverhandlung erfolgt nach der Behandlung einer Lektüre, bei der es um eine Schuldfrage geht, z.B.: *Ballad of the Sad Cafe, Of Mice and Men, Lord of the Flies, The Great Gatsby, An Inspector Calls.*

Der „Fall" sollte kontrovers sein, damit gegensätzliche Meinungen auftreten und formuliert werden. Grundlegendes Vokabular zum Gerichtsverfahren sollte eingeführt sein (siehe unten). Übertreibungen, Humor, absurde Einlagen und Sequenzen usw. sind bei der Gerichtsverhandlung durchaus angebracht. Vor Gericht darf gelacht werden. Ein Tier, ein Werkzeug, ein Gebäude usw. kann z.B. als Zeuge aussagen.

Vom Richter/Richterin muss die Verhandlung straff, evtl. gar autoritär geführt werden. Alle Beteiligten sollen gehört werden (d.h. alle Schüler müssen aktiv teilnehmen).

Role-Cards deuten die Rolle oder die Charakterisierung der Rolle nur an. Die Rolle muss von dem betreffenden Schüler individuell ausgefüllt werden.

List of characters

1. Judge = Teacher
2. Little Red Ridinghood
3. Grandmother
4. Mr Hunter, the accused
5. Mrs Hunter
6. Mrs Wolf
7. Miss Wolf, 18 years old
8. Public Prosecutor
9. Barrister
10. Police Inspector
11. The Knife
12. Doctor
13. Wood Cutter 1 (He's a friend of Mr Wolf.)
14. Wood Cutter 2 (He doesn't like Mr Wolf, because Mr Wolf hit him once when they were quarrelling in a pub.)
15. Policeman (He has to keep order in the courtroom.)
16. Reporter (He represents a tabloid paper. He is trying to interrupt the case by asking provocative questions. After the trial he's going to interview the participants ...)
17. (and more) Members of the Jury (They may ask questions at any time ...)

Role-cards

Little Red Ridinghood

GRANDMOTHER: You know the fairy-tale. You do and state everything in order to get a NOT GUILTY for Mr Hunter: He has saved your life and you are very grateful to him.

MR HUNTER: You are the acccused. You have killed Mr Wolf. You claim that, of course, it was an act of self-defence. Only by killing him could you save Little Red Ridinghood and Grandmother.

MRS HUNTER: Of course, you are terribly shocked that your brave and honest husband is accused of killing Mr Wolf. You love your husband dearly.

MRS WOLF: You are really shocked by the death of your husband who was killed by Mr Hunter. You are VERY emotional, and you tend to shout, so sob, to insult Mr and Mrs Hunter.

MISS WOLF: You are shocked at your father's death. But you left home one year ago, since you couldn't stand your father's brutality any longer.

PUBLIC PROSECUTOR: You must prove that Mr Hunter is guilty of killing Mr Wolf.

BARRISTER: You must defend Mr Hunter so that he will leave this court as a "free man". For you, of course, it is obvious that Mr Hunter acted in self-defence. He saved the lives of both Little Red Ridinghood and Grandmother. You know that Mr Wolf was a VERY bad man.

POLICE INSPECTOR: You inspected the whole case and carried out the investigation. You were called to grandmother's house after Mr Wolf's death.

POLICEMAN: You are responsible for law and order in the court-room. You have to guard the accused, Mr Hunter.

DOCTOR: You were called to save Mr Wolf's life after his belly had been cut open by Mr Hunter. You saw the scene in Grandmother's house.

WOODCUTTER 1: You were/are a friend of Mr Wolf's. You saw Little Red Ridinghood talking to Mr Wolf. You believe that she tried to seduce him. Eating her was the only way for Mr Wolf to get away from her.

MEMBER OF THE JURY: You must decide whether Mr Hunter is guilty or not guilty (of killing Mr Wolf). You may ask the witnesses any questions you like.

THE KNIFE: Mr Hunter used you to cut open Mr Wolf's belly. You are the tool that killed Mr Wolf. You are shocked, since before you had only cut bread or cheese.

The Case of Little Red Ridinghood

Vocabulary

- law, law and order
- legal, illegal
- to observe laws, to observe rules (befolgen, einhalten)
- a violation of a law
- to commit a crime (ein Verbrechen begehen)
- permission
- justice
- court, to appear in court
- judge
- judgement
- sentence (Strafe, Urteilsspruch)
- life sentence (lebenslängliche Freiheitsstrafe)
- to sentence (verurteilen)
- public prosecutor
- prosecution
- witness for the prosecution
- lawyer, solicitor, barrister
- trial, to try (vor Gericht stellen; verhandeln)
- to stand trial
- to examine, to crossexamine, to interrogate (verhören)
- jury, to sit on the jury
- defence, to defend
- client
- to accuse, to accuse sb of murder
- the accused (der Angeklagte)
- charge (Anklage, Tatverdacht)
- a charge of murder, to be charged with murder

- guilt
- guilty (of a crime), not guilty, innocent
- fine (Geldstrafe)
- to fine (mit einer Geldstrafe belegen)
- to punish
- to convict (verurteilen)
- verdict (Urteilsspruch)
- to clear (freisprechen), to be cleared of a charge
- prison, jail
- evidence (Beweismaterial; beweiskräftige Aussage)
- to give evidence in court (vor Gericht aussagen)
- witness
- witness-box (Zeugenstand)
- to testify against/in favour of sb (gegen/für jdn. aussagen)
- proof
- to deny
- to confess, confession
- to protest one's innocence (seine Unschuld beteuern)
- self-defence (Notwehr)
- to act in self-defence
- "Objection, your honour!" (Einspruch, Euer Ehren)
- Objection overruled/sustained (Einspruch abgelehnt/Dem Einspruch wird stattgegeben.)

Schooltown

Lernstufe: Beginners and Advanced
Kontext: freies Sprechen, nach dem Weg fragen, „Simulation"
Material: von den Schülern gemalte Straßen- und Hinweisschilder, von den Oberstufenschülern entworfene Rollenkarten (Karteikarten) in großer Anzahl (mindestens 5 pro Teilnehmer), „rote Karten", evtl. Kamera und/oder Aufnahmegerät mit Mikrofon
Dauer: Vorbereitung für die Mittel- bzw. Unterstufenklasse: 1/2 Stunde Vorbereitung für die Oberstufengruppe: 2 Stunden, für die Durchführung: 1 Stunde

What to do

1. **Preparation of the beginners' class:**
   Ask the students to draw the following signposts (without telling them what the signs will be used for): *High Street, Fulford Road, London Road, Oxford Street* (and some further street-names, if needed); *castle, The Hungry Lion Restaurant, station, hospital, bookshop, greengrocer, school, cinema, museum, bank, post-office, supermarket* (and any further buildings or institutions that you want to have in Schooltown).

2. **Preparation of the A-level students:**
   a) Tell them what you are intending to do. "I want you to create, to produce, to present an English-speaking town for class 5/6/7, and for one lesson we are going to make this town come alive. You will be the citizens living and working in the town, a doctor, a post-office clerk, a policeman, a teacher, the station master, somebody working in the museum or in the cinema. The younger pupils will be asked e.g. to go to the station and enquire about the departure times of trains; then the station master will have to tell them. Or a young boy breaks his leg, and he is taken to the hospital, and there we will need a nurse or a doctor. Or somebody just happens to know the price of apples at the grocer's.

   You will have to be present in Schooltown and answer the questions of the "young" pupils and help them whenever they are faced with problems. But the "young" pupils don't really know what they are going to do in Schooltown. Thus they need role-cards, cards that tell them what to do. The cards will send them from one place to another . If they are in the museum they might enquire about Robin Hood or you can ask them questions, too, which they have to answer. When the conversation is over, you give them another role-card and they must go somewhere else. (*Examples of role-cards are given below.*) It is now your job to write these role-cards."

b) The students must be informed about the buildings and institutions that exist in Schooltown (see above). They write the rolecards – individually, in pairs or in small groups. They should find lots of activities for the "young" pupils, tell them where to go and what to do. Of course, some of the activities should be funny or even "naughty". Ask the students to correct each other's English and don't forget to tell them to keep their handwriting up to a certain standard of legibility.

c) Discuss with the students who is going to take on which role. The teacher should know which roles are needed, but, of course, the group might have further ideas: doctor, bookseller, bank clerk, guard in the museum etc. In Schooltown these citizens will stay in their buildings/shops/institutions and wait for "customers". It is advisable to have some common people, too, who happen to be passing by or be walking along a street and try to start some conversation with the "younger" pupils/inhabitants of the town. You may also introduce a person who continuously keeps asking other people what time it is. In order to preserve law and order, at least two police officers are needed. They show a "red card" whenever the pupils use German. A photographer and a reporter are present. They should take "real" photos and make "real" interviews, thus creating a "real" atmosphere. Make sure that the A-level students are not simply asked to carry out your instructions: They should be co-organizers whose ideas and comments ought to be taken up.

d) Since for some A-level students the presentation of "Schooltown" still is a rather vague idea, some situations that may appear can be role-played. Take some role-cards and make the students act out the situation given on the card.

You should also make the students aware of the fact that the "younger" pupils' command of English might not be very good. Thus the A-level

students should not use difficult constructions, they should keep to simple words and phrases. This, by the way, is a good practice for intercultural communication. Often when meeting foreign people English is used as lingua franca, but often the language must be kept simple in order to achieve some successful communication.
3. **Presentation of Schooltown:**
   a) Prepare the room (together with the A-level students). Streets must be formed, it must be arranged where to locate the various buildings and shops. Put the signposts up and put the students into their positions and distribute the role-cards among them.

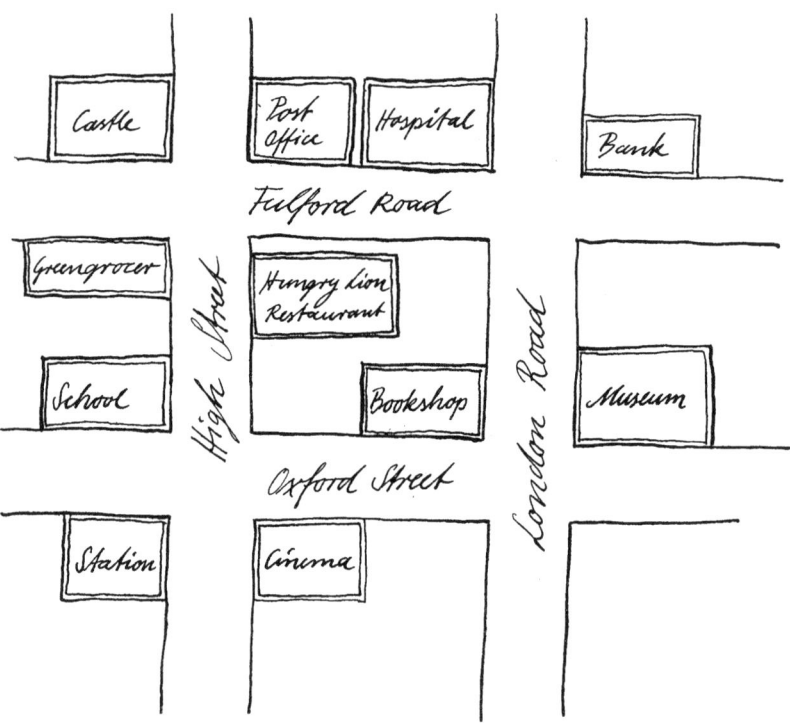

b) Now let the "younger" pupils enter the room and explain to them what they have to do (see above). Inform them about the fact that they must not speak German – or they will be punished by the police. Hand out the first role-cards, and get the pupils going.

If you would like some kind of competition, you may tell them that in the end both the role-cards that have been handed in at various institutions and the "red cards" will be counted: The class is the winner when they have collected more role-cards than "red cards".

c) While "Schooltown" is in progress, it is the teacher's task to coordinate everything. Pupils who don't know what to do, how to communicate etc. are to be encouraged. If there are not enough role-cards, cards must be collected from the various "citizens" and institutions and handed out again to the "pupils".

We hope that by producing this kind of language activity the illusion of an English-speaking town can be maintained for a whole lesson.

Bemerkung

Für diese Simulation eines englischsprachigen Städtchens empfiehlt sich eine Zusammenarbeit zwischen dem Lehrer einer 5./6./7. Klasse und dem Leiter eines Oberstufenkurses. Eine „Personalunion" ist natürlich auch möglich. Insgesamt ist es vorteilhaft, wenn die eigentliche Durchführung von „Schooltown" in einem größeren Raum (Aula?) stattfindet.

Suggested role-cards

1. Go to the school. On your way ask three people what they are doing in Schooltown. When you are at school, talk to the teacher. Find out when school starts in the morning and when school is over. Which subjects are taught at school? Do the pupils wear school uniforms? How many pupils are there and how many teachers?
2. There is a reporter in town. Find him. Ask him what he is doing and why he is doing it. Does he work for a newspaper or for a radio station? What is his name? How old is he? Where is he from? Find out many details about him and his job. Then talk to some friends and tell them about the reporter.
3. Go to the Museum and tell the people there what you know about Robin Hood.
4. You have broken your leg. Shout for help. Tell the people about your problem. They must help you to get to the hospital. At the hospital talk to the doctor. We hope that he will help you.
5. Go to the restaurant and talk to the waitress there. What can you eat there? What can you drink there? How much are the drinks? Does the waitress like her job? When does she start work? How many hours does she work?
6. You are a bad boy/girl. Whenever you meet another boy or girl, you shout at him or her: "You are stupid! You are nuts! You are an idiot!" Go to the post-office and tell the people there that they are stupid, too.
7. You want to travel to London. Go to the station and ask about the times when trains leave for London. How long does it take to get to London? When you are back from London, you must tell one of your friends about this trip. What did you see/visit in London? What did you buy? Did you like it there?
8. You have a very bad cold. Go to the museum and ask for help there. If they cannot help you, go to the hospital and tell the doctor about your cold.
9. Walk up and down all the streets and count how many people you meet. Tell the number to the teacher at the school. When you are at school, ask the teacher about the town: How many people live here? Which sights can you visit?
10. Find the restaurant and walk up to the waiter and tell him that the food and the drinks are terrible and far too expensive ... (It's a lousy place!)
11. You are very nervous, because you must catch a train. Therefore you ask everyone you meet for the way to the station. When you finally get to the station, you are, of course, late. Your train has left. You are terribly upset, you shout at the station master ...
12. You are a little boy/girl. You have lost your parents. Where are they? You are trying to find them. Of course, you keep crying, sobbing, tears are running down your face ... Maybe the people in the supermarket can help you.

© Cornelsen Verlag Scriptor, Berlin • Fundgrube Englisch handlungsorientiert

Schooltown

13. Ask the reporter what he thinks about football and find out where you can buy his newspaper.
14. Go to the bank and ask the clerk what she was doing during her holidays. Try to steal some money from the bank. But mind, you might get caught by the police.
15. Somebody has fallen down in the street. Has he had an accident? Go and call the policemen and the doctor to help this person.
16. Go to the bookshop and ask the bookseller for some good books.
17. Ask for the way to the supermarket. Buy some food there to prepare a meal for five friends. You must also buy some drinks.
18. Go to the school and tell your teacher why you can't come to school today.
19. Yesterday you left your bag behind in the restaurant. Go there and ask if the bag is still there. You must describe your bag and its contents.
20. You are a very bad person. Shoot down the photographer and try to take her camera. Watch out for police!

© Cornelsen Verlag Scriptor, Berlin • Fundgrube Englisch handlungsorientiert

Possible Roles to be taken over by A-level students

1. Teacher at school
2. Reporter
3. Photographer
4. Warden in Museum
5. Doctor at Hospital
6. Waitress at Restaurant
7. Shop assistant at supermarket
8. Official at station
9. Post-office clerk
10. Person who keeps asking what time it is
11. Two police officers
12. Passer-by
13. Bank clerk
14. Greengrocer
15. Friendly tourist
16. Erratic tourist (he insults everybody)
17. Bookseller
18. Newspaperseller
19. Ticketseller in Schooltown's ticket-agency
20. Roadsweeper

5 Dabbling in Poetry

Put It in a Picture

Lernstufe: Lower Intermediate
Kontext: Leseverstehen, topic: nursery rhymes and poems for children
Material: Texte, Buntstifte, Papier
Dauer: 1 Stunde

What to do
1. Ask your students which children's rhymes they can remember, let them recite some. Do they know any in English?
2. Hand out copies of the three nursery rhymes. Let the students work on them on their own using a dictionary or talking to the other students until they feel they know what all three texts are about.
3. Let them choose one of the texts and illustrate it.
4. Ask them to hang their drawing up along the wall.

Bemerkung
Nursery rhymes are verses for singing or reciting with young children. Like fairy tales, nursery rhymes have been passed down by word of mouth since the Middle Ages. The most famous collection is "Mother Goose's Melody" (1780 or earlier).

A Little Squirrel
I saw a little squirrel,
Sitting in a tree;
He was eating a nut
And wouldn't look at me.
Anon.

Hey Diddle Diddle,
Hey diddle diddle,
The cat and the fiddle,
The cow jumped over the moon.
The little dog laughed
To see such fun,
And the dish ran away with the spoon.

I Had a Little Nut Tree,
Nothing would it bear
But a silver nutmeg
And a golden pear;
The King of Spain's daughter
Came to visit me,
And all because of
My little nut tree.

Edward Lear
"The Owl and the Pussy-Cat"

Lernstufe: Lower Intermediate
Kontext: Gedichte lesen, kreatives Schreiben, szenisches Spiel
Material: Overheadfolie (Bild/Lückentext), Overheadstifte, Overheadprojektor, Gedichttext, Anleitung zum szenischen Spiel, Wörterbücher
Dauer: ab 3 Stunden

Edward Lear (1812–1888)
Edward Lear was born in London as the youngest of 20 children. At the age of 15, he had to start earning his living, and he got a job drawing parrots in the zoo. He was such an excellent artist that he was soon engaged as a house-artist by the Earl of Derby. Later he gave drawing lessons to Queen Victoria. He used to write nonsense poems for the Earl of Derby's grandchildren and illustrated them himself with nonsense drawings. These were so popular that he put them together in "A Book of Nonsense". This was followed by many more books which included longer poems such as "The Owl and the Pussy-Cat", "The Pobble who had no Toes" and "The Jumblies", as well as countless limericks, whose popularity is largely due to Lear. He was also a writer of travel books and a gifted landscape artist.

What to do

1. Your students take a close look at the following picture (transparency) and make suggestions as to • who these two are • where they are • why they are there • what they have got with them • where they want to go • why they want to go there

The Owl and the Pussy-Cat went _____
in _____,
They took _____,
wrapped up _____.
The owl looked up _____,
and sang _____,
"O lovely Pussy, o Pussy my love,
what a beautiful Pussy you are!"
Pussy said to the Owl, "You _____!
How _____!
O let us _____,
but _____?"
They sailed away _____
to the _____,
and there in _____,
with a ring at the end of his nose,
with a ring at the end of his nose.
"Dear Pig, _____
_____?" Said the Piggy, "I will."
So took it _____
by the Turkey _____.
They dined _____,
which they ate _____;
and hand in hand, _____,
they danced by the light of the moon,
they danced by the light of the moon.

E. Lear "The Owl and the Pussy-Cat"　　　　　　　　　　　　　　　　73

2. Make a transparency of the fragmentary text on page 72 (one for every three students). 3 or 4 students get one transparency and an overhead pen. They complete the text as they find most interesting.
3. Have your students present their texts, using their transparencies.
4. Now hand out the original poem and read it aloud to them.
5. Ask them to present "Play your part" (see page 74). Give them the instructions how to do it.

The Owl and the Pussy-Cat went to sea

In a beautiful pea-green boat,
They took some honey, and plenty of money,
Wrapped up in a five-pound note.
The Owl looked up to the stars above,
And sang to a small guitar,
'O lovely Pussy! O Pussy, my love,
What a beautiful Pussy you are,
You are,
You are!
What a beautiful Pussy you are!'

Pussy said to the Owl, 'You elegant fowl!
How charmingly sweet you sing!
O let us be married! too long we have tarried:
But what shall we do for a ring?'
They sailed away, for a year and a day,
To the land where the Bong-Tree grows,
And there in a wood a Piggy-wig stood,
With a ring at the end of his nose,
His nose,
His nose,
With a ring at the end of his nose.

'Dear Pig, are you willing to sell for one shilling
Your ring?' Said the Piggy, 'I will.'
So they took it away, and were married next day
By the Turkey who lives on the hill.
They dined on mince, and slices of quince,
Which they ate with a runcible spoon;
And hand in hand, on the edge of the sand,
They danced by the light of the moon,
The moon,
The moon,
They danced by the light of the moon.　　　　　　　　*Edward Lear, 1871*

© Cornelsen Verlag Scriptor, Berlin • Fundgrube Englisch handlungsorientiert

Play your Part!

Read the text, make sure you understand all the words or phrases. Then produce a script for the group. But be careful – you must follow these 3 instructions!
- No changes in the text are allowed. The text remains authentic all the way.
- **Either:**
  There is a narrator, who reads the whole text. The other characters mime their roles. The narrator must leave them time to do this.
  Or:
  There is a narrator who reads the text, leaving out the parts in direct speech, which are spoken by the characters themselves.
- It is up to you to make your own stage-props.
  Or:
  One narrator speaks the parts that have to do with the "whole" story, 2 other narrators speak the parts concerning the owl or the pussycat, and 2 others speak the parts of the owl and the pussycat.

© Cornelsen Verlag Scriptor, Berlin • Fundgrube Englisch handlungsorientiert

Beispieltext
(wurde von Schülerinnen ausgefüllt)

The Owl and the Pussy-Cat went __to America__
in __a little boat,__
They took __some honey, a guitar and clothes__
wrapped up __in some old newspapers__
The owl looked up __and saw very grey clouds__
and sang __a love song__
"O lovely Pussy, o Pussy my love,
what a beautiful Pussy you are!"

Pussy said to the Owl, "You __can sing very well__!
How __did you get this voice__!
O let us __sing together__,
but __not too loud . O.K.__?"
They sailed away __in the little boat__
to the __land of their dreams__
and there in __a big house (where) a pig lived__,
with a ring at the end of his nose,
with a ring at the end of his nose.

"Dear Pig, __will you let us stay for a night in your house__?" Said the Piggy, "I will."
So they took it __to a meal cooked__
by the Turkey __in America__
They dined __in a big dining-room__
which they ate __Turkey with potatoes__
and hand in hand, __they danced around the table__
they danced by the light of the moon,
they danced by the light of the moon.

"The Rainbow Fairies"

Lernstufe: Intermediate
Kontext: kreatives Schreiben, darstellendes Spiel
Material: Gedicht "The Rainbow Fairies", Buntstifte, bunte Tücher, eine Schnur
Dauer: 2 Stunden

What to do

1. Draw this on the board:

2. Ask your pupils to think about a rainbow and to tell you
   – words that **describe** a rainbow   – other words you can use to **talk about** rainbows
3. Make 2 lists like this on the board. These are merely suggestions of words pupils might offer:
   – bright, green   – drops of water, shower, sun
4. Tell your pupils they are going to read a poem about a rainbow. It begins like this:
   "Two little clouds, one summer's day …"
   What do they think happens? They should draw a picture or write a little text beginning with the line "Two little clouds …"
   Some words on the board taken from the poem can help them.
5. After they have read out their poems or hung them up with the drawings, hand out the original poem and read it aloud to them.
6. Ask them to mime it. Get them to stretch a string between 2 chairs and hang coloured scarves over it, as a "stage-prop". Perhaps they have got some more ideas of their own.
7. Now ask them to write a story or a poem about some other weather "speciality", e.g. a flash of lightning, a thunderclap, snow, etc.

> **The Rainbow Fairies**
>
> Two little clouds, one summer's day,
> Went flying through the sky;
> They went so fast they bumped their heads,
> And both began to cry.
>
> Old Father Sun looked out and said:
> 'Oh, never mind, my dears,
> I'll send my little fairy folk
> To dry your falling tears.'
>
> One fairy came in violet,
> And one wore indigo;
> In blue, green, yellow, orange, red,
> They made a pretty row.
>
> They wiped the cloud-tears all away,
> And then from out the sky,
> Upon a line the sunbeams made,
> They hung their gowns to dry.
>
> *Anon.*

© Cornelsen Verlag Scriptor, Berlin • Fundgrube Englisch handlungsorientiert

Relativity

Lernstufe: Intermediate
Kontext: talking about perception; creative writing
Material: Kopien des Lückentexts mit den jumbled words, Wörterbücher
Dauer: 1–2 Stunden

What to do

1. Bring an ant into the class. Show it to the children asking them what they believe the ant can see.
2. Put it on your desk between books and duster and sponge and pieces of chalk etc. and ask the children what they believe all these items look like to the ant. (Set the poor insect free immediately afterwards!) Ask

them about small pets they have and about what they believe their family and their rooms look like to the pets. Ask them about the time when they were very small themselves.
3. Distribute the copies with the gap-poem "The Fly" and the jumbled letters to each pupil and tell them to fill in the blanks. Ask one pupil to read the complete poem aloud, check with the class whether the gaps have been filled correctly and let the students exchange their views of the poem. Finally let one of them read the poem again.
4. Ask them to add one more stanza to Walter de la Mare's (1873–1956) poem. They may work in partner teams or individually, as they wish.
5. Ask them to write a poem in a similar vein, but with a reversal of size, i.e. with something big observing the world. The pupils can work individually in class or at home; give them the choice between writing two or three stanzas; or they can team up in groups of three, each pupil producing one stanza individually and then joining it with two others in

---

The Fly

How large unto the _____ fly

Must little things appear! –

A rosebud like a _____ bed,

Its _____ like a spear;

A dewdrop like a _____ -glass,

A hair like _____ wire;

The smallest grain of mustard-seed

As fierce as coals of _____ ;

A loaf of _____ , a lofty hill;

A wasp, a cruel leopard;

And specks of salt as bright to see

As lambskins to a _____ .

Walter de la Mare, 1945

Unjumble the following words and fill them in the gaps of the poem:

h – r – e – e – t – a – f
e – i – r – f
r – d – b – a – e
e – e – p – h – h – d – r – s
k – l – r – i – c – p – e
i – o – g – k – o – n – l
n – t – y – i
e – l – d – g – o – n

a convincing manner. Or they can work in groups, collecting comparisons (like: "a hair like golden wire") and jotting them down at first, then fitting them into a poem.
6. Tell them that illustrations are welcome. Have all the poems fastened along the wall and let everybody read them. Collect them in a folder and add it to the class library.

Bemerkung

In dieser Einheit geht es darum, sich aktiv mit der Relativität von Perspektive, Größe und Wahrnehmung zu beschäftigen, indem die alltägliche Wahrnehmung von Menschen mit anderen Blickwinkeln und Formen der optischen Wahrnehmung konfrontiert wird.

Imitating Jabberwocky

Lernstufe: Advanced
Kontext: kreatives Schreiben; readers' theatre; exploring genre: the ballad
Material: Kopien von Lewis Carrolls "Jabberwocky" (z.T. komplett, z.T. nur die ersten drei Strophen); Kopien von je einem Drittel von "The Daemon Lover" für je ein Drittel der Klasse; keine Wörterbücher während der Arbeit mit "Jabberwocky"; Wörterbücher für "The Daemon Lover"; ggf. eine Videokamera zur Aufnahme der (szenischen) Lesungen.
Dauer: 2–3 Doppelstunden

Lewis Carroll (1832–1898)
Lewis Carroll is the pseudonym of Charles Lutwidge Dodgson, a lecturer in mathematics in Oxford and competent photographer who became famous for "Alice's Adventures in Wonderland" (1865), a book based on an impromptu story that he had told a friend's daughters on a boat trip. Among his other works are "Through the Looking-Glass and What Alice found there" (1871). The lasting success of his books is attributed to the fact that he did not attempt to teach his young readers anything.

What to do

1. Tell the class about Lewis Carroll.
2. Describe the three different tasks to work on (see below) and ask the students to decide which group they would like to join: A: the translators, B: the poets, or C: the theatre company.
3. Give the members of group A and C a copy of the poem each (see page 81). The members of group B only get the first three stanzas. Make sure the groups are out of earshot of each other.

Group A

- Read through the text on your own.
- Then take turns reading a stanza aloud so as to get the feeling of the poem.
- Translate the poem into intelligible English, but keep the ballad form.

Group B

- These are the first three stanzas of a poem of seven stanzas; read them carefully on your own.
- Now take turns reading a stanza aloud each so that you get into the rhythm and tone of the poem.
- Then complete the ballad by adding four more stanzas in the same vein.

Group C

- Read through the text carefully.
- Take turns reading it several times aloud and develop ideas for a dramatic reading of the poem on stage (readers' theatre).
- Discuss ways of staging the poem.
- Prepare a performance for your classmates.

4. Ask the groups to present the results of their work and film the performance (group C) if possible.
5. Announce that the class will work on a different ballad and distribute copies of the first, second and third group of stanzas of "The Daemon Lover" (see page 82) to group A, B and C respectively. Leave out the title and the last stanza.

6. Give each group the same task:

- Read through your part of the ballad carefully.
- Try to find out what happens in the parts of the poem that you do not know.
- Write the complete story (including what you believe to be the contents of the parts of the ballad unknown to you) in prose as a modern story.
- Now "jabberwocky" your part, i. e. replace some words or parts with nonsense words.
- Prepare a dramatic reading of your "jabberwockied" part in which all members of your group participate.

7. Ask the class to get together in a circle and to do their Jabberwocky reading in the order of the original poem and read the last stanza of the poem yourself. Arrange to videotape, if possible.
8. Let each group read their prose version to the plenary.
9. Collect all the products of this teaching unit and the two original poems in a folder.

Bemerkung

Die Anregung zu dem Unterrichtsvorschlag stammt aus einem literaturdidaktischen Seminar, in dem Studierende simulierend Unterricht mit Jabber*wocky* ausprobierten und sehr fantasievolle und witzige Bearbeitungen hervorbrachten. So wählte z. B. die Gruppe, die *Jabberwocky* in Szene setzen sollte, die Form eines Handpuppenspiels mit einer Nagelfeile als *vorpal sword* und einem Taschenregenschirm als *Tumtum tree*, an dem sinnend Jabberwocky als eine behandschuhte Hand lehnte.

Jabberwocky

'Twas brillig, and the slithy toves
Did gyre and gimble in the wabe;
All mimsy were the borogoves,
And the mome raths outgrabe.

"Beware the Jabberwock, my son!
The jaws that bite, the claws that catch!
Beware the Jubjub bird, and shun
The frumious Bandersnatch!"

He took his vorpal sword in hand;
Long time the manxome foe he sought –
So rested he by the Tumtum tree,
And stood awhile in thought.

And, as in uffish thought he stood,
The Jabberwock, with eyes of flame,
Came whiffling through the tulgey wood,
And burbled as it came!

One, two! One, two! And through and through
The vorpal blade went snicker-snack!
He left it dead, and with its head
He went galumphing back.

"And hast thou slain the Jabberwock?
Come to my arms, my beamish boy!
O frabjous day! Callooh! Callay!"
He chortled in his joy.

'Twas brillig, and the slithy toves
Did gyre and gimble in the wabe;
All mimsy were the borogoves,
And the mome raths outgrabe.

Lewis Carroll, 1871

The Daemon Lover

'O where have you been, my long, long love,
　This long seven years and more?'
'O I'm come to seek my former vows
　Ye granted me before.'

'O hold your tongue of your former vows,
　For they will breed sad strife;
O hold your tongue of your former vows,
　For I am become a wife.'

He turned him right and round about,
　And the tear blinded his ee:
'I wad never hae trodden on Irish ground,
　If it had not been for thee.'

'I might hae had a king's daughter,
　Far, far beyond the sea;
I might have had a king's daughter,
　Had it not been for love o thee.'

'If ye might have had a king's daughter,
　Yersel ye had to blame;
Ye might have taken the king's daughter,
　For ye kend that I was nane.'

*　*　*

'If I was to leave my husband dear,
　And my two babes also,
O what have you to take me to,
　If with you I should go?'

'I hae seven ships upon the sea –
　The eighth brought me to land –
With four-and-twenty bold mariners,
　And music on every hand.'

She has taken up her two little babes,
　Kissd them baith cheek and chin:
'O fair ye weel, my ain two babes,
　For I'll never see you again.'

She set her foot upon the ship,
　No mariners could she behold;
But the sails were o' the taffetie,
　And the masts o' the beaten gold.

She had not sailed a league, a league,
　A league but barely three,
When dismal grew his countenance,
　And drumlie grew his ee.

*　*　*

They had not sailed a league, a league,
　A league but barely three,
Until she espied his cloven foot,
　And she wept right bitterlie.

'O hold your tongue of your weeping,' says he,
　'Of your weeping now let me be;
I will shew you how the lilies grow
　On the banks of Italy.'

'O what hills are yon, yon pleasant hills,
　That the sun shines sweetly on?'
'O yon are the hills of heaven,' he said,
　'Where you will never win.'

'O whaten a mountain is yon,' she said,
　'All so dreary wi frost and snow?'
'O yon is the mountain of hell,' he cried,
　'Where you and I will go.'

*　*　*

He strack the tap-mast wi his hand,
　The fore'mast wi his knee,
And he brake that gallant ship in twain,
　And sank her in the sea.

　　　　　　　　　　　　Anon.

Christopher Marlowe
"The Passionate Shepherd to His Love"

Lernstufe: Upper Intermediate/Advanced
Kontext: Gedichte lesen, kreatives Schreiben, Interpretieren (Wandlung von Sprache, Werten, Kultur); topics: love, values
Material: viele Bilder aus Zeitschriften, die geeignet sind, Gefühle und Leidenschaft zu illustrieren, z.b. Fußballspiele, Schmuck, Autos, küssende Menschen, Farben, Musik, Hobbys, Bücher etc., Overheadfolie für Aufgabe 2, Overheadprojektor, Gedichttext
Dauer: 3–4 Stunden

Christopher Marlowe (1564–1593)
Marlowe, son of a shoemaker, was academically so brilliant that he was awarded a scholarship to study at Cambridge. He became an agent (spy) for Walsingham, the head of Elizabeth I's secret service. He was killed in a fight at a pub in Deptford, but there is still no evidence that this was because of his activities as a spy – there is also some speculation that it was because of his homosexuality and his blatant atheism. Theory is that it was really what it seemed – death in a drunken brawl. Marlowe was really famous as a playwright – "Tamburlaine the Great", "The Famous Tragedy of the Rich Jew of Malta" and "The Tragicall History of D. Faustus" being his most famous works. The latter inspired many later writers and composers – Goethe, Thomas Mann, Richard Wagner and Franz Liszt for example.

What to do

1. Spread the pictures out across some desks and invite each student to choose the picture which, in their opinion, gives a very good example of passion. They should then get into groups and explain to each other why they have picked that particular picture.
2. Show the transparency (page 84) and ask your students:
   What comes into your minds on reading the words? • What do you think the text could be about? • What kind of text do you think he wrote?
   • Which person uses these words in the text?
   They should note down their ideas.

3. Hand out the poem (page 85) and read it aloud to your students. Ask them whether they like it and if it was what they expected to hear. They may use their notes they took in activity 2.
4. Draw this diagram on the board.

What the shepherd promises	What a lover could promise nowadays

5. Then ask your students to read the poem again and tell them that it is an old poem in which a shepherd, talking to the woman he loves, tries to persuade her to be his love.
Your students should find out what he promises her and write it in the left hand column. And in the other column they should write down promises somebody would make nowadays in a similar situation. Have some examples presented to the whole class.
6. Ask your students to imagine a car mechanic, madly in love. What sort of a poem would he write? They should write one or two stanzas. Should some of your students prefer to choose a different job (waitress, chimney sweep, etc.) they are free to do so.

© Cornelsen Verlag Scriptor, Berlin • Fundgrube Englisch handlungsorientiert

The Passionate Shepherd to His Love

Come live with me and be my love
And we will all the pleasures prove
That hills and valleys, dales and fields,
And all the craggy mountains yields.

There we will sit upon the rocks,
And see the shepherds feed their flocks,
By shallow rivers to whose falls
Melodious birds sing madrigals.

And I will make thee beds of roses
With a thousand fragrant posies,
A cap of flowers, and a kirtle
Embroidered all with leaves of myrtle;

A gown made of the finest wool
Which from our pretty lambs we pull;
Fair lined slippers for the cold,
With buckles of the purest gold;

A belt of straw and ivy buds,
With coral clasps and amber studs:
And if these pleasures may thee move,
Come live with me and be my love.

The shepherds' swains shall dance and sing
For thy delight each May morning:
If these delights thy mind may move,
Then live with me and be my love.

Christopher Marlowe, 1589

This is an example one of our students wrote.

A Passionate Car Mechanic to His Love

Come live with me and be my love
And we will all the motors prove
The brakes and tyres, wires and light,
That all the parts are alright

There we will lie under the cars
To check the oil and check the gas
And car, truck, bike and bus
With engine-sounds say thanks to us

An overall of dark blue wool
Which you can wash, push and pull
Fur-lined boots for the ground
Which make a cheerful banging sound

And I will make thee beds of scraps
With a thousand hammer raps
A splash of oil on your overall
Looks like an embroidered shawl

If you will all the motors prove
Then come with me and be my love

Peter T.

Robert Browning
"Home Thoughts, from Abroad"

Lernstufe: Advanced
Kontext: englische Literatur, Gedichte; topics: love for one's country, homesickness, nostalgia
Material: Gedichttext ohne Titel als Overheadfolie, Overheadprojektor, Gedichttext mit Titel (Kopien), evtl. den Biographie-Text kopieren, Parodietext (Kopien)
Dauer: 2–3 Stunden

Robert Browning (1812–1889)

Robert Browning, who wrote verse from an early age, enjoyed only moderate recognition for a long time. After a visit to Italy in 1838, he published many of the poems for which he is now well-known for example "My Last Duchess", "Home Thoughts, from Abroad", "Porphyria's Lover". In 1844 he returned from a second visit to Italy to take part in the chorus of admiration which greeted the publication of Elizabeth Barrett's "Poems" that same year. Elizabeth Barrett (1806–1861), whose father was a strict tyrant, had been a successful writer of verse ("Sonnets from the Portuguese" and "Aurora Leigh") for several years before she published her volume of "Poems". Since early childhood she had suffered from very bad health. Robert Browning was a great admirer of her works, and, although they had never met, he wrote to her "I do, as I say, love these books with all my heart – and I love you too". They began to write to each other (their correspondence was published too!), and fell in love after their first meeting in May 1845. They were married secretly in September 1845, as they were sure Elizabeth's father would not agree to their marriage. They travelled to Italy a week later and lived in Florence until Elizabeth's death in 1861. After her death, Browning returned to England with their son. His popularity increased immensely, and he produced a remarkable amount of literary works ("The ring and the book", "Balaustion's Adventure") until his death in 1889, during a visit to his son in Venice.

What to do

1. Ask your students to imagine that they are away from home for several years. Which season do they think they would miss most? Which aspects of that particular season would they long for most?
2. Collect their suggestions on the board under the respective headings.

Winter	Spring	Summer	Autumn

3. Show them the transparency of the poem (page 88) – without the title – and read it aloud to them. Then ask 2–3 students to read it out aloud as well. Ask them how they like it, what effect it has on them. Can they understand how Browning feels? Or do they think he's overdoing it? Are there any lines they find particularly impressive/soppy/…

4. Ask them to find a title for the poem. Collect these on the board and have a vote for the favourite.
5. Now give them the original title and ask them if they can accept it. Do they think it is a suitable title?
6. Get your students to think about the reason why Browning left England. Then hand out his biography and the text of the poem. Where can the students find links?
7. Give your students the parody "Home Truths, from Abroad" by an anonymous writer. They should compare it with the original and find out where the differences lie, and what the characteristics of a parody are. If necessary, you could give them the following definition of parody:

> A humorous imitation of serious writing. It follows the form of the original, but often changes the sense to ridicule the writer's "style".

8. Ask them to write 6 lines of a parody on the original themselves. Or, as a variation, they can begin "Oh, to be in Germany …".

Home-Thoughts, from Abroad

Oh, to be in England
Now that April's there,
And whoever wakes in England
Sees, some morning, unaware,
That the lowest boughs and the brushwood sheaf
Round the elm-tree bole are in tiny leaf,
While the chaffinch sings on the orchard bough
In England – now!

And after April, when May follows,
And the whitethroat builds, and all the swallows!
Hark, where my blossomed pear-tree in the hedge
Leans to the field and scatters on the clover
Blossoms and dewdrops – at the bent spray's edge –
That's the wise thrush; he sings each song twice over,
Lest you should think he never could recapture
The first fine careless rapture!
And though the fields look rough with hoary dew,
All will be gay when noontide wakes anew
The buttercups, the little children's dower –
Far brighter than this gaudy melon-flower!   *Robert Browning, 1845*

> **Home Truths, from Abroad**
>
> Oh, to be in England
> Now that April's there,
> And whoever wakes in England
> Sees some morning, in despair,
> There's a horrible fog i' the heart o' the town,
> And the greasy pavement is damp and brown;
> While the rain-drop falls from the laden bough,
> In England – now!
>
> And after April when May follows,
> How foolish seem the returning swallows.
> Hark! how the east wind sweeps along the street,
> And how we give one universal sneeze!
> The hapless lambs at thought of mint-sauce bleat,
> And ducks are conscious of the coming peas.
>
> Lest you should think the Spring is really present,
> A biting frost will come to make things pleasant,
> And though the reckless flowers begin to blow,
> They'd better far have nestled down below;
> And English spring sets men and women frowning,
> Despite the rhapsodies of Robert Browning.
>
> Anon.

© Cornelsen Verlag Scriptor, Berlin • Fundgrube Englisch handlungsorientiert

Percy Bysshe Shelley "Ozymandias"

Lernstufe: Advanced
Kontext: englische Literatur, Gedichte lesen, kreatives Schreiben; topics: ambition, power and passions
Material: 2 Overheadfolien, Overheadprojektor, Abdeckschablonen, Gedicht, Hintergrundtext
Dauer: 2 Stunden

Percy Bysshe Shelley (1792–1822)
Shelley was a poet of the Romantic Movement whose private life was every bit as fascinating as his poetry. When he was 19 he had to leave Oxford University because of a pamphlet he had published called "The Necessity of Atheism". He promptly ran away to Scotland with a 16-year-old girl whom he married. Three years later he eloped with another 16-year-old. His wife drowned herself and he married Mary, later to become famous as the author of "Frankenstein". He was drowned in a sailing accident in Italy and when his body was washed up 10 days later, it was burnt on the beach by his friend, the famous poet Lord Byron. Shelley's poems are inspired by his dream of mankind free of authority. Yet it was his short poems ("Ode to the West Wind", "To a Skylark" and "Ozymandias") which have been more widely known and loved. "Ozymandias" is said to be the best-known short poem in the English language.

Vorbemerkung

Als Bildmaterial können Sie das Foto (S. 91) verwenden. Vergrößern Sie es auf das gewünschte Format und ziehen Sie davon eine Overheadfolie. Da die Schüler Spekulationen zu dem Bild anstellen sollen, sind dazu drei Schablonen vorgesehen, um das Bild in drei Phasen zeigen zu können. Diese Schablonen finden Sie in der Reihenfolge von 1 bis 3 auf dem „Schnittmuster" (S. 91). Machen Sie davon 3 Kopien in der gleichen Größe wie das Foto. Schneiden Sie jeweils die angegebene Linie aus und legen Sie die Schablonen dann in der Reihenfolge 1 bis 3 auf das Foto. Bei der ersten Schablone ist dann beispielsweise nur das rechte Knie sichtbar.

What to do

1. Show the transparency to your students by lifting the masks gradually. With each mask elicit responses from your students as to who and what this picture could show. Give them time to think about it, remember that each time you take away a mask the scene will change, obliging the students to reconsider their ideas.
2. Collect the ideas on the blackboard.
3. When the picture is wholly visible ask your students to describe how they feel about it. Ask them to find a title for the picture.
4. Dictate the following words from the poem:
   passion   sneer   sunk   colossal   shattered
   mighty   desert   antique   pedestal   decay

P. B. Shelley "Ozymandias"

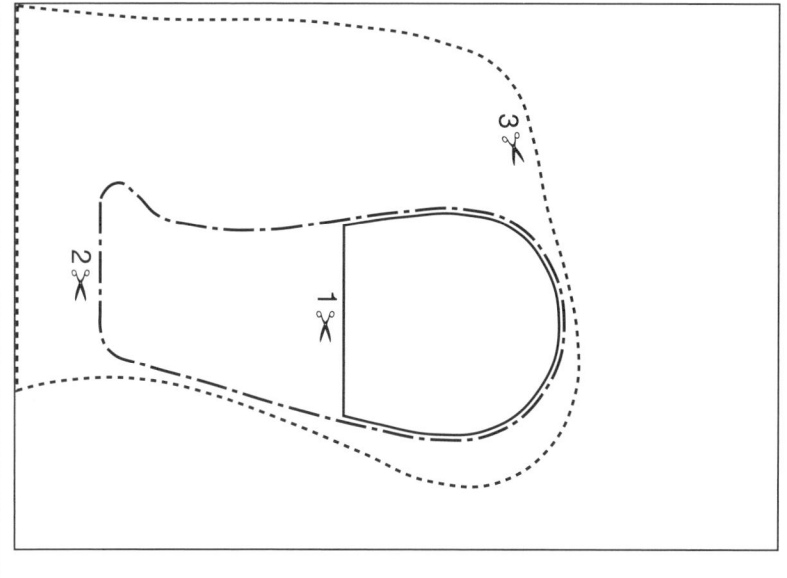

© Cornelsen Verlag Scriptor, Berlin • Fundgrube Englisch handlungsorientiert

Now ask them to rank these words according to their degree of transience. Having done this they should explain their decision.

5. Hand out the information text about Rameses II (see page 93) and ask them to speculate on what the poem they are going to read could be about.
6. Now give them the poem and read it aloud several times. The text is not quite simple as it seems to be so it is advisable to read it in a way that facilitates understanding.

Ozymandias

I met a traveller from an antique land,
Who said – "Two vast and trunkless legs of stone
Stand in the desert. ... Near them, on the sand,
Half sunk, a shattered visage lies, whose frown,
And wrinkled lip, and sneer of cold command,
Tell that its sculptor well those passions read
Which yet survive, stamped on these lifeless things,
The hand that mocked them and the heart that fed;
And on the pedestal these words appear:
My name is Ozymandias, King of Kings,
Look on my works, ye Mighty, and despair!
Nothing beside remains. Round the decay
Of that colossal wreck, boundless and bare
The lone and level sands stretch far away."

Percy Bysshe Shelley, 1817

---

7. Show them the second transparency with the excerpt from the poem (see page 93). Ask them which passions the poet means, do they still survive today? Can they think of any examples?
8. The students write a six-line poem using the acrostic about another person who had similar ambitions or dreams.

M
I
G
H
T
Y

> Ozymandias is the Greek name for the mighty Egyptian Pharaoh Rameses II, who reigned from 1290–1224 BC. Rameses built more than half of the temple tombs that still exist in Egypt today. The most famous are those of Abydos and Abu Simbel, as well as the Ramesseum, near Thebes, on the West Bank of the Nile, where there is also a colossal granite statue of Rameses. The name Ozymandias is derived from Rameses' first name Oser-ma-re.

> ... whose frown,
> And wrinkled lip, and sneer of cold command,
> Tell that its sculptor well those passions read
> which yet survive, stamped on these lifeless things,
> The hand that mocked them and the heart that fed;

9. When they have finished the students should swap their poems and try to guess who the other poem is about.

Poemtelling

Lernstufe: Advanced
Kontext: Poesie und Alltagssprache; Krieg
Material: Kopien zweier thematisch verwandter Gedichte für jeweils die Hälfte der Klasse; Wörterbücher
Dauer: 1–2 Stunden

What to do

1. Pair the students.
2. Give one of the partners Owen's poem, the other Hardy's.
3. Tell them to take their time and study their texts carefully and to look up unknown words in the dictionaries or ask you for help.
4. Ask them to return the poems to you and to tell their partner about their poem so that the he/she gets a vivid impression of it.
5. Distribute the texts again, this time in reverse order, so that everybody has the other poem.
6. Ask the class to get together in a circle and to talk about what they experienced.

Futility

Move him into the sun –
Gently its touch awoke him once,
At home, whispering of fields half-sown.
Always it woke him, even in France,
Until this morning and this snow.
If anything might rouse him now
The kind old sun will know.

Think how it wakes the seeds –
Woke once the clays of a cold star.
Are limbs, so dear achieved, are sides
Full-nerved, still warm, too hard to stir?
Was it for this the clay grew tall? –
O what made fatuous sunbeams toil
To break earth's sleep at all?

Wilfred Owen, 1918

The Man He Killed

Had he and I but met
By some old ancient inn,
We should have sat us down to wet
Right many a nipperkin!

But ranged as infantry,
And staring face to face,
I shot at him as he at me,
And killed him in his place.

I shot him dead because –
Because he was my foe,
Just so: my foe of course he was;
That's clear enough; although

He thought he'd ‚list, perhaps,
Off-hand like – just as I –
Was out of work – had sold his traps –
No other reason why.

Yes; quaint and curious war is!
You shoot a fellow down
You'd treat if met where any bar is,
Or help to half-a-crown.

Thomas Hardy, 1902

Bemerkung
Diese Aufgabe wurde angeregt durch Susan Bassnett, Peter Grundy (1993). *Language through Literature*. Burnt Mill, Harlow, Essex: Longman, page 60: "The Unexpected". In diesem Vorschlag geht es erstens darum, Unterschiede zwischen gebundener lyischer Form und berichtender Inhaltsangabe herauszuarbeiten. Zweitens ist das Verfahren eine *pre-reading activity*, die Erwartungen an lyrische Texte weckt. Drittens bietet es eine Möglichkeit, sich intensiv mit der – vielleicht von der eigenen abweichenden – Textrezeption eines Anderen zu beschäftigen. Und schließlich zwingt die Aufgabe zu einer intensiven Auseinandersetzung mit den Texten und bereitet damit ein produktives Abschlussgespräch vor.

William Carlos Williams "The Artist"

Lernstufe: Advanced
Kontext: outsiders, gender, art
Material: drei Karteikarten mit Schlüsselwörtern; OH-Folie mit dem Gedicht; je Schüler eine Kopie des Gedichts ohne Autor und Titel
Dauer: 1–2 Doppelstunden

William Carlos Williams (1883–1963)

William Carlos Williams was born in New Jersey, in the small community Rutherford that was to be his lifelong home. His father was English, his mother a Puerto Rican who had studied painting in Paris. He was educated at home and in Switzerland and France, studied medicine at the University of Pennsylvania and during six decades was both a poet and a pediatrician. This combination was very much in accordance with his conviction that poetry should be in direct touch with locality, people and objects and not withdrawn from reality. The poem was written late in his life when a series of strokes had made it already difficult for him to write. It is composed in the "triadic line" characteristic of many of Williams' later works. "To construct the 'triadic line' Williams arranged relatively short feet, of uneven length, in gradually descending steps across the page, establishing a musical pace (...) that gives weight to silent pauses as well as to the words, and accords an even time interval to each of the segments (*Selected letters*, pp. 326–27)". (*The Norton Anthology of American Literature*, vol. 2, New York, London: W.W. Norton 1979, page 1436.)

The Artist

Mr. T.
    bareheaded
        in a soiled undershirt

his hair standing out
    on all sides
        stood on his toes

heels together
    arms gracefully
        for the moment

curled above his head.
    Then he whirled about
        bounded

into the air
    and with an *entrechat*
        perfectly achieved

completed the figure.
    My mother
        taken by surprise

where she sat
    in her invalid's chair
        was left speechless.

Bravo! she cried at last
    and clapped her hands.
        The man's wife

came from the kitchen:
    What goes on here? she said.
        But the show was over.

William Carlos Williams, 1962

What to do

1. There are, of course, many ways of getting into the text. Two of them are outlined here.
   a) Divide the class into three groups and hand out a card to each with the following words respectively:

card 1	card 2	card 3
gracefully undershirt soiled entrechat*	invalid mother clapped her hands	wife kitchen the show is over

   * Ballet figure in which the dancer's feet are rapidly crossed several times in the air.

   The groups are given the task to portray a person around the words on their card.
   b) Or: Write the words of the above task on the board in a jumbled manner and ask the pupils to speculate about the poem, its people, its subject. Note: If you choose this way of approaching the text, please skip the next two steps and go on with the presentation of the poem.
2. Ask each of the three groups to present their character to the others.
3. This step serves to bring together the three characters and thus to approach Williams' poem more closely.
   Arrange the class in groups of three (or six, if you want larger groups), each consisting of one (or two) member(s) of each of the original three groups needed for step 1 a) and 2 above respectively. The tasks for the groups are: "Invent a situation in which the three characters meet. Rehearse the meeting." Ask volunteer groups to act out the meeting in front of the class.
4. Read the poem to the class once. Read it out once again, this time displaying the poem with its triadic structure on an overhead transparency. Give the class time to read the poem silently again once or twice before encouraging the students to express their ideas, feelings, responses. Ask the pupils to exchange their mental images of the characters, of their age, their appearance, their (former/present) profession and their habits and likes and dislikes.
5. Williams was always concerned about the locality of his writing. He wanted his literature to be related very directly to concrete situations.

This step is an attempt to visualize the poem's place. It can be done in pairs. Tell your students to clarify the following points: Where does the poem take place? Where is the mother in relation to the artist? Where is the kitchen? Where is the wife? What is she doing in the kitchen? What is the place of the first person character (the lyrical "I"), the observer of the scene? When they have developed a concrete idea of where the poem takes place they will be ready to tackle the following task: "Take a bird's eye view of the poem's place and draw a rough outline indicating the room, the kitchen and the position of the people mentioned. Do not forget the observer." Have the students stick their plans to the wall, look at what the others produced and discuss the different plans.

6. This last step rounds off the work with the poem by drawing attention to its context. Hand out a sheet of paper to each student with the poem's text copied into the middle without title and author. Ask the class to make the poem part of a letter written by the first person observer to a friend. The letter should contain what went on before the poem begins, leave the poem as the middle part, and end with what follows after its ending. The pupils are free to choose between Williams' triadic manner or prose.

Zig-Zag-Translations

Lernstufe: Intermediate/Advanced
Kontext: language awareness; (literarisches) Übersetzen
Material: einsprachige Wörterbücher; zwei in Umfang und Schwierigkeitsgrad vergleichbare Gedichte für je die Hälfte der Klasse
Dauer: 1 Stunde

What to do

1. Divide the class into pairs. Both partners must have either the same mother-tongue or learn the same foreign language (in addition to English).
2. Hand each of the two a different poem of roughly the same size and difficulty. They must not show the text to each other.

3. Give them enough time to translate the poem from English into their mother-tongue or their second foreign language.
4. Make them swap their translations – but not the original English poems.
5. Let them translate the translated texts back into English.
6. Let the partners compare their original English versions with the first translations and the re-translations.
7. Make the class get together again and read some of the texts, translations and re-translations. Be sure to include readings in minority languages in the class.
8. Discuss the difficulties the partner teams encountered and the discoveries they made.

Bemerkung

Dieses Übersetzungsverfahren eignet sich für Klassen, in denen mehrere Herkunfts- und/oder Fremdsprachen gesprochen werden. Die Sprachen, die in das Verfahren einbezogen werden, müssen mindestens von zwei Mitgliedern der Klasse gesprochen werden. Aber die Übersetzungs-Rückübersetzungs-Übung kann natürlich auch von zwei deutschen Schülern durchgeführt werden.

Das Verfahren lässt sich auch auf Prosatexte, Gebrauchsanweisungen, Zeitungsartikel und viele andere Textarten und -sorten übertragen. Wenn es die mehrsprachige Situation in der Klasse erlaubt, kann der Vorgang um einen oder mehrere Übersetzungsdurchgänge erweitert werden.

The Leopard

Gentle hunter
His tail plays on the ground
While he crushes the skull.

Beautiful death
Who puts on a spotted robe
When he goes to his victim.

Playful killer
Whose loving embrace
Splits the antelope's heart.

Anon. Yoruba

The Sick Rose

Rose, thou art sick!
The invisible worm
That flies in the night,
In the howling storm,

Has found out thy bed
Of crimson joy:
And his dark secret love
Does thy life destroy.

William Blake, 1794

6 Once there was ...

The Gunpowder Plot

Lernstufe: Intermediate
Kontext: Landeskunde, Lese- oder Hörverstehen, kreatives Schreiben, storytelling
Material: Wenn die Aufgabe als Leseaufgabe verstanden wird, dann benötigen die Schüler je eine Kopie des Textes mit den Fragen, aber *ohne* die eingekästelten Antworten, die vorher mit Tipp-Ex entfernt wurden. Overheadfolie mit Antworten aus dem Original der Geschichte; Overheadprojektor
Dauer: 1 Stunde

What to do

1. Give each of your students a copy of "The Gunpowder Plot" and read the text aloud. When you get to the first question allow them several minutes to write their answers.
2. Continue in this way till the story is finished.
3. Ask them to get into groups of 4 and to compare their versions of the story.
4. When they have finished show them the transparency with the extracts from the original text. This doesn't mean that their stories are not every bit as good as the original but it is important to acquaint them with famous folk stories that every British child knows.
5. Ask the students whether there was any version in one of their groups that they preferred. If so, have it read out to the whole class.

Bemerkung

Der Text kann auch als Höraufgabe verwendet werden. Dann wird er vorgelesen und nach jeder Frage erhalten die Schüler Zeit, die Antwort zu notieren. Sie setzen sich dann in Gruppen zusammen und vergleichen ihre Ideen. Um jedoch auch das Original kennenlernen zu können, müssten ih-

The Gunpowder Plot

nen die Ausschnitte aus der wirklichen Geschichte erzählt werden. Dazu dienen Ihnen die eingerahmten Teile in der Geschichte.

Bemerkung
Sie können anschließend Ihren Schülerinnen und Schülern erzählen, wie die Briten tatsächlich den Tag feiern, und eventuell mit ihnen eine Lektüre zu dem Thema lesen. Manche SchülerInnen werden eventuell den Film „V for Vendetta" kennen, der, wenn auch etwas entfernt, Bezug auf den „Gunpowder Plot" nimmt.

Text
A long time ago, at the very beginning of the 17th century, only sixty years after the Reformation, Protestants and Catholics in England were still having great problems with one another.

What did they do to each other?

> Catholics were not allowed to celebrate Mass, many priests had been killed, others had run away to France or Spain. Some Catholics had started rebellions which were never successful. Their leaders usually ended up with their heads stuck on London Bridge.

There was a Protestant king on the throne. He was actually from Scotland, so nobody in England really liked him very much. The King tolerated Catholics at first – he was much more frightened of witches! He was afraid they might try to kill him.

What happened to women who were thought to be witches?

> They were tortured, burnt at the stake and drowned.

In 1604, a group of Catholics decided that King James I was not giving them enough rights.

Which rights did they want to have?

> They wanted to be able to celebrate Mass freely, as King James had promised. They also wanted the priests back in England.

They met one night in one of their houses. The word for these men is "plotters", because they planned, or plotted, to do something bad to the King. One of the plotters, a fanatical Catholic whose name was Guido Fawkes, had been a captain in the Spanish army. He was an expert in explosives.

What kind of a person was he?

Nobody really knows very much about him. In any case he was not one of the main plotters but he was prepared to die for his faith.

The plotters had a brilliant idea. They would kill the King when he came to open Parliament on 5 November 1605.

How did they want to do this?

First they wanted to dig a tunnel beneath the House of Lords. But the walls were too thick. Then they rented a cellar under the Houses of Parliament.

They secretly organized thirty barrels of gunpowder and put them in the cellar under the room where the King would sit. But one of the plotters had a brother-in-law who was a Member of Parliament, and he didn't want him to be killed. So he wrote him a warning letter in code.

What did he write in his letter?

He only told him not to go to the opening of Parliament.

When this man got this very strange letter, he suspected there was going to be an attack on the King, and so he warned the King's chief minister. On the night of 4 November, soldiers of the King inspected all the cellars underneath the Houses of Parliament and discovered Guy Fawkes, who was guarding the gunpowder. He was tortured horribly until he told them the names of the plotters and what they had planned. Some of the plotters were killed in a fight with soldiers, but Guy Fawkes and seven others were hanged, drawn and quartered in 1606.

Since 1605 the cellars under the Houses of Parliament are searched every year the night before the opening of Parliament. The British love rituals!

Every year, on 5 November, people in Great Britain, particularly children, celebrate Guy Fawkes Day.

How do they do this?

The children make a dummy – a sort of doll – out of straw and paper. They put old clothes on it and carry it through the streets, calling "Penny for the Guy!" With the money they get they buy fireworks. When it gets dark people all over Britain light bonfires – either in their own gardens or in a park in the town – and burn the guy. Then they let off the fireworks.

A Modern Myth in Halves

Lernstufe: Lower Intermediate
Kontext: storytelling
Material: Kopien der senkrecht gefalteten Geschichte
Dauer: 1 Stunde

Vorbereitung
Fertigen Sie eine vergrößerte Kopie der Geschichte an, sodass sie eine DIN-A4-Seite füllt. Falten Sie nun die Geschichte senkrecht in der Mitte, überschreiben Sie die linke Hälfte mit A, die rechte mit B und kopieren Sie beide Hälften getrennt auf DIN-A4-Bögen. Bei einer Arbeit in Dreiergruppen sollte die Zahl der Kopien einem Drittel Ihrer Schülerzahl entsprechen, d. h. bei dreißig Kindern sollten Sie zehn Kopien machen, fünf von A und fünf von B, sodass je fünf Dreiergruppen an derselben Aufgabe arbeiten.

What to do

1. Ask your pupils to get together in groups of three, give each group one of the halves and ask them to complete the story by putting it on a sheet of paper and writing the lines so that the story makes sense to them. Make sure that the teams working on the A-half are well separated from the B-teams.
2. One of the ways of exchanging the results would be to ask some of the teams to read out their solutions. It is much more interesting to forget about the printed text at this stage and to collect the text halves the pupils have produced in separate A-boxes and B-boxes. Now ask one pupil to take one text half out of the A-box and another to take one out of the B-box. Make the two pupils sit next to each other and adjust the text halves so that the complete story appears to them. Ask them to take turns in reading out the full text in front of them. After three or four such readings read out the original version. Pin that version as well as the A- and the B-halves produced to the wall so that they can be read by everybody during the break.
3. Ask the teams to formulate a sentence expressing the moral of the story.
4. Tell them another modern myth and ask them if they know any such stories.

A family from Birmingham travelled to Australia on holiday. They hired a car and drove into the desert. In Australia you must be very careful because kangaroos sometimes cross the road. The family were driving through the desert when all of a sudden a kangaroo jumped in front of them. It was too late to stop the car, so it hit the poor animal and knocked it to the ground. The family stepped out of the car to see what had happened. The kangaroo lay on the ground, lifeless. While he was looking at the animal, the father thought: "This would make an exciting picture for the photograph album." But he did not want a sad picture. Suddenly he had a funny idea. He took off his jacket and put it on the kangaroo. That would make people laugh! He picked up his camera to take the picture when the kangaroo opened its eyes, jumped up and disappeared into the desert. It was wearing the man's jacket. And in that jacket were the car keys, credit cards and the return tickets to England. Neither the kangaroo nor the jacket were ever seen again.

Bemerkung
Die obige Geschichte ist eine Adaption von "The Kangaroo in the Jacket" in Andrew Wright (1995), *Storytelling with Children,* Oxford University Press. Das Verfahren 1./2. eignet sich auch für Lehrbuch- und Sachtexte, Teile von Lektüren und andere Prosatexte. Um A- und B-Teams gerechte Anteile der Geschichte zu geben, ist es ratsam, wie im obigen Beispiel die Geschichte ohne Absätze durchgängig zu tippen und im Blocksatz oder zentriert zu formatieren. Das Verfahren ist auch für Gedichte vorstellbar, wobei dann Zentrierung unerlässlich scheint.

From Word to Story

Lernstufe: Lower Intermediate
Kontext: storytelling, Wortschatz
Material: Wortkarten, auf Karton geklebt und ausgeschnitten
Dauer: beliebig

What to do
1. Divide the class into groups of not less than 5 and not more than 10. Have them sit in circles.
2. Hand out all the cards – depending on the size of the group, each player will have between 3 and 6 cards.
3. The first player (a volunteer!) begins to tell a story, using one of the words. His neighbour continues, also using one card, and so on, until all cards are used (each may only be used once!).

Bemerkung
Mit weniger Wortkarten kann dieser Aufgabentyp auch schon in früheren Jahrgängen eingesetzt werden. Dann wird beim Erzählen ein Text entstehen, der kürzer ist und nicht alle Merkmale einer *„story"* aufweist.
Diese Aufgabe ermöglicht es, dass jeder beliebige Wortschatz wiederholt werden kann. Die Auswahl der Wörter kann sich nach einem Fantasiethema richten, nach der letzten Lektüre oder auch nach den Themen der letzten Lehrbuchkapitel. Die Auswahl der Wörter trifft die Lehrkraft, wenn der Aufgabentyp den Schülern nicht geläufig sein sollte. Später können sie bei

picnic basket	heavy	wicked
sandwiches	kill	hook
sun	pirate	adventure
perfect	fairy	alarm clock
enjoy	crocodile	muddle
spot	tree	darling
statue	shadow	laugh
expensive	mouse-trap	worm
spray	arrest	amazing
terrified	tickle	angrily

© Cornelsen Verlag Scriptor, Berlin • Fundgrube Englisch handlungsorientiert

der Auswahl beteiligt werden, bis sie selbstständig die Wortkarten erstellen. Die Herstellung kann in den einzelnen Gruppen nach verschiedenen Themen erfolgen (z.B. die letzten Themen des Lehrbuches) und nach Benutzung zwischen den Gruppen ausgetauscht werden.

Suniti Namjoshi "Bird Woman"

Lernstufe: Intermediate
Kontext: Erziehung, Geschlechterverhältnisse, Anpassung
Material: große Bögen, z.B. Packpapier- oder Tapetenrolle
Dauer: 2–3 Stunden

Suniti Namjoshi (born in 1941)
Born in India, Suniti Namjoshi has taught at different universities both in India and in Canada. She has been a member of the Department of English at the University of Toronto since 1972. Some of her texts were written in England where she spent some time in Devon. In 1981 her *Feminist Fables* were published by Sheba Feminist Publishing House in London. It contains "Bird Woman", reprinted in the Cornelsen collection *Her Own Story (Best.- Nr. 52087)*. Among Namjoshi's other publications are *The Blue Donkey Fables* (The Women's Press 1988). Namjoshi has repeatedly picked up the subject of norm and deviation and the irritation caused by difference. She prefers didactic genres like fables, fairy tales, parables. These are simple on a linguistic level, usually brief (some of them no more than a few lines), and to the point. They make easy but interesting reading even for younger readers.

About the story
"Bird Woman" begins with the magic words of a fairy tale: "Once there was …". It tells the story of a little girl who grows wings. Three times – again a magic element of the genre – the neighbours urge the girl's parents to do something about her unusual development, to stop it. The parents, however, simply teach their daughter how to fly. The context of the *Feminist Fables* and of *Her Own Story* suggest a feminist reading. The insistence of the neighbours to have the child's wings cut serves as a metaphor for he pressure put on girls to conform to a given image and to reduce their

natural possibilities, to consider their strength and gifts as impediment to the development prescribed to them. A feminist reading is, however, just one of the possible ways of making sense of the text. The fable may just as profitably be approached in a more open manner as referring to any pressure put on individuals to conform to society's expectations and to the difficulties those who deviate have to face.

Bird Woman

Once there was a child who sprouted wings. They sprang from her shoulder blades, and at first they were vestigial. But they grew rapidly, and in no time at all she had a sizable wing span. The neighbours were horrified. "You must have them cut," they said to her parents. "Why?" said her parents. "Well, it's obvious," said the neighbours. "No," said the parents, and this seemed so final that the neighbours left. But a few weeks later the neighbours were back. "If you won't have them cut, at least have them clipped." "Why?" said the parents. "Well, at least it shows that you're doing something." "No," said the parents, and the neighbours left. Then for the third time the neighbours appeared. "On at least two occasions you have sent us away," they informed the parents, „but think of that child. What are you doing to the poor little thing?" "We are teaching her to fly," said the parents quietly.

Suniti Namajoshi, 1981

What to do

1. Brainstorming can serve to get the class into the story. Write "humans with wings" or "humans flying" in the centre of the blackboard and write the group's associations around the centre. Initiate a classroom conversation around the following statement: "It is said that humankind has longed to be able to fly from the beginning of its existence. Can you think why? Do you share this desire?"

2. Tell the class to close their eyes, to make themselves comfortable and to let their minds drift and to get ready for a fantasy flight. Speak the following sentences in a slow manner. Pause after each sentence: "Imagine you are standing on the top of a mountain. Suddenly you can feel your arms transforming into wings. The wings are growing rapidly. They are getting big and strong. Now they nearly touch the ground. You are a bit scared. But at the same time you feel exhilarated and ready to try them out. Now you open them wide. You bend forward. Get on tiptoe. Spread your wings and take off. What do you feel? What do you see? What happens?" (You may want to accompany this phase by some background music to make the pupils relax, but music might have the disadvantage of influencing the pupils' visions.) Ask them to return to the ground. Give them twenty minutes in which to write an answer to the following question: "You have been granted wings for 24 hours. How will you spend the time?" The pupils' productions should then be fastened to the wall and the class be given time to study them.
3. Tell the story, changing the text so that there is no indication as to the gender of the child. Do not mention author or title. Tell the story freely but keep to the three-stage structure. If you do not trust your memory, prepare a story skeleton (see below). The oral presentation enables you to insert new words and structures into the text and to circumscribe them and explain them. You can either simplify the story or make it more sophisticated. It may be useful to stop at certain points and ask the class to speculate about the progression of the story.

Story skeleton

baby sprouting wings
at first small, vestigial
grow quickly
horrified neighbours: "Cut wings!"
parents: "Why?"
neighbours: "Clip wings! Do something!"
neighbours again: "What are you doing to the poor child?"
"We are teaching our child to fly."

Storytelling (model)

Once upon a time there was a baby who started growing wings – it *sprouted* wings. They sprouted from the child's shoulderblades. At first they were very small, you could hardly see them, they were just *vestigial*, like a chicken's. But soon they began to grow and they grew wider and stronger every day. The neighbours were shocked. "You must have them cut immediately", they told the parents.

(Can you imagine why the neighbours were horrified? What would you do if your child started growing wings? How will the parents in the story react?)

"Why should we want to cut the wings?" the parents asked. But the neighbours just stared at them and shook their heads in disbelief. "How can you even ask such a question? It's obvious!" "No", said the parents and sent the neighbours away. But a few weeks later they were back again. This time they said: "If you don't want to have the child's wings cut, at least have them clipped. At least do something!" Once again the parents would not listen and sent them away. But the neighbours came back a third time. This time they asked the parents to think of the child. "What are you doing to the poor little thing?" they asked.

(What did the parents reply?)

The parents answered quietly: "We are teaching our child to fly."

4. After the story has been told, the class is divided into groups, each working on the same tasks. Write these on the board or hand them out on cards or show them on an overhead transparency. Each group also receives a big sheet of paper (e.g. wallpaper) on which to write down the result of the last task.

> **Group tasks**
>
> Exchange your views of the story.
>
> Whose side are you on: the neighbours' or the parents'?
>
> None of the parties involved gives reasons for their behaviour. Imagine a debate between parents and neighbours. What are the arguments of the first, what are those of the latter?
>
> Write down what you think is the message of the story in one sentence in big, bold letters.

Pin the big message sheets to the board or wall, visible to everybody.

5. Ask each group to present the sentence with their idea of the message of the story. Let the class discuss the differences between the group messages. Then split the class into halves. Cast lots to decide which half is to take the side of the parents and which that of the neighbours. Organise a debate between the two groups or ask one of the pupils to chair the discussion.
6. Now tell the class that you gave them a fake version. Let them speculate what you might have changed. Read out the original version, again without author and title. Ask for comments: "What do you think of the difference?" "Does it make you see the story in a different light?" Inform the class about author and title and context of the story: its appearance as a feminist fable, the Indian background of the author. Ask again whether this information influences their understanding of the story.
7. This task can be solved individually at home or as pair work during the lesson. Tell the class to prepare a speech on the basis of the story. They may choose from the possibilities below or make a speech on another topic around the concept of education and gender that they feel strongly about. Their argument need not correspond to their own sex.
Possible topics: • The plight of girls' education and the restrictions it imposes on young women. • The plight of boys' education and the restrictions it imposes on young men. • Gender education versus free child development.
8. A fictitious letter of the winged child now grown-up to its parents is another way of dealing with the story. This can be done individually or in groups. The pupils are given this task: "Twenty years have passed. The Bird Woman has grown up. Try to identify with her and write a letter to her parents either thanking them or reproaching them for the way they let her grow up and develop."
9. The story is declared a fable by the author. As such it represents a way of indirect speaking, transferring its subject to a different narrative plane and expecting the readers to reverse that process. In the indirectness of what is *said* and the task to transfer this to what is *meant* the fable resembles the metaphor. "Flying" is the moment of contention of the story. The semantic field around this idea has brought forth a number of metaphors – to fly into a temper, to fly into a rage, high-flown ideals, high-flown language, a door flying open, rumours flying around, high-flier etc. – that could be collected with the help of different dictionaries of idiomatic usage. The findings could be compared to similar expressions in the mother tongues of the students.

7 Getting into Fiction and Getting on with It

O. Henry "By Courier"

Lernstufe: Advanced
Kontext: Sprachregister, Soziolekte; Sprache und Gesellschaft; literarisches Übersetzen; *staging a story*
Material: Kopien der Geschichte für alle; Wörterbücher, möglichst auch ein Slangwörterbuch und ein idiomatisches Wörterbuch; evtl. eine Videokamera
Dauer: 2–3 Doppelstunden

"By Courier" ist die Geschichte zweier Liebender, die ein Missverständnis beinahe für immer getrennt hätte, das glücklicherweise in letzter Minute aber aufgeklärt wird. Dabei spielt der Bote des Titels eine zentrale Rolle, denn er vermittelt die Verständigung zwischen den Zerstrittenen. Diese Verständigung erzeugt aber ihrerseits Verständigungsprobleme, denn der Bote, *streetwise,* aber ungebildet, versteht die wohlhabend-wohlerzogenen, aber weniger weisen Liebenden nicht immer, sondern muss ihre Sprache in die seine übersetzen, während Auftraggeber und Adressatin seine Botschaften wieder in ihr Register rückübertragen müssen. In diesem Spiel mit Register und Soziolekt liegt eine interessante Möglichkeit für den Sprachunterricht.

O. Henry (1862–1910)

O. Henry is the pseudonym of the American short story writer William Sydney Porter. He was born in Greensboro, North Carolina, the son of a physician. After leaving school at the age of 15 he worked in his uncle's drugstore, then on a ranch, in a general land office and in a bank in Austin, Texas. In 1896 he was charged with embezzling funds and fled to Honduras. His wife's fatal illness brought him back and after her death in 1898 he was sentenced to five years' imprisonment. On his release after just over three years he went to New York where some of his best stories are set. He became one of the most popular American storytellers of his time.

What to do

1. Distribute copies of the story (see pages 114–116) to the class and ask the students to read the text individually. This may also be done as a homework in preparation for the lesson.
2. Discuss the story in class. Discuss the setting, the social and financial standing of the couple and the courier, their living conditions, clothes, food, hobbies, education etc.
3. Tell the class to get together in three or four groups and to work on task A or B.
4. Each of the presentations should be reviewed by the audience. Ask those who watch to take notes for a review during the play and to write the review at home. Lay down the rule that the feelings of the actors and actresses must not be hurt, but that honesty must prevail at the same time.
5. Enjoy the performances. Videotape them if possible.
6. Have some reviews read out and discussed in the following lesson, at least one for each performance.
7. Collect all the written products in a folder entitled "By Courier".

A

Turn the story into a one-act play set in contemporary urban Germany.

Re-write/translate the dialogue freely.

Provide the play with stage directions.

Perform it in front of the class.

B

Discuss a transfer of the story into contemporary urban Germany.

Translate and re-create it accordingly.

Perform it as a readers' theatre (i. e. you perform it by reading your role, without learning the text by heart) with a narrator and the three characters and possibly a flashback to the scene that separated the lovers.

By Courier

It was neither the season nor the hour when the park had frequenters; and it is likely that the young lady, who was seated on one of the benches at the side of the walk, had merely obeyed a sudden impulse to sit for a while and enjoy a foretaste of coming spring.
5 She rested there, pensive and still. A certain melancholy that touched her countenance must have been of recent birth, for it had not yet altered the fine and youthful contours of her cheek, nor subdued the arch though resolute curve of her lips.
A tall young man came striding through the park along the path near which 10 she sat. Behind him tagged a boy carrying a suit-case. At sight of the young lady, the man's face changed to red and back to pale again. He watched her countenance as he drew nearer, with hope and anxiety mingled on his own. He passed within a few yards of her, but he saw no evidence that she was aware of his presence or existence.
15 Some fifty yards further on he suddenly stopped and sat on a bench at one side. The boy dropped the suit-case and stared at him with wondering, shrewd eyes. The young man took out his handkerchief and wiped his brow. It was a good handkerchief, a good brow, and the young man was good to look at. He said to the boy:
20 "I want you to take a message to that young lady on that bench. Tell her I am on my way to the station, to leave for San Francisco, where I shall join that Alaska moose-hunting expedition. Tell her that, since she has commanded me neither to speak nor to write to her, I take this means of making one last appeal to her sense of justice, for the sake of what has 25 been. Tell her that to condemn and discard one who has not deserved such treatment, without giving him her reasons or a chance to explain is contrary to her nature as I believe it to be. Tell her that I have thus, to a certain degree, disobeyed her injunctions, in the hope that she may yet be inclined to see justice done. Go, and tell her that."
30 The young man dropped a half-dollar into the boy's hand. The boy looked at him for a moment with bright, canny eyes out of a dirty, intelligent face, and then set off at a run. He approached the lady on the bench a little doubtfully, but unembarrassed. He touched the brim of an old plaid bicycle cap perched on the back of his head. The lady looked at him coolly, without prejudice or 35 favor.
"Lady," he said, "dat gent on de oder bench sent yer a song and dance by me. If yer don't know the guy, and he's tryin' to do de Johnny act, say de word, and I'll call a cop in t'ree minutes. If yer does know him, and he's on de square, w'y I'll spiel yer de bunch of hot air he sent yer."

40 The young lady betrayed a faint interest.
"A song and dance!" she said, in a deliberate, sweet voice that seemed to clothe her words in a diaphanous garment of impalpable irony. "A new idea – in the troubadour line, I suppose. I – used to know the gentleman who sent you so I think it will hardly be necessary to call the police. You may
45 execute your song and dance, but do not sing too loudly. It is a little early yet for open-air vaudeville, and we might attract attention."
"Awe," said the boy, with a shrug down the length of him, "yer know what I mean, lady. 'Tain't a turn, it's wind. He told me to tell yer he's got his collars and cuffs in dat grip for a scoot clean out to 'Frisco. Den he's goin' to shoot
50 snow-birds in de Klondike. He says yer told him not to send 'round no more pink notes nor come hangin' over de garden gate, and he takes dis means of puttin' yer wise. He says yer refereed him out like a has-been, and never give him no chance to kick at de decision. He says yer swiped him, and never said why."
55 The slightly awakened interest in the young lady's eyes did not abate. Perhaps it was caused by either the originality or the audacity of the snow-bird hunter, in thus circumventing her express commands against the ordinary modes of communication. She fixed her eye on a statue standing disconsolate in the dishevelled park, and spoke into the transmitter:
60 "Tell the gentleman that I need not repeat to him a description of my ideals. He knows what they have been and what they still are. So far as they touch on this case, absolute loyalty and truth are the ones paramount. Tell him that I have studied my own heart as well as one can, and I know its weakness as well as I do its needs. That is why I decline to hear his pleas, whatever
65 they may be. I did not condemn him through hearsay or doubtful evidence, and that is why I made no charge. But, since he persists in hearing what he already well knows, you may convey the matter.
Tell him that I entered the conservatory that evening from the rear, to cut a rose for my mother. Tell him I saw him and Miss Ashburton beneath the
70 pink oleander. The tableau was pretty, but the pose and juxtaposition were too eloquent and too evident to require explanation. I left the conservatory and, at the same time, the rose and my ideal. You may carry that song and dance to your impresario."
"I'm shy on one word, lady. Jux–jux–put me wise on that, will yer?"
75 "Juxtaposition – or you may call it propinquity – or, if you like, being rather too near for one maintaining the position of an ideal."
The gravel spun from beneath the boy's feet. He stood by the other bench. The man's eyes interrogated him, hungrily. The boy's were shining with the impersonal zeal of the translator.

80 "De lady says dat she's on to de fact dat gals is dead easy when a feller some spielin' ghost stories and tryin' to make up, and dat's why she won't listen to no soft-soap. She says she caught yer dead to rights, huggin' a bunch o' calico in de hot-house. She side-stepped in to pull some posies and yer was squeezin' der oder gal to beat de band. She says it looked cute,
85 all right all right, but it made her sick. She says yer better git busy, and make a sneak for de train."
The young man gave a low whistle and his eyes flashed with a sudden thought. His hand flew to the inside pocket of his coat, and drew out a handful of letters. Selecting one, he handed it to the boy, following it with a
90 silver dollar from his vest-pocket.
"Give that letter to the lady," he said, "and ask her to read it. Tell her that it should explain the situation. Tell her that, if she had mingled a little trust with her conception of the ideal, much heartache might have been avoided. Tell her that loyalty she prizes so much has never wavered. Tell her I am
95 waiting for an answer."
The messenger stood before the lady.
"De gent says he's had de ski-bunk put on him widout no cause. He says he's no bum guy; and, lady, yer read dat letter, and I'll bet yer he's a white sport, all right."
100 The young lady unfolded the letter, somewhat doubtfully, and read it.

DEAR DR. ARNOLD: I want to thank you for your most kind and opportune aid to my daughter last Friday evening, when she was overcome by an attack of her old heart-trouble in the conservatory at Mrs. Waldron's reception. Had you not been near to catch her as she fell and to render
105 proper attention, we might have lost her. I would be glad if you would call and undertake the treatment of her case.
Gratefully yours,
ROBERT ASHBURTON.

The young lady refolded the letter, and handed it to the boy.
110 "De gent wants an answer," said the messenger. "What's de word?"
The lady's eyes suddenly flashed on him, bright, smiling and wet.
"Tell that guy on the other bench," she said, with a happy, tremulous laugh, "that this girl wants him."

Puzzling W. Somerset Maugham's "The Outstation"

Lernstufe: Advanced
Kontext: Literatur, Geschichte: Empire/Asien, Human Interest Story
Material: Arbeitsblätter zum Text-Puzzle, evtl. Rollenkarten für die abschließende Gerichtsverhandlung, evtl. Landkarte Asien
Dauer: 4–6 Stunden

What to do

1. Start off with a "guided fantasy" using the following text as a basic structure. (Make the students close their eyes and be absolutely quiet, then start telling them about their journey …).
Well, at last the holidays have started, and off you are to the (nearest) airport (Frankfurt or Tegel or Fulsbüttel …), and you board a plane. You relax in your seat and after take-off you listen to some of your favourite music as you cruise high above the clouds. After a while you can see some sea, far below, and some stretches of desert, and the stewardess appears and you are offered something to drink. Eventually you doze off, dreaming happy dreams. It is just before landing that you wake up, and after touch-down you step outside, and hot, humid air strikes you; you observe the palm-trees, there are flowers everywhere, a lush vegetation, and people dressed in casual clothes, you feel hot, but comfortable and you are carried off in a bus to the landing-stage. You board the boat. The launch takes you to the mouth of a river, and you go up-stream. The sky is blue, dappled with little white clouds. The green of the mangroves and the nipahs glistens in the sun. On each side of the river stretches the pathless jungle, and, in the distance, silhouetted against the sky, is the rugged outline of a mountain. It is still quite early in the morning, and the air is fresh. You seem to enter a friendly land, and you have a sense of spacious freedom. You watch the banks for monkeys sitting on the branches of the tangled trees … It takes hours, it takes days before you get to your final destination, a bungalow, surrounded by a garden that is not very well kept … There are some more houses, well, not exactly houses, rather huts, shabby huts, run-down huts.

2. Ask the students how they feel after this journey, how they feel about their destination. What had they expected during the flight, during the boat trip up the river? Have their expectations been met? What is going to happen to them now? The students should exchange their views, their hopes, their fears ...
3. After this "warm-up" activity ask the students where they have landed, where they are. From the guided fantasy it is evident that they are somewhere in the tropical jungle. Maugham's text is actually set in Borneo, and the final destination might be a place like Kapit or Belaga in Sarawak. A map of Asia would help to locate the setting of the story.
4. You should tell the students now that you are going to discuss a piece of English literature with them and that this story is set in this place in Malaya or Borneo. Such questions as to why English people wrote stories about Borneo and why the British had been there ought to be raised, and the students are to be given some information on the British in South-East Asia and on the structure of the administration of the Empire, i. e. the terms "Resident" or "District Officer" (and their tasks and duties) should be introduced.

Some background information
During the 19th century there happened a gradual extension of British influence on Malaya. 1819 saw the foundation of Singapore as the most important straits settlement and trading-post. Various British interventions in peninsular Malaya, finally, led to general colonial rule in the Federated Malay States by the turn of the century. North Borneo (today's Sarawak) where Maugham's story is set, was ruled by James and later Vyner Brooke, the "white Rajahs", James having obtained his "country" as a gift from the Sultan of Brunei for helping him crush an insurrection. When Maugham travelled in South-East Asia in the early twenties, the Brooke administration already heavily relied on British colonial personnel. Warburton seems to be such a colonial official serving as "resident" (he resided there, in this place!) or "district officer" in a remote part of Borneo. British colonial rule depended on these "civil servants" who – as "representatives of the crown" – governed the "natives" in a certain area or region. They were in charge of jurisdiction, the police, finance, of maintenance of public roads, buildings, communication etc.
It was only after World War II that these parts of the world gained independence from European colonial rule. 1963 saw the inauguration of

Malaysia, comprising peninsular Malaya and the regions of Sarawak and Sabah on Borneo. Singapore opted to become a state of its own.
The "natives" mentioned in Maugham's story are Dayaks, an indigenous Borneo people consisting of various tribes. They used to be notorious for their head-hunting. Maugham equates them with the Malays (he calls them "Malays"!) which is not correct. Malay kampongs (villages) on Borneo were only situated at the coast.

5. Hand out worksheet 1 (see pages 122–123) to the students. Tell them to read the given fragments (A–I) of this story. In these passages two different people, the story's protagonists, are described and the students are to find out which person is described/characterized in which extract. (The students may work individually or in pairs.)
6. Discuss the students' solutions. The students should give reasons for their choice. At an early stage in the discussion you may introduce the two names "Warburton" and "Cooper" so that it becomes easier to identify the two characters. It is to be wished for that there are some disagreements among the students, so that they will have to stand up for and defend their views. While arguing for their choices, the students gradually engage in a characterisation of the two "heroes" of the story. It should become clear that Warburton has an upper-class background. In conventional (outdated) interpretations of this story he is praised as a "gentleman" who even in rather awkward surroundings keeps up the "gentleman ideal", but, in a way, he is rather a snob. His presence in Borneo can be explained by referring to passage E: Apparently he has gambling debts. Towards the "natives", however, he feels rather sympathetic.
Cooper, on the other hand, comes from a lower middle-class or even working-class background. He is dirty, negligent and never comes to grips with the situation and the behaviour of the local people.
If you wish, you can support the findings of the students by listing the characteristics of both Warburton and Cooper in a contrastive manner on the blackboard.
By the way, Warburton is characterized in extracts A, D, E, F, I; Cooper is described in B, C, G, H.
7. Due to the fact that there is such a contrast between the two characters it becomes obvious that a "clash" between the two protagonists will be unavoidable. Well, ask the students how – far away from "civilization" in

the Borneo jungles – these two "white men" will get along with each other. What is going to happen there? If they clash, why does it happen? Could they think of any solution, any way out? The students should speculate on possible developments of the plot.

You may also ask two of the students to role-play a situation with one student taking Warburton's, the other one taking Cooper's role. You could tell them to make up a scene in which e.g. Warburton complains about Cooper's clothes and his brutal behaviour towards the natives. Or you may make the students write letters, impersonating either Warburton or Cooper, in which they rail about each other: *I've got a new colleague. He is terrible ...* or: *I've got a new post – and a new "boss": a terrible snob.*

8. Hand out Worksheet 2 (see pages 124–126). Tell the students to work out the plot by establishing the correct order, the logical sequence of the given extracts (1–8).
9. Let the students discuss their choice of ordering the extracts. The correct solution, actually, is 7–1–4–6–3–8–5–2, and generally there should be no disagreement concerning the beginning (7–1) and the end (5–2). The rough outline of the plot can easily be established. In between, however, when the plot is leading up to its climax, there are various stages whose possible sequence is not obvious, and judging the plot from the logic of the extracts an even better order – than the "correct" one 4–6–3–8 – would be 6–4–8–3 or 6–8–4–3. As you may see, the task of ordering the passages leaves enough vagueness for interpretation and disagreement. And that is the intention! In the course of working out the deveploment of the plot, the finding of the correct version does not matter. The students should be encouraged to argue, to speculate, to find reasons for their choice of sequencing, and by doing so, re-create the structure of the plot.
10. Once the students have established the plot, there remains one vital question to be solved: What is going to happen to Cooper's murderer? As for Warburton, as a resident or district officer he represents the law, and it is his duty to convict and sentence the murderer; on the other hand, he seems to be relieved, having got rid of Cooper. Well, ask the students how Warburton is going to act and to decide. They ought to dispute this issue. Don't tell them the ending of the story. Leave it open, and if they should wish to find out about it, provide them with the whole

text of Maugham's story or with just the last three or four pages. They may read the end themselves.

11. If you wish to continue this unit on Maugham's short story "The Outstation", you may now organize a court trial (along the lines described in the activity THE CASE OF LITTLE RED RIDINGHOOD, see pages 59–63). It is advisable for the teacher to act as the judge (Mr Warburton?), thus keeping law and order in the courtroom (and in the classroom).

The following roles may be taken by the students:

1. prosecutor
2. barrister to defend the accused Abas
3. Abas, accused of murdering Cooper
4. Warburton's "boy" (Abas' uncle)
5. the kris
6. Abas' mother
7. girl from the village who heard/saw(?) what was going on when Cooper was killed
8. Cooper's ghost
9. wise, old man from the village
10. Hassan, same age as Abas and his rival, he would like to see Abas convicted
11. policeman 1(he found the dead body)
12. member of the jury 1
13. policeman 2 (he is to keep order in the courtroom)
14. member of the jury 2
15. journalist (who asks all kinds of questions)

Bemerkung

Hier handelt es sich um eine Form von Literaturbehandlung, in der der eigentliche Text nur in Fragmenten benutzt wird. Bis zum Ende der Stunde bzw. der Unterrichtseinheit sollte den Schülern der Titel der behandelten Kurzgeschichte – *The Outstation* – nicht verraten werden. Dem Lehrer sei jedoch die Lektüre des gesamten Textes selbstverständlich empfohlen: vgl. Somerset Maugham: *Collected Short Stories, Vol. 4,* Penguin, S. 338–365. Vielleicht ist es nicht ganz unproblematisch, Maughams Kurzgeschichte unkommentiert zu behandeln. Zu offensichtlich sind die kolonialistisch-rassistischen Untertöne. Die Hauptpersonen sind Weiße, sind britische Kolonialbeamte, die anscheinend „ganz natürlich" herrschen, verwalten, richten usw. Die grundsätzliche Frage, was eigentlich die Europäer dort im Dschungel von Borneo treiben, warum sie überhaupt dort sind, wird nicht gestellt. Die „Eingeborenen" werden von Maugham kaum wahrgenommen, spielen eine untergeordnete, fast rein atmosphärische Rolle; ihre Probleme, ihre Wünsche, Hoffnungen, Ängste werden nicht thematisiert.

A
He went into his room, where his things were as neatly laid out as if he had an English valet, undressed, and, walking down the stairs to the bath-house, sluiced himself with cool water. The only concession he made to the climate was to wear a white dinner jacket; but otherwise, in a boiled shirt and a high collar, silk stocks and patent-leather shoes, he dressed as formally as though he were dining at his club in Pall Mall. A careful host, he went into the dining-room to see that the table was properly laid. The napkins were folded into elaborate shapes. Shaded candles in silver candlesticks shed a soft light.

B
Cooper seemed to be about thirty. He was a tall, thin fellow, with a sallow face in which there was not a spot of colour. He had a large, hooked nose and blue eyes. When entering the bungalow, he had taken off his topee and flung it to a waiting boy. Mr Warburton noticed that his large skull, covered with short, brown hair, contrasted somewhat oddly with a weak, small chin. He was dressed in khaki shorts and a khaki shirt, but they were shabby and soiled; and his topee had not been cleaned for days.

C
He was honest, just, painstaking, but he had no sympathy for the natives. It bitterly amused Mr Warburton to observe that this man who looked upon himself as every man's equal should look upon so many men as his own inferiors. He was hard, he had no patience with the native mind, and he was a bully. Mr Warburton very quickly realised that the Malays disliked and feared him.

D
"When I lived in London I moved in circles in which it would have been just as eccentric not to dress for dinner every night as not to have a bath every morning. When I came to Borneo I saw no reason to discontinue so good a habit. For three years during the war I never saw a white man. I never omitted to dress on a single occasion on which I was well enough to come to dinner. You have not been very long in this country, believe me, there is no way to maintain the proper pride which you should have in yourself. When a white man surrenders in the slightest degree to the influences that surround him he very soon loses his self-respect, and when he loses his self-respect you may be quite sure the natives will soon cease to respect him."

E
After all he was a good fellow. He was always ready to back a bill for an impecunious nobleman, and if you were in a tight corner you could safely count on him for a hundred pounds. He gave good dinners. He happened to be a gambler, an unlucky one, but he was a good loser, and it was impossible not to admire the coolness with which he lost five hundred pounds at a sitting. His passion for cards, almost as strong as his passion for titles, was the cause of his undoing.

F
He liked to sit in judgement on his fellow men. It pleased him to compose quarrels between rival chiefs. When the head-hunters were troublesome in the old days he set out to chastise them with a thrill of pride in his own behaviour. He became a skilful administrator. He was strict, just and honest. And little by little he conceived a deep love for the Malays. He interested himself in their habits and customs. He was never tired of listening to their talk. He admired their virtues ...

G
He was untidy and none too clean. His face and hands were covered with little red blotches where mosquitoes had bitten him and he had scratched himself till blood came. His long, thin face bore a sullen look.

H
Cooper abused the boy Abas of stealing some of his clothes, and when the boy denied the theft took him by the scruff of the neck and kicked him down the steps of the bungalow. The boy demanded his wages and Cooper flung at his head every word of abuse he knew. Next morning the boy waylaid him outside the Fort when he was walking to his office, and again demanded his wages. Cooper struck him in the face with his clenched fist. The boy fell to the ground and got up with blood streaming from his nose.

I
He read his *Times* every morning, did his work at the office, took his exercise, dressed for dinner, dined and sat by the river smoking his cheroot.

For the teacher: Some words and expressions might not be known:
A: valet: a man's personal servant
  to sluice: waschen, abspritzen
  Pall Mall: street in London (Westminster) where the most famous clubs were and are located
B: sallow: fahl, blässlich
  topee: hard hat for protecting the head in tropical sunshine
  khaki: cloth of yellow-brown colour, especially as worn by soldiers
C: painstaking: gewissenhaft, sorgfältig, gründlich
E: impecunious: having little or no money
  undoing: the cause of someone's ruin, failure
F: to chastise: to punish
  to conceive: (hier) fassen
G: sullen: verdrießlich, mürrisch
H: by the scruff of the neck: am Genick
  to waylay: auflauern
I: cheroot: local cigarette/cigar

1
On the first Sunday after Cooper's arrival he asked him to dinner. He did everything ceremoniously, and though they had met on the previous day in the office and later, on the Fort veranda where they drank a gin and bitters together at 6 o'clock, he sent a polite note across to the bungalow by the boy. Cooper, however unwillingly, came in evening dress and Mr Warburton, though gratified that his wish was respected, noticed with disdain that the young man's clothes were badly cut and his shirt ill-fitting. But Mr Warburton was in a good temper that evening.

"By the way," he said to him, as he shook hands, "I've talked to my head-boy about finding you someone and he recommends his nephew. I've seen him and he seems a bright and willing lad. Would you like to see him?"

"I don't mind."

"He's waiting now."

Mr Warburton called his boy and told him to send for his nephew. In a moment a tall, slender youth of twenty appeared. He had large dark eyes and a good profile. He answered to the name of Abas. Mr Warburton looked on him with approval, and his manner insensibly softened as he spoke to him in fluent and idiomatic Malay.

2
Cooper was lying in the bed, with his mouth open, and a kris sticking in his heart. He had been killed in his sleep. Mr Warburton started, but not because he had not expected to see just such a sight, he started because he felt in himself a sudden glow of exultation. A great burden had been lifted from his shoulders.

Cooper was quite cold. Mr Warburton took the kris out of the wound, it had been thrust in with such force that he had to use an effort to get it out, and looked at it. He recognised it. It was a kris that a dealer had offered him some weeks before, and which he knew Cooper had bought.

"Where's Abas?" he asked sternly.

"Abas is in the village of his mother's brother."

3
"I understand that you are again having trouble with your servants. Abas, my head-boy's nephew, complains that you have held back his wages for three months. I consider it a most arbitrary proceeding. The lad wishes to leave you, and I certainly do not blame him. I must insist on your paying what is due to him."

"I don't choose that he should leave me. I am holding back his wages as a pledge of his good behaviour."

"You do not know the Malay character. The Malays are very sensitive to injury and ridicule. They are passionate and revengeful. It is my duty to warn you that if you drive this boy beyond a certain point you run a great risk."

Cooper gave a contemptuous chuckle.

"What do you think he'll do?"

"I think he'll kill you."

4
The two men now held no communication with one another. They broke the time-honoured custom sharing, notwithstanding personal dislike, a drink at six o' clock with any white man who happened to be at the station. Each lived in his own house as though the other did not exist. Now that Cooper had fallen into the work, it was necessary for them to have little to do with one another in the office. Mr Warburton used his orderly to send any message he had to give to his assistant, and his instructions he sent by a formal letter. They saw one another constantly, that was inevitable, but did not exchange half a dozen words in a week. The fact that they could not avoid catching sight of one another got on their nerves. They brooded over their antagonism, and Mr Warburton, taking his daily walk, could think of nothing but how much he detested his assistant.

5
The idiot! Hesitation for a little was in Mr Warburton's mind. Did the man know in what peril he was? He supposed he ought to send for him. But each time he had tried to reason with Cooper, Cooper had insulted him. Anger, furious anger welled up suddenly in Mr Warburton's heart, so that the veins on his temples stood out and he clenched his fists. The cad had had his warning. Now let him take what was coming to him. It was no business of his, and if anything happened it was not his fault.

6
"You disliked me from the first moment I came here. You've done everything you could to make the place impossible for me because I don't lick your boots for you. You got your knife into me because I wouldn't flatter you."
Cooper, spluttering with rage, was nearing dangerous ground, and Mr Warburton's eyes grew on a sudden colder and more piercing.
"You are wrong. I thought you were a cad, but I was perfectly satisfied with the way you did your work."
"You snob. You damned snob. You thought me a cad because I hadn't been to Eton. Oh, they told me in K. S. what to expect. Why, don't you know that you're the laughing-stock of the whole country? I could hardly help bursting into a roar of laughter when you told me your celebrated story about the Prince of Wales. My God, how they shouted at the club when they told it. By God, I'd rather be the cad I am than the snob you are."
He got Mr Warburton on the raw.
"If you don't get out of my house this minute I shall knock you down," he cried.
The other came a little closer to him and put his face in his.
"Touch me, touch me," he said. "By God, I'd like to see you hit me. Do you want to say it again? Snob. Snob."
Cooper was three inches taller than Mr Warburton, a strong, muscular young man. Mr Warburton was fat and fifty-four. His clenched fist shot out.

7

The new assistant arrived in the afternoon. When the Resident, Mr Warburton, was told that the prahu was in sight he put on his solar topee and went down to the landing-stage. The guard, eight little Dayak soldiers, stood to attention as he passed. He noted with satisfaction that their bearing was martial, their uniforms neat and clean, and their guns shining. They were a credit to him. From the landing-stage he watched the bend of the river round which in a moment the boat would sweep. He awaited the newcomer with mingled feelings. There was more work in the district than one man could properly do, and during his periodical tours of the country under his charge it had been inconvenient to leave the station in the hands of a native clerk, but he had been so long the only white man there that he could not face the arrival of another without misgiving. He was accustomed to loneliness.

8

"*My dear Warburton,*

I do not want to answer your letter officially, and so I am writing you a few lines myself. I know Cooper is a rough diamond, but he is capable, and he should be given every chance. I think you are a little too much inclined to attach importance to a man's social position. You must remember that times have changed. Of course it's a very good thing for a man to be a gentleman, but it's better that he should be competent and hard-working. I think if you'll exercise a little tolerance you'll get on very well with Cooper.

Yours very sincerely,
Richard Temple."

For the teacher: Some words and expressions might not be known to the students:

1: disdain: Verachtung
2: kris: a Malay dagger
   to thrust: stoßen
3: arbitrary: willkürlich
   pledge: Versprechen, Zeichen
   contemptuous: verächtlich, geringschätzig
4: notwithstanding: in spite of
   to detest: verachten
5: peril: danger
   to well up: anschwellen, emporsteigen
   cad: person of low manners (nicht mehr üblich)
6: to get/to touch s.o. on the raw: jemanden an seinem wunden Punkt berühren
7: prahu: Malay boat

Ray Bradbury "The Veldt"

Lernstufe: Upper Intermediate/Advanced
Kontext: englische Literatur, Short Story; topic: childhood and adolescence
Material: Text der Geschichte
Dauer: 7 Stunden

Ray Bradbury (1920)
Ray Bradbury was born into a working-class family in Illinois and spent most of his youth moving forth between Waukegan, Illinois and Los Angeles. On leaving High School he decided not to go to College, but began writing short stories, poems and radio plays. Although often described as a science-fiction author, he rejects this title, claiming to be fantasy-writer. His most famous works are probably *The Martian Chronicles*, which earned him an asteroid named in his honour (*9766 Bradbury*), as well as a crater on the moon (*Dandelion Crater*), and *The Illustrated Man*. He also wrote *Fahrenheit 451*, which was made into a very successful film in 1966.

What to do

1. Ask your students to imagine that they feel they are being neglected or badly treated by one or both of their parents and that they are desperately looking for a way out of their misery.
   What decision would they make? How would they try to change or improve their situation? How do they think their parent(s) would react?
   Ask them to write a short note to a person they trust, describing the situation and saying what they have planned to do. Explain that they may never see this person again, so they can be perfectly frank.
2. Take the (anonymous) notes, mix them and ask the students to draw one, being careful not to draw their own. They should then try to jot down how they feel, having read the note. Then the notes should be read out in class, with a general discussion about the reactions to them.
3. Ask your students to imagine that they are living in the 22nd century. Automation has ensured that life in the home has been made as pleasant

as possible. There are some apparatus which look after one's physical welfare and others that take care of one's mental well-being. Ask them to close their eyes and imagine what their home looks like inside. After a minute or two, they should describe their "fantastic" surroundings.
4. Following this, the students read the first page of "The Veldt" up to "... with a soft automaticity".

The Veldt

"George, I wish you'd look at the nursery."
"What's wrong with it?"
"I don't know."
"Well, then."
"I just want you to look at it, is all, or call a psychologist in to look at it."
"What would a psychologist want with a nursery?"
"You know very well what he'd want." His wife paused in the middle of the kitchen and watched the stove busy humming to itself, making supper for four.
"It's just that the nursery is different now than it was."
"All right, let's have a look."
They walked down the hall of their soundproofed Happylife Home, which had cost them thirty thousand dollars installed, this house which clothed and fed and rocked them to sleep and played and sang and was good to them. Their approach sensitized a switch somewhere and the nursery light flicked on when they came within ten feet of it. Similarly, behind them, in the halls, lights went on and off as they left them behind with a soft automaticity.

---

5. Divide your class into 3 groups, each group having a different part of the story to read.
   - Group A has the text from "Well," said George Hadley. to "... Sorry, no."
   - Group B has the text from "The lions were coming ..." to "Now, Lydia ..."
   - Group C has the text from "You've got to tell Wendy ..." to "'Of course not,'" he said.

The students read their text on their own, then get together as a group and talk about their text, until they are quite sure everyone has understood it. The students are then regrouped so that each group consists of 3 members (A, B and C), each of whom has read a different part of the story. The members of the group tell each other what they know. When the students all feel they know what has happened up to this point, one group can tell the story to the class, asking for advice on parts they may have misunderstood or left out.

It is advisable to tell the students to read the parts they have "heard" as homework.

"Well," said George Hadley.
They stood on the thatched floor of the nursery. It was forty feet across by forty feet long and thirty feet high; it had cost half again as much as the rest of the house. "But nothing's too good for our children," George had said.
The nursery was silent. It was empty as a jungle glade at hot high noon. The walls were blank and two dimensional. Now, as George and Lydia Hadley stood in the center of the room, the walls began to purr and recede into crystalline distance, it seemed, and presently an African veldt appeared, in three dimensions; on all sides, in colors reproduced to the final pebble and bit of straw. The ceiling above them became a deep sky with a hot yellow sun.
George Hadley felt the perspiration start on his brow.
"Let's get out of the sun," he said. "This is a little too real. But I don't see anything wrong."
"Wait a moment, you'll see," said his wife.
Now the hidden odorophonics were beginning to blow a wind of odor at the two people in the middle of the baked veldtland. The hot straw smell of lion grass, the cool green smell of the hidden water hole, the great rusty smell of animals, the smell of dust like a red paprika in the hot air. And now the sounds: the thump of distant antelope feet on grassy sod, the papery rustling of vultures. A shadow passed through the sky. The shadow bickered on George Hadley's upturned, sweating face.
"Filthy creatures," he heard his wife say.
"The vultures."
"You see, there are the lions, far over, that way. Now they're on their way to the water hole. They've just been eating." said Lydia. "I don't know what."
"Some animal." George Hadley put his hand up to shield off the burning light from his squinted eyes. "A zebra or a baby giraffe, maybe."
"Are you sure?" His wife sounded peculiarly tense.
"No, it's a little late to be sure," he said, amused. "Nothing over there I can see but cleaned bone, and the vultures dropping for what's left."
"Did you hear that scream?" she asked.
"No."
"About a minute ago?"
"Sorry, no."

The lions were coming. And again George Hadley was filled with admiration for the mechanical genius who had conceived this room. A miracle of efficiency selling for an absurdly low price. Every home should have one. Oh, occasionally they frightened you with their clinical accuracy, they startled you, gave *you a* twinge, but most of the time what fun for everyone, not only your own son and daughter, but for yourself when you felt like a quick jaunt to a foreign land, a quick change of scenery. Well, here it was!

And here were the lions now, fifteen feet away, so real, so feverishly and startlingly real that you could feel the prickling fur on your hand, and your mouth was stuffed with the dusty upholstery smell of their heated pelts, and the yellow of them was in your eyes like the yellow of an exquisite French tapestry, the yellows of lions and summer grass, and the sound of the matted lion lungs exhaling on the silent noontide, and the smell of meat from the panting, dripping mouths.

The lions stood looking at George and Lydia Hadley with terrible green-yellow eyes.

"Watch out!" screamed Lydia.

The lions came running at them.

Lydia bolted and ran. Instinctively, George sprang after her. Outside, in the hall, with the door slammed he was laughing and she was crying, and they both stood appalled at the other's reaction.

"George!"

"Lydia! Oh, my dear poor sweet Lydia!"

"They almost got us!"

"Walls, Lydia, remember; crystal walls, that's all they are. Oh, they look real, I must admit – Africa in your parlor – but it's all dimensional superractionary, supersensitive color film and mental tape film behind glass screens. It's all odorophonics and sonics, Lydia. Here's my handkerchief."

"I'm afraid." She came to him and put her body against him and cried steadily. "Did you see? Did you feel? It's too real."

"Now, Lydia ..."

"You've got to tell Wendy and Peter not to read any more on Africa."

"Of course – of course." He patted her.

"Promise?"

"Sure."

"And lock the nursery for a few days until I get my nerves settled."

"You know how difficult Peter is about that. When I punished him a month ago by locking the nursery for even a few hours – the tantrum he threw! And Wendy too. They live for the nursery."

"It's got to be locked, that's all there is to it."

"All right." Reluctantly he locked the huge door. "You've been working too hard. You need a rest."
"I don't know – I don't know," she said, blowing her nose, sitting down in a chair that immediately began to rock and comfort her. "Maybe I don't have enough to do. Maybe I have time to think too much. Why don't we shut the whole house off for a few days and take a vacation?"
"You mean you want to fry my eggs for me?!"
"Yes." She nodded.
"And dam my socks?"
"Yes." A frantic, watery-eyed nodding.
"And sweep the house?"
"Yes, yes – oh, yes!"
"But I thought that's why we bought this house, so we wouldn't have to do anything?"
"That's just it. I feel like I don't belong here. The house is wife and mother now and nursemaid. Can I compete with an African veldt? Can I give a bath and scrub the children as efficiently or quickly as the automatic scrub bath can? I can not. And it isn't just me. It's you. You've been awfully nervous lately."
"I suppose I have been smoking too much."
"You look as if you didn't know what to do with yourself in this house, either. You smoke a little more every morning and drink a little more every afternoon and need a little more sedative every night. You're beginning to feel unnecessary, too."
"Am I?" He paused and tried to feel into himself to see what was really there.
"Oh, George!" She looked beyond him, at the nursery door. "Those lions can't get out of there, can they?"
He looked at the door and saw it tremble as if something had jumped against it from the other side.
"Of course not," he said.

6. Tell your students that what they will find on

   A are statements made by grown-ups about themselves and their children, and on
   B snatches of conversation between children and parents.

   Ask them to try to imagine what these children are like and what sort of relationship they and their parents have. Are the grown-ups justified in talking about the children like this? Can the student sympathize with one or other of the 2 parties? This could lead you to quite a lively discussion, after which the students should read on in the text up to "They went to the fuse box together and threw the switch that killed the nursery."

A

"They were awfully young ... for death thoughts. Or, no, you were never too young, really. Long before you knew what death was you were wishing it on someone else."

"We've given the children everything they ever wanted. Is this our reward ...?"

"Children are carpets, they should be stepped on occasionally!" "We've never lifted a hand. They're insufferable – let's admit it. They come and go when they like; they treat us as if we were offspring. They're spoiled and we're spoiled."

"... You'll have to change your life. Like too many others, you've built it around creature comforts."

"The usual violences, a tendency towards a slight paranoia here or there, usual in children because they feel persecuted by parents constantly, ..."

"We've been contemplating our mechanical, electronic navels for too long. My God, how we need a breath of honest air!"

B

"There's no Africa in the nursery," said Peter simply. "Oh, come now, Peter. We know better."

"Wendy'll look and come tell us," said Peter. "She doesn't have to tell me. I've seen it."
"I'm sure you're mistaken, Father."
"I'm not, Peter. Come along now."

"Father?" said Peter.
"Yes."
Peter looked at his shoes. He never looked at his father any more, nor at his mother. "You aren't going to lock up the nursery for good, are you?"
"That all depends."

"I don't want to do anything but look, listen and smell; what else is there to do?"

---

7. Ask them to reconsider their opinion of the Hadley family. Have they changed their minds? What do they expect to happen as a result of the nursery being "killed"? Finally, the students read the conclusion.

At dinner they ate alone, for Wendy and Peter were at a special plastic carnival across town and had televised home to say they'd be late, to go ahead eating. So George Hadley, bemused, sat watching the dining-room table produce warm dishes of food from its mechanical interior.
"We forgot the ketchup," he said.
"Sorry," said a small voice within the table, and ketchup appeared.
As for the nursery, thought George Hadley, it won't hurt for the children to be locked out of it awhile. Too much of anything isn't good for anyone. And it was clearly indicated that the children had been spending a little too much time on Africa. That sun. He could feel it on his neck, still, like a hot paw. And the lions. And the smell of blood. Remarkable how the nursery caught the telepathic emanations of the children's minds and created life to fill their every desire. The children thought lions, and there were lions. The children thought zebras, and there were zebras. Sun – sun. Giraffes – giraffes. Death and death.
That *last*. He chewed tastelessly on the meat that the table had cut for him. Death thoughts. They were awfully young, Wendy and Peter, for death thoughts. Or, no, you were never too young, really. Long before you knew what death was you were wishing it on someone else. When you were two years old you were shooting people with cap pistols.
But this – the long, hot African veldt – the awful death in the jaws of a lion. And repeated again and again.
"Where are you going?"
He didn't answer Lydia. Preoccupied, he let the lights glow softly on ahead of him, extinguish behind him as he padded to the nursery door. He listened against it. Far away, a lion roared.
He unlocked the door and opened it. Just before he stepped inside, he heard a faraway scream. And then another war from the lions, which subsided quickly.
He stepped into Africa. How many times in the last year had he opened this door and found Wonderland, Alice, the Mock Turtle, or Aladdin and his Magical Lamp, or Jack Pumpkinhead of Oz, or Dr Doolittle, or the cow jumping over a very real-appearing moon – all the delightful contraptions of a make-believe world. How often had he seen Pegasus flying in the sky ceiling, or seen fountains of red fireworks, or heard angel voices singing. But now, this yellow hot Africa, this bake oven with murder in the heat. Perhaps Lydia was right. Perhaps they needed a little vacation from the fantasy which was growing a bit too real for ten-year-old children. It was all right to exercise one's mind with gymnastic fantasies, but when the lively child mind settled on one pattern ...?
It seemed that, at a distance, for the past month, he had heard lions roaring, and smelled their strong odor seeping as far away as his study door. But, being busy, he had paid it no attention.
George Hadley stood on the African grassland alone. The lions looked up from

their feeding, watching him. The only flaw to the illusion was the open door through which he could see his wife, far down the dark hall, like a framed picture, eating her dinner abstractedly.
"Go away," he said to the lions.
They did not go.
He knew the principle of the room exactly. You sent out your thoughts. Whatever you thought would appear.
"Let's have Aladdin and his lamp," he snapped.
The veldtland remained; the lions remained.
"Come on, room! I demand Aladdin!" he said.
Nothing happened. The lions mumbled in their baked pelts.
"Aladdin!"
He went back to dinner. "The fool room's out of order," he said. "It won't respond."
"Or – "
"Or what?"
"Or it *can't* respond," said Lydia, "because the children have thought about Africa and lions and killing so many days that the room's in a rut."
"Could be."
"Or Peter's set it to remain that way."
"Set it?"
"He may have got into the machinery and fixed something."
"Peter doesn't know machinery."
"He's a wise one for ten. That I. Q. of his – "
"Nevertheless – "
"Hello, Mom. Hello, Dad."
The Hadleys turned. Wendy and Peter were coming in the front door, cheeks like peppermint candy, eyes like bright blue agate marbles, a smell of ozone on their jumpers from their trip in the helicopter.
"You're just in time for supper," said both parents.
"We're full of strawberry ice cream and hot dogs," said the children, holding hands. "But we'll sit and watch."
"Yes, come tell us about the nursery," said George Hadley.
The brother and sister blinked at him and then at each other. "Nursery?"
"All about Africa and everything," said the father with false joviality.
"I don't understand," said Peter.
"Your mother and I were just traveling through Africa with rod and reel; Tom Swift and his Electric Lion," said George Hadley.
"There's no Africa in the nursery," said Peter simply.
"Oh, come now, Peter. We know better."
"I don't remember any Africa," said Peter to Wendy. "Do you?"
"No."

"Run see and come tell."
She obeyed.
"Wendy, come back here!" said George Hadley, but she was gone. The house lights followed her like a flock of fireflies. Too late, he realized he had forgotten to lock the nursery door after his last inspection.
"Wendy'll look and come tell us," said Peter.
"She doesn't have to tell me. I've seen it."
"I'm sure you're mistaken, Father."
"I'm not, Peter. Come along now."
But Wendy was back. "It's not Africa," she said breathlessly.
"We'll see about this," said George Hadley, and they all walked down the hall together and opened the nursery door.
There was a green, lovely forest, a lovely river, a purple mountain, high voices singing, and Rima, lovely and mysterious, lurking in the trees with colorful flights of butterflies, like animated bouquets, lingering in her long hair. The African veldtland was gone. The lions were gone. Only Rima was here now, singing a song so beautiful that it brought tears to your eyes.
George Hadley looked in at the changed scene. "Go to bed," he said to the children.
They opened their mouths.
"You heard me," he said.
They went off to the air closet, where a wind sucked them like brown leaves up the flue to their slumber rooms.
George Hadley walked through the singing glade and picked up something that lay in the corner near where the lions had been. He walked slowly back to his wife.
"What is that?" she asked.
"An old wallet of mine," he said.
He showed it to her. The smell of hot grass was on it and the smell of a lion. There were drops of saliva on it, it had been chewed, and there were blood smears on both sides.
He closed the nursery door and locked it, tight.
In the middle of the night he was still awake and he knew his wife was awake.
"Do you think Wendy changed it?" she said at last, in the dark room.
"Of course."
"Made it from a veldt into a forest and put Rima there instead of lions?"
"Yes."
"Why?"
"I don't know. But it's staying locked until I find out."
"How did your wallet get there?"
"I don't know anything," he said, "except that I'm beginning to be sorry we bought that room for the children. If children are neurotic at all, a room like

that – "

"It's supposed to help them work off their neuroses in a healthful way."

"I'm starting to wonder." He stared at the ceiling.

"We've given the children everything they ever wanted. Is this our reward – secrecy, disobedience?"

"Who was it said, 'Children are – carpets, they should be stepped on occasionally'? We've never lifted a hand. They're insufferable – let's admit it. They come and go when they like; they treat us as if we were offspring. They're spoiled and we're spoiled."

"They've been acting funny ever since you forbade them to take the rocket to New York a few months ago."

"They're not old enough to do that alone, I explained."

"Nevertheless, I've noticed they've been decidedly cool toward us since."

"I think I'll have David McClean come tomorrow morning to have a look at Africa."

"But it's not Africa now, it's Green Mansions country and Rima."

"I have a feeling it'll be Africa again before then."

A moment later they heard the screams.

Two screams. Two people screaming from downstairs. And then a roar of lions.

"Wendy and Peter aren't in their rooms," said his wife.

He lay in his bed with his beating heart. "No," he said.

"They've broken into the nursery."

"Those screams – they sound familiar."

"Do they?"

"Yes, awfully."

And although their beds tried very hard, the two adults couldn't be rocked to sleep for another hour. A smell of cats was in the night air.

"Father?" said Peter.

"Yes."

Peter looked at his shoes. He never looked at his father anymore, nor at his mother. "You aren't going to lock up the nursery for good, are you?"

"That all depends."

"On what?" snapped Peter.

"On you and your sister. If you intersperse this Africa with a little variety – oh, Sweden perhaps, or Denmark or China – "

"I thought we were free to play as we wished."

"You are, within reasonable bounds."

"What's wrong with Africa, Father?"

"Oh, so now you admit you have been conjuring up Africa, do you?"

"I wouldn't want the nursery locked up," said Peter coldly.

"Ever."

"Matter of fact, we're thinking of turning the whole house off for about a month. Live sort of a carefree one-for-all existence."
"That sounds dreadful! Would I have to tie my own shoes instead of letting the shoe tier do it? And brush my own teeth and comb my hair and give myself a bath?"
"It would be fun for a change, don't you think?"
"No, it would be horrid. I didn't like it when you took out the picture painter last month."
"That's because I wanted you to learn to paint all by yourself, son."
"I don't want to do anything but look and listen and smell; what else is there to do?"
"All right, go play in Africa."
"Will you shut off the house sometime soon?"
"We're considering it."
"I don't think you'd better consider it any more, Father!"
"I won't have any threats from my son!"
"Very well." And Peter strolled off to the nursery.
"Am I on time?" said David McClean.
"Breakfast?" asked George Hadley.
"Thanks, had some. What's the trouble?"
"David, you're a psychologist."
"I should hope so."
"Well, then, have a look at our nursery. You saw it a year ago when you dropped by; did you notice anything peculiar about it then?"
"Can't say I did; the usual violences, a tendency toward a slight paranoia here or there, usual in children because they feel persecuted by parents constantly, but, oh, really nothing."
They walked down the hall. "I locked the nursery up," explained the father, "and the children broke back into it during the night. I let them stay so they could form the patterns for you to see."
There was a terrible screaming from the nursery.
"There it is," said George Hadley. "See what you make of it."
They walked in on the children without rapping. The screams had faded. The lions were feeding.
"Run outside a moment, children," said George Hadley.
"No, don't change the mental combination. Leave the walls as they are. Get!"
With the children gone, the two men stood studying the lions clustered at a distance, eating with great relish whatever it was they had caught.
"I wish I knew what it was," said George Hadley. "Sometimes I can almost see. Do you think if I brought high-powered binoculars here and –"
David McClean laughed dryly. "Hardly." He turned to study all four walls. "How long has this been going on?"

"A little over a month."
"It certainly doesn't feel good."
"I want facts, not feelings."
"My dear George, a psychologist never saw a fact in his life. He only hears about feelings; vague things. This doesn't feel good, I tell you. Trust my hunches and my instincts. I have a nose for something bad. This is very bad. My advice to you is to have the whole damn room torn down and your children brought to me every day during the next year for treatment."
"Is it that bad?"
"I'm afraid so. One of the original uses of these nurseries was so that we could study the patterns left on the walls by the child's mind, study at our leisure, and help the child. In this case, however, the room has become a channel toward – destructive thoughts, instead of a release away from them."
"Didn't you sense this before?"
"I sensed only that you had spoiled your children more than most. And now you're letting them down in some way. What way?"
"I wouldn't let them go to New York."
"What else?"
"I've taken a few machines from the house and threatened them, a month ago, with closing up the nursery unless they did their homework. I did close it for a few days to show I meant business."
"Ah ha!"
"Does that mean anything?"
"Everything. Where before they had a Santa Claus now they have a Scrooge. Children prefer Santas. You've let this room and this house replace you and your wife in your children's affections. This room is their mother and father, far more important in their lives than their real parents. And now you come along and want to shut it off. No wonder there's hatred here. You can feel it coming out of the sky. Feel that sun. George, you'll have to change your life. Like too many others, you've built it around creature comforts. Why, you'd starve tomorrow if something went wrong in your kitchen. You wouldn't know how to tap an egg. Nevertheless, turn everything off. Start new. It'll take time. But we'll make good children out of bad in a year, wait and see."
"But won't the shock be too much for the children, shutting the room up abruptly, for good?"
"I don't want them going any deeper into this, that's all." The lions were finished with their red feast.
The lions were standing on the edge of the clearing watching the two men.
"Now *I'm* feeling persecuted," said McClean. "Let's get out of here. I never have cared for these damned rooms. Make me nervous."
"The lions look real, don't they?" said George Hadley. "I don't suppose there's any way –"

"What?"
"– that they could become real?"
"Not that I know."
"Some flaw in the machinery, a tampering or something?"
"No."
They went to the door.
"I don't imagine the room will like being turned off," said the father.
"Nothing ever likes to die – even a room."
"I wonder if it hates me for wanting to switch it off?"
"Paranoia is thick around here today," said David McClean. "You can follow it like a spoor. Hello." He bent and picked up a bloody scarf. "This yours?"
"No." George Hadley's face was rigid. "It belongs to Lydia."
They went to the fuse box together and threw the switch that killed the nursery.

The two children were in hysterics. They screamed and pranced and threw things. They yelled and sobbed and swore and jumped at the furniture.
"You can't do that to the nursery, you can't!"
"Now, children."
The children flung themselves onto a couch, weeping. "George," said Lydia Hadley, "turn on the nursery, just for a few moments. You can't be so abrupt."
"No."
"You can't be so cruel."
"Lydia, it's off, and it stays off. And the whole damn house dies as of here and now. The more I see of the mess we've put ourselves in, the more it sickens me. We've been contemplating our mechanical, electronic navels for too long. My God, how we need a breath of honest air!"
And he marched about the house turning off the voice clocks, the stoves, the heaters, the shoe shiners, the shoe lacers, the body scrubbers and swabbers and massagers, and every other machine he could put his hand to.
The house was full of dead bodies, it seemed. It felt like a mechanical cemetery. So silent. None of the humming hidden energy of machines waiting to function at the tap of a button.
"Don't let them do it!" wailed Peter at the ceiling, as if he was talking to the house, the nursery. "Don't let Father kill everything." He turned to his father. "Oh, I hate you!"
"Insults won't get you anywhere."
"I wish you were dead!"
"We were, for a long while. Now we're going to really start living. Instead of being handled and massaged, we're going to live."

Wendy was still crying and Peter joined her again. "Just a moment, just one moment, just another moment of nursery," they wailed.
"Oh, George," said the wife, "it can't hurt."
"All right – all right, if they'll only just shut up. One minute, mind you, and then off forever."
"Daddy, Daddy, Daddy!" sang the children, smiling with wet faces.
"And then we're going on a vacation. David McClean is coming back in half an hour to help us move out and get to the airport. I'm going to dress. You turn the nursery on for a minute, Lydia, just a minute, mind you."
And the three of them went babbling off while he let himself be vacuumed upstairs through the air flue and set about dressing himself. A minute later Lydia appeared.
"I'll be glad when we get away," she sighed.
"Did you leave them in the nursery?"
"I wanted to dress, too. Oh, that horrid Africa. What can they see in it?"
"Well, in five minutes we'll be on our way to Iowa. Lord, how did we ever get in this house? What prompted us to buy a nightmare?"
"Pride, money, foolishness."
"I think we'd better get downstairs before those kids get engrossed with those damned beasts again."
Just then they heard the children calling, "Daddy, Mommy, come quick – quick!"
They went downstairs in the air flue and ran down the hall. The children were nowhere in sight. "Wendy? Peter!"
They ran into the nursery. The veldtland was empty save for the lions waiting, looking at them. "Peter, Wendy?"
The door slammed.
"Wendy, Peter!"
George Hadley and his wife whirled and ran back to the door.
"Open the door!" cried George Hadley, trying the knob.
"Why, they've locked it from the outside! Peter!" He beat at the door. "Open up!"
He heard Peter's voice outside, against the door.
"Don't let them switch off the nursery and the house," he was saying.
Mr and Mrs George Hadley beat at the door. "Now, don't be ridiculous, children. It's time to go. Mr McClean'll be here in a minute and ..."
And then they heard the sounds.
The lions on three sides of them, in the yellow veldt grass, padding through the dry straw, rumbling and roaring in their throats.
The lions.
Mr Hadley looked at his wife and they turned and looked back at the beasts edging slowly forward, crouching, tails stiff. Mr and Mrs Hadley screamed.
And suddenly they realized why those other screams had sounded familiar.

> "Well, here I am," said David McClean in the nursery doorway. "Oh, hello." He stared at the two children seated in the center of the open glade eating a little picnic lunch. Beyond them was the water hole and the yellow veldtland; above was the hot sun. He began to perspire. "Where are your father and mother?" The children looked up and smiled. "Oh, they'll be here directly."
> "Good, we must get going." At a distance Mr McClean saw the lions fighting and clawing and then quieting down to feed in silence under the shady trees. He squinted at the lions with his hand up to his eyes.
> Now the lions were done feeding. They moved to the water hole to drink.
> A shadow flickered over Mr McClean's hot face. Many shadows flickered. The vultures were dropping down the blazing sky.
> "A cup of tea?" asked Wendy in the silence.

8. To round off the story you could offer one of the following activities.
   - Ask them to write an epitaph for the parents' gravestone.
   - Ask them to form groups and write a short newspaper article on the event as could appear in different newspapers, e.g. in "The Sun", "Daily Mirror", "The Times", "The Guardian", "Morning Star".
   - Ask them to speculate on what might have/could have happened if the parents had reacted differently. "If George had/hadn't ..." (This exercise offers a little refreshment in grammar!)

Oscar Wilde "The Nightingale and the Rose"

Lernstufe: Advanced
Kontext: englische Literatur, Short story; topic: love
Material: Karten mit je 1 Aufgabe (1 Satz pro Gruppe); sie sollten vorzugsweise den Schülern in einem Umschlag angeboten werden, der mit Rosenbildern oder Rosenpapier beklebt ist. Text, evtl. Musikkassette, Dictionary of Quotations, Zeitschriften, Scheren, Kleber, Pappe, Overheadfolie, Overheadprojektor
Dauer: mindestens 3–4 Stunden

Oscar Wilde (1854–1900)
Oscar Wilde was born in Dublin, as the son of Sir William and Lady Jane Wilde. He studied at Trinity College, Dublin and Magdalen College, Oxford

and was a brilliant student. He was always a colourful figure, famous for wearing velvet knee-breeches and collecting peacock's feathers.
In 1884 he married and in 1888 he published a collection of fairy-stories he had written for his two sons, "The Happy Prince and Other Tales". "The Nightingale and the Rose" is one of these stories. The novel "The Picture of Dorian Gray" followed in 1890, after which Wilde found his real vocation – as playwriter. His last play was his greatest masterpiece: "The Importance of Being Earnest" 1895.
Oscar Wilde was a homosexual at a time when this was forbidden by law. The Marquis of Queensberry, father of Wilde's lover Lord Alfred Douglas, publicly insulted Wilde, who sued him for libel. Unfortunately Wilde lost the case and was prosecuted for homosexuality and sentenced to two years hard labour. On his release from prison he moved to France, where he died in poverty three years later. Oscar Wilde was a very controversial figure in his day – he shocked Victorian society, which hated him for blatantly exposing its double standards. He caused furore with his brilliant wit – when asked by a U. S. Customs Officer if he had anything to declare, he is said to have answered "Only my genius."
"The Nightingale and the Rose" tells the story of a nightingale who sings of love night after night. One day she overhears a student weeping, because the girl he loves will only dance with him at a ball, if he brings her a red rose – and he cannot find one anywhere. The nightingale is so impressed by this "true" lover, that she resolves to help, even at the cost of her own life. The only way to get a red rose is for her to press her breast against the thorn of a white one, singing until her life's blood flows into it, turning it red. The student knows nothing of her sacrifice and when he brings his love the red rose, she turns him down in favour of someone else, who will give her jewels. The student is disillusioned with love which "is always ... making one believe things that are not true" and throws the rose onto the street, where it is crushed by a cart.

What to do

1. Ask your students to work in pairs or groups, hand out the envelopes with the tasks. Have a Dictionary of Quotations at the ready in case they need one.
2. Each group/pair chooses one of the tasks and begins to work on it. Should some students wish to do the "musical" task but aren't quite

sure of the tune, it might be helpful to ask the music teacher to play it on a piano and record it on a cassette.
3. Students present their results. Depending on the task they can write a song about roses and sing it to the class, • read their text, illustrating it with pictures and quotations or song-lines on transparencies, • act out their text, • have a poetry reading and show their poems on a transparency to facilitate understanding, • create a frieze of Valentine's Day cards.
4. Give the students the quotation from the first page of the story "The Nightingale and the Rose": **"Here at last is a true lover"** and ask them to say what they **think** a true lover is. Is there such a thing as a true lover? • How does one recognize a true lover?
5. In Oscar Wilde's story this sentence is spoken by a nightingale. Ask your students to speculate on the following: Why does a **nightingale** say this? • Who does she say it to? • Who is the person she is speaking about? Collect the most interesting ideas on a transparency, and keep them until the end of the story, when you will give them a second look.
6. Hand out the first part of the story. Ask your students to read as far as "But the tree shook its head" and to do task no. 1. They may do it in pairs.
7. While your students are reading out their "descriptions", write these on a transparency and have a vote on the ones they like best.
8. Let your students read on at their own pace. Then they work on task no. 2 (see page 146). Collect their ideas orally.
9. Give the students the next part of the story up to "and he leaned down and plucked it". Ask them, when they have finished, to note down the feelings they had while they were reading. They should then talk to their neighbours about their reaction to the events in the story, looking for similarities or differences of opinion. This is task no. 3.
10. Show the transparency, on which the student goes to his loved one's house and ask for suggestions about her reaction.
11. Give your students the end of the story to read.
12. Show them the transparency with the speculations from 5 and ask them to revise their opinions.
13. Ask them to discuss what possible moral the story might have and to write their favourite version.

Tasks

Please decide as a group on one of the following tasks. You will have to present your results to the whole class.

1. Using these bars of music, write a song about a rose and sing it aloud. (If you are no good at reading music, you may go outside and listen to the tune on cassette!)

2. Think of lines from at least 3 songs or of 3 quotations you know that have to do with roses, and work them into an interesting text. It can be a radio-play, a short essay, article in a magazine or anything else you can think of. (If you are at loss for quotations, there are dictionaries of quotations to help you.)

3. Write a short poem about a rose/roses. It can be in free verse or rhyming, Haiku or a sonnet – anything you like. Haiku is a short Japanese poem, which consists of 17 syllables, like this:
    5 mornings crisp and cold
    7 mist hanging in the tree-tops
    5 autumn gilds the fields

4. You are the advertising agency responsible for the publicity work for the Rosegrowers' Association. Design a Valentine's Day card with a difference – not forgetting who is paying you!

The Nightingale and the Rose

"S H E said that she would dance with me if I brought her red roses," cried the young Student, "but in all my garden there is no red rose."
From her nest in the holm-oak tree the Nightingale heard him, and she looked out through the leaves and wondered.
"No red rose in all my garden!" he cried, and his beautiful eyes filled with tears. "Ah, on what little things does happiness depend! I have read all that the wise men have written, and all the secrets of philosophy are mine, yet for want of a red rose is my life made wretched."
"Here at last is a true lover," said the Nightingale. "Night after night have I sung of him though I knew him not: night after night have I told his story to the stars and now I see him. His hair is dark as the hyacinth-blossom, and his lips are red as the rose of his desire, but passion has made his face like pale ivory and sorrow has set her seal upon his brow."
"The Prince gives a ball tomorrow night," murmured the young Student, "and my love will be of the company. If I bring her a red rose she will dance with me till dawn. If I bring her a red rose, I shall hold her in my arms, and she will lean her head upon my shoulder and her hand will be clasped in mine. But there is no red rose in my garden, so I shall sit lonely and she will pass me by. She will have no heed of me, and my heart will break."
"Here, indeed, is the true lover," said the Nightingale. "What I sing of, he suffers: what is joy to me, to him is pain. Surely love is a wonderful thing. It is more precious than emeralds and dearer than fine opals. Pearls and pomegranates cannot buy it, nor it is set forth in the market-place. It may not be purchased of the merchants, nor can it be weighed out in the balance for gold."
"The musicians will sit in their gallery," said the young Student, "and play upon their stringed instruments, and my love will dance to the sounds of the harp and the violin. She will dance so lightly that her feet will not touch the floor, and the courtiers in their gay dresses will throng round her. But with me she will not dance, for I have no red rose to give her"; and he flung himself down on the grass, and buried his face in his hands, and wept.
"Why is he weeping?" asked a little Green Lizard, as he ran past him with his tail in the air.
"Why, indeed?" said a Butterfly, who was fluttering about after a sunbeam.
"Why, indeed?" whispered a Daisy to his neighbour, in a soft, low voice.
"He is weeping for a red rose," said the Nightingale.
"For a red rose?" they cried; "how very ridiculous!" and the little Lizard, who was something of a cynic, laughed outright.
But the Nightingale understood the secret of the Student's sorrow, and she sat silent in the oak-tree, and thought about the mystery of Love.
Suddenly she spread out her brown wings for flight, and soared into the air.

She passed through the grove like a shadow and like a shadow she sailed across the garden.
In the centre of the grass-plot was standing a beautiful rose-tree, and when she saw it she flew over to it, and lit upon a spray.
"Give me a red rose," she cried, "and I will sing you my sweetest song."
But the Tree shook its head.

> **Task 1:** "My roses are white," it answered; "as white as _____ and whiter than _____." How did the tree describe its roses? Think up some examples. Do the same with yellow and red roses.

"My roses are white," it answered; "as white as the foam of the sea, and whiter than the snow on the mountain. But go to my brother who grows round the old sun-dial, and perhaps he will give you what you want."
So the Nightingale flew over to the Rose-tree that was growing round the old sun-dial.
"Give me a red rose," she cried, "and I will sing you my sweetest song."
But the Tree shook its head.
"My roses are yellow," it answered; "as yellow as the hair of the mermaiden who sits upon an amber throne, and yellower than the daffodil that blooms in the meadow before the mower comes with his scythe. But go to my brother who grows beneath the Student's window, and perhaps he will give you what you want."
So the Nightingale flew over to the Rose-tree that was growing beneath the Student's window.
"Give me a red rose," she cried, "and I will sing you my sweetest song."
But the Tree shook its head.
"My roses are red," it answered; "as red as the feet of the dove, and redder than the great fans of coral that wave and wave in the ocean-cavern. But the winter has chilled my veins, and the frost has nipped my buds, and the storm has broken my branches, and I shall have no roses at all this year."
"One red rose is all I want," cried the Nightingale, "only one red rose! Is there no way by which I can get it?"
"There is a way," answered the Tree; "but it is so terrible that I dare not tell it to you."
"Tell it to me," said the Nightingale, "I am not afraid."

> **Task 2:** What do you think the Nightingale had to do?

"If you want a red rose," said the the Tree, "you must build it out of music by moonlight, and stain it with your own heart's-blood. You must sing to me with your breast against a thorn. All night long you must sing to me, and the thorn must pierce your heart, and your life-blood must flow into my veins, and become mine."
"Death is a great price to pay for a red rose," cried the Nightingale, "and Life is very dear to all. It is pleasant to sit in the green wood, and to watch the Sun in his chariot of gold, and the Moon in her chariot of pearl. Sweet is the scent of the hawthorn, and sweet are the bluebells that hide in the valley, and the heather that blows on the hill. Yet Love is better than Life, and what is the heart of a bird compared to the heart of a man?"
So she spread her brown wings for flight, and soared into the air. She swept over the garden like a shadow, and like a shadow she sailed through the grove.
The young Student was still lying on the grass, where she had left him, and the tears were not yet dry in his beautiful eyes.
"Be happy," cried the Nightingale, "be happy; you shall have your red rose. I will build it out of music by moonlight, and stain it with my own heart's-blood. All that I ask of you in return is that you will be a true lover, for Love is wiser than Philosophy, though he is wise, and mightier than Power, though he is mighty. Flame-coloured are his wings, and coloured like flame is his body. His lips are sweet as honey, and his breath is like frankincense."
The Student looked up from the grass, and listened, but he could not understand what the Nightingale was saying to him, for he only knew the things that are written down in books.
But the Oak-tree understood, and he felt sad, for he was very fond of the little Nightingale who had built her nest in his branches.
"Sing me one last song," he whispered; "I shall feel lonely when you are gone."
So the Nightingale sang to the Oak-tree, and her voice was like water bubbling from a silver jar.
When she had finished her song, the Student got up, and pulled a note-book and a lead-pencil out of his pocket.
"She has form," he said to himself, as he walked away through the grove – "that cannot be denied to her; but has she got feeling? I am afraid not. In fact, she is like most artists; she is all style without any sincerity. She would not sacrifice herself for others. She thinks merely of music, and everybody knows that the arts are selfish. Still, it must be admitted that she has some beautiful notes in her voice. What a pity it is that they do not mean anything, or do any practical good!" And he went into his room, and lay down on his little pallet-bed, and began to think of his love; and, after a time, he fell asleep.
And when the moon shone in the heavens the Nightingale flew to the Rose-

tree, and set her breast against the thorn. All night long she sang, with her breast against the thorn, and the cold crystal Moon leaned down and listened. All night long she sang, and the thorn went deeper and deeper into her breast, and her life-blood ebbed away from her.
She sang first of the birth of love in the heart of a boy and a girl. And on the topmost spray of the Rose-tree there blossomed a marvellous rose, petal following petal, as song followed song. Pale was it, at first, as the mist that hangs over the river – pale as the feet of the morning, and silver as the wings of the dawn. As the shadow of a rose in a mirror of silver, as the shadow of a rose in a water-pool, so was the rose that blossomed on the topmost spray of the Tree.
But the Tree cried to the Nightingale to press closer against the thorn. "Press closer, little Nightingale," cried the Tree, "or the Day will come before the rose is finished."
So the Nightingale pressed closer against the thorn, and louder and louder grew her song, for she sang of the birth of passion in the soul of a man and a maid.
And a delicate flush of pink came to the leaves of the rose, like the flush in the face of the bridegroom when he kisses the lips of the bride. But the thorn had not yet reached her heart, so the rose's heart remained white, for only a Nightingale's heart's-blood can crimson the heart of a rose.
And the Tree cried to the Nightingale to press closer against the thorn. "Press closer, little Nightingale," cried the Tree, "or the Day will come before the rose is finished."
So the Nightingale pressed closer against the thorn, and the thorn touched her heart, and a fierce pang of pain shot through her. Bitter, bitter was the pain, and wilder and wilder grew her song, for she sang of the Love that is perfected by Death, of the Love that dies not in the tomb.
And the marvellous rose became crimson, like the rose of the eastern sky. Crimson was the girdle of petals, and crimson as a ruby was the heart.
But the Nightingale's voice grew fainter, and her little wings began to beat, and a film came over her eyes. Fainter and fainter grew her song, and she felt something choking in her throat.
Then she gave one last burst of music. The white Moon heard it, and she forgot the dawn, and lingered on in the sky. The red rose heard it, and it trembled all over with ecstasy, and opened its petals to the cold morning air. Echo bore it to her purple cavern in the hills, and woke the sleeping shepherds from their dreams. It floated though the reeds of the river, and they carried its message to the sea.
"Look, look!" cried the Tree, "the rose is finished now"; but the Nightingale made no answer, for she was lying dead in the long grass, with the thorn in her heart.

And at noon the Student opened his window and looked out.
"Why, what a wonderful piece of luck!" he cried; "here is a red rose! I have never seen any rose like it in all my life. It is so beautiful that I am sure it has a long Latin name", and he leaned down and plucked it.
Then he put on his hat, and ran up to the Professor's house with the rose in his hand. The daughter of the Professor was sitting in the door-way winding blue silk on a reel, and her little dog was lying at her feet.
"You said that you would dance with me if I brought you a red rose," cried the Student. "Here is the reddest rose in all the world. You will wear it tonight next your heart, and as we dance together it will tell you how I love you."

Task 3: How does she react? What does she say?

But the girl frowned. "I am afraid it will not go with my dress," she answered; "and, besides, the Chamberlain's nephew has sent me some real jewels, and everybody knows that jewels cost far more than flowers."
"Well, upon my word, you are very ungrateful," said the Student angrily; and he threw the rose into the street, where it fell into the gutter, and a cart-wheel went over it.
"Ungrateful!" said the girl. "I tell you what, you are very rude; and, after all, who are you? Only a Student. Why, I don't believe you have even got silver buckles to your shoes as the Chamberlain's nephew has"; and she got up from her chair and went into the house.
"What silly thing Love is!" said the Student as he walked away. "It is not half as useful as Logic, for it does not prove anything, and it is always telling one of things that are not going to happen, and making one believe things that are not true. In fact, it is quite unpractical, and, as in this age to be practical is everything, I shall go back to Philosophy and study Metaphysics."
So he returned to his room and pulled out a great dusty book, and began to read.

Carson McCullers: "The Member of the Wedding"

Lernstufe: Advanced
Kontext: englische Literatur, Romane lesen, Meinungen äußern, Wortschatzarbeit; topic: initiation, adolescence
Material: „The Member of the Wedding" (Bantam Books, New York, ISBN 0-553-25051-5), 1 Arbeitsbogen mit Wortpuzzle, 1 Overheadfolie mit Lösung, 1 Overheadfolie (Stern), Overheadprojektor, Lückentext, die ersten zwei Seiten bzw. Seiten 16–25 des Romans
Dauer: je 2 Stunden

Carson McCullers (1917–1967)

Carson McCullers was an American novelist whose theme was usually the struggle of individuals against spiritual isolation and of their (often vain) attempts to win love and recognition. She dramatized "The Member of the Wedding" which ran successfully on Broadway for several years.

"The Member of the Wedding" is about 13-year-old Frankie and spans the short space of time leading up to the wedding of the girl's brother. Within these three days we get an insight into the emotional turmoil Frankie is experiencing: her feeling of not belonging, her fear of being "different" and unloved, her longing to have a close friend to confide in. And within these three days she makes remarkable progress on the social and psychological level. The novel is widely regarded as being one of the very few stories of initiation with a female protagonist.

What to do

Pages 1–2
- Hand out the word puzzle. Tell your students to read the first two pages of the novel very closely. Eleven words from these pages are hidden in the puzzle (page 151). They are written vertically, horizontally but some of them can be read backwards or from bottom to top.
- When they have finished they can check their answers with the transparency.

C. McCullers: "The Member of the Wedding" 151

- Then the students should read the text again and find the sentences the words occur in. They should make sure they understand the meaning of the words (they may use a dictionary if necessary) and then they fill out the blanks in the sentences (gap-text).
- When the students have corrected their gap-text, each of them should try to write a sentence of their own containing as many of the eleven words as possible.

Pages 16–25
- Show your students the transparency of the star and ask them, working in pairs, to
  a) find the words that describe different things Frankie is afraid of
  b) collect them in the star (page 153) under the right headings, giving the page, the line and the catchwords.
  The students either draw their star on a very large sheet of paper or they cut the star out of cardboard.
- When they have finished they hang up their stars and all of them compare their results.

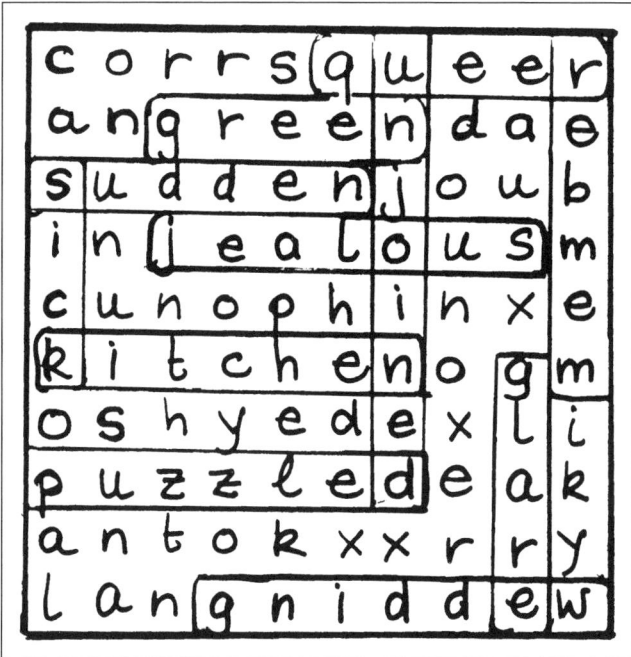

The Member of the Wedding

Please fill in the gaps with some of the words you have found in the puzzle.

1. The old lady went to the church every Saturday morning, in the hope of seeing a _____, with a bride in a long white dress.
2. In some countries, the _____ is the most important room in the house.
3. Her husband was so _____ that she was afraid he would kill her, if he saw her looking at another man.
4. The political prisoner was interrogated under the _____ of a 150 Watt lamp.
5. You usually have to be a _____ of a tennis club, if you want to use its courts.
6. They were shocked to hear of the _____ death of one of their best friends.
7. When the boy changed schools he didn't know anyone at first, so he felt a bit _____.
8. The child didn't know how to wind up its toy, so it stared at it with a _____ look on its face.
9. She was _____ and tired of hearing the same complaints every day.
10. Did you ever go up to the top of the Leaning Tower of Pisa? You can feel quite _____ when you look down on the way!

© Cornelsen Verlag Scriptor, Berlin • Fundgrube Englisch handlungsorientiert

C. McCullers: "The Member of the Wedding" 153

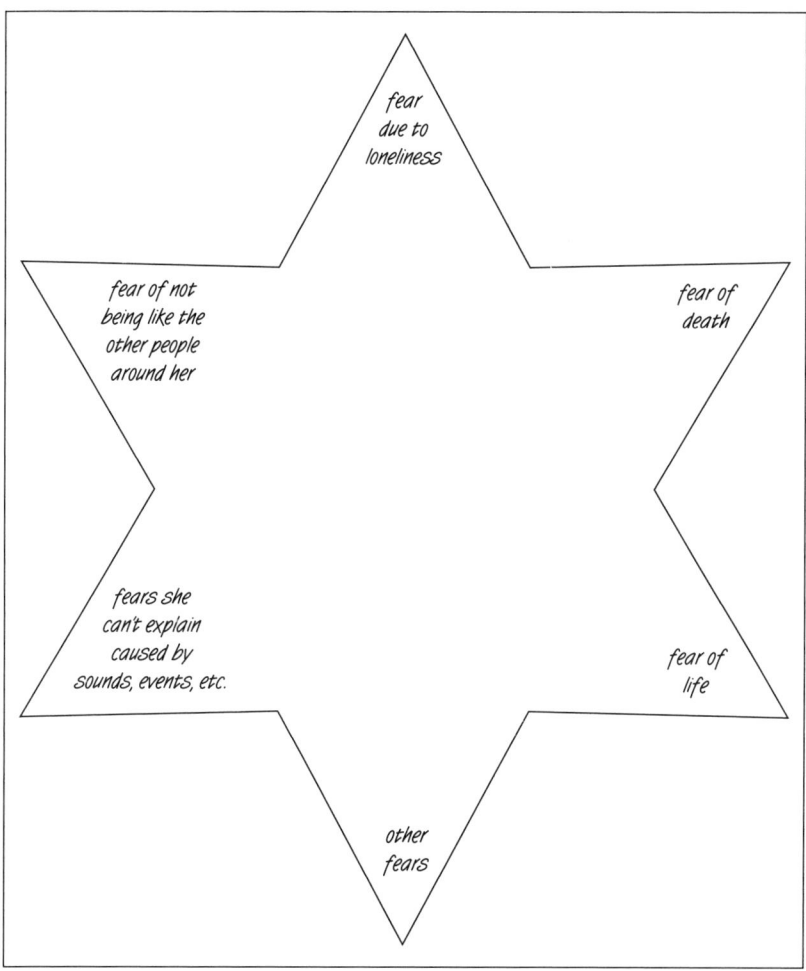

© Cornelsen Verlag Scriptor, Berlin • Fundgrube Englisch handlungsorientiert

8 Use your Eyes!

Discovery Trip

Lernstufe: Lower Intermediate
Kontext: Dialoge schreiben/sprechen, role-play, kreatives Schreiben, Wortschatzarbeit (inhaltlicher Kontext variabel, s. Variationen)
Material: 1 Bild pro Schüler bzw. Overhead-Folie
Dauer: 1–2 Stunden

What to do

1. Either give each student the picture (see page 15) or show it to them as a transparency.
2. Ask them to imagine that they are sitting in the plane:
   "Look down – what do you see below you? • Do you like what you see? • Would you like to be down there? • Why? Or why not? • Who do you see? Have a little chat with somebody down there."
3. Tell your students to
   take a partner and talk about what they have written. They should perform one of the dialogues using the rest of the text as an introduction.
   or
   pin their texts on the wall and go around reading what their classmates have written.

Bemerkung

Natürlich können auch andere Transportmittel „benutzt" werden (wie ein Zug, ein Raumschiff, ein Planwagen etc.), die sich in anderen Umgebungen bewegen, z. B. in einer Eskimosiedlung, im Wilden Westen, im australischen Busch, im Dschungel ...

Discovery Trip

Up My Street

Lernstufe: Lower Intermediate
Kontext: kreatives Schreiben, sprechen, Beschreibung, Rollenspiel; Wortschatz: home
Material: Papier und Buntstifte oder Wachskreiden
Dauer: 1–2 Stunden

What to do

1. Ask each student to draw some sort of housing (for different people and for animals, etc.).
2. Collect the pictures and redistribute them among the students, making sure nobody gets his own drawing.
3. Ask the students to make notes about their "home", saying who lives there, what it looks like, etc.
4. Ask the pupils to form groups of three and, using their pictures and notes, develop a conversation between 3 new neighbours.
5. Have the students present this as a sketch or tape it.

Biography

Lernstufe: Lower Intermediate
Kontext: schreiben, Wortschatzarbeit; Thema: Lebensgeschichte
Material: verschiedene Bilder aus Illustrierten, große Bögen Papier, Klebstoff
Dauer: 1–2 Stunden

What to do

1. Ask your students to work in groups. Give each group a set of pictures, paper and glue.
2. Tell them to put the pictures in an order that could tell somebody's life story and to stick them on the paper as a sort of photo album.

3. The students should find a suitable heading or a short (explanatory) text for each picture.
4. The students should hang up their exhibits.

Bemerkung
Es macht den Schülern großen Spaß, auch die Lebensgeschichten von Gegenständen zu erfinden, z.B. für ein Tier, eine Pflanze, ein Auto, ein Haus, ein Spielzeug, eine Maschine.

Picture Gallery

Lernstufe: Intermediate
Kontext: kreatives Schreiben, erzählen
Material: 1 Klassensatz Bilder aus Illustrierten
Dauer: 1 Stunde

What to do

1. Give each of your students a picture – tell them not to show it to anyone else.
2. Ask them to write down 10–12 words which occur to them in connection with the picture.
3. When they have finished you collect their pictures and their lists.
4. Shuffle the word-lists and hand them out again, making sure that nobody gets her own.
5. The students then should write a text about the mental pictures which these words have evoked in their mind's eye.
6. Shortly before they have finished, hang up the pictures and invite the students to pin their texts under the picture they think most suitable. There will be some surprises.

Note: The students should not be expected to find the picture their word-list belongs to, so it is possible that one picture will be allotted to several texts, whereas another will have none.

Bemerkung:
Für diese Aufgabe können natürlich auch Bilder benutzt werden, die sich eng an das Thema anlehnen, das zuletzt im Mittelpunkt des Unterrichtsgeschehens gestanden hat. Auf diese Weise kann der dabei eingeführte Wortschatz wiederholt und in der Anwendung gefestigt werden.

What's My Line?

Lernstufe: Upper Intermediate
Kontext: sprechen, Charakterisierung von Personen, kreatives Schreiben, Rollenspiel
Material: Bild einer Person für jede Gruppe, Dieses Bild kann aus einer Zeitschrift ausgeschnitten und auf ein Stück Pappe gelebt werden. (Dies kann den Schülern als Hausaufgabe übertragen werden.) Die Bilder werden ausgelegt.
Dauer: 2 Stunden

What to do

1. Ask the pupils to work in 4 – 6 groups and to choose a picture. Tell them to give their person a name. Taking it in turns, they should also write: where he/she lives • something about his/her family • what his/her job is • what hobbies and interests he/she has • things he/she likes and hates, etc.
Each student should write this down and all the other information that follows.
2. Using their notes the students form groups of As, Bs, Cs etc. They write dialogues for a role-play in a given situation: "You all meet in an airport lounge where you have already been waiting for two hours for the plane to take off. The pilots have gone on strike indefinitely."

Bemerkung
Schüler höherer Klassen werden über die Situation in Nr. 2 selbst entscheiden können.

Fantasy Flight

Lernstufe: Upper Intermediate
Kontext: erzählen, Ideenaustausch initiieren, kreatives Schreiben, Wortschatzarbeit
Material: Bild (wahlweise Collage)
Dauer: 2–3 Stunden

What to do

1. Ask the students to form groups of 3.
2. Show each group the picture for 30 seconds. Make sure the others don't see it.
3. Ask the students to write down what they have seen, giving each other help within their own group.
4. Collect all the words on the board.
5. Write down some categories like buildings, nature, work, travel, etc. and invite the students to put their words under the correct heading on the blackboard.

© Cornelsen Verlag Scriptor, Berlin • Fundgrube Englisch handlungsorientiert

6. Have the students speculate upon the connections these categories have to one another in the picture.
7. Tell them to work individually, and write down their own personal answers to your questions.
   Where are you in the picture? • What can you smell around you? • Close your eyes. What do you hear? • What's the weather like? • How do you feel at the moment? • Are you alone?
8. Ask the students to discuss their ideas within their group.

Bemerkung
In kleinen Lerngruppen kann die Aufgabe 7 auch mündlich gemacht werden.

Still Life

Lernstufe: Upper Intermediate
Kontext: kreatives Schreiben, erzählen
Material: Foto
Dauer: 2 Stunden

What to do

1. Ask the students to form groups of 3.
2. Tell them to look at the picture for a minute or two without saying anything. They can make notes if they like.
3. The students should then discuss their immediate impressions, with one student acting as a secretary to write down all the ideas.
4. The group should come to an agreement which interpretation they find the most acceptable. Ask them to do this within a certain length of time. These questions could help them come to a decision:
   What time of the day is it? Is this important? • Is it taking place in a private home? A café, hotel or restaurant? • What is going on to the right and to the left of the picture? • What sort of music is playing? • What has happened up to now?

5. When the groups have finished, have one student from each group move to another to find out how they have interpreted the picture.

© Cornelsen Verlag Scriptor, Berlin • Fundgrube Englisch handlungsorientiert

A follow-up task could be to have the students imagine there is some connection between them and the picture, e.g.: "The plate which hasn't been used is yours. Why is it still untouched?" Or: "You have interrupted your meal. Why? Why didn't you wait for the other person before you started to eat?"

Sticky Situations

Lernstufe: Intermediate
Kontext: Problemlösung, sprechen, kreatives Schreiben
Material: Bildkarten, die auf Pappe geklebt und ausgeschnitten sind; Karten, die eine problematische Situation wiedergeben; Papier und Schreibgerät
Dauer: 1–2 Stunden

What to do

1. The students get into groups of three or four.
2. Spread the picture cards face down on your table.
3. A student from each group draws any three cards and collects a situation card from you.
4. Within their groups the students discuss the situation and consider how to solve the problem, using the three objects shown on their picture cards.
5. The students write down their solution and present it to the rest of the class. They either pin up their texts with the situation and picture cards on the wall and the others walk around reading them. Or the students *tell* their class about the problem and their solution using their notes. They should avoid *reading* a text, may, however, make use of the overhead projector and transparencies to explain the problem and their suggestions for its solution.

Situation cards

You're out on the open sea in a rowing-boat and suddenly a storm rises. All at once you see a boy sitting on a rocky island, calling for help. You can't get to the island in the boat because the waves are too big and too dangerous. How do you save him?

In the Amazon Jungle you see a man who has just jumped out of a plane. He is using a parachute. At first you think he is going to land on the ground, but then you see that he is directly above a swamp. How do you save him?

You're walking along a railway-line when you suddenly hear a cry for help. You see a young woman tied to the tracks. At the same time you hear the whistle of a train coming. How do you save her?

© Cornelsen Verlag Scriptor, Berlin • Fundgrube Englisch handlungsorientiert

Sticky Situations 163

Inside a Picture

Lernstufe: Lower Intermediate
Kontext: Wortschatzarbeit, kreatives Schreiben
Material: ein Bild als Postkarte oder als Overheadfolie
Dauer: 1-2 Stunden

What to do

1. Ask your students to collect all the words they can think of when looking at this picture. They will probably collect all sorts of nouns. Tell them to find verbs, adjectives and adverbs that go with them.

Pieter Bruegel d.Ä.: Der Sturz des Ikarus, 1558

© Cornelsen Verlag Scriptor, Berlin • Fundgrube Englisch handlungsorientiert

2. The students are supposed to play a part in this picture. Ask them to find a point of entry. These questions might help them:

> Where can you get into the picture? How do you get into it? By clapping your hands, by singing a song, by speaking a code word? What can you see from where you are in the picture? What can you hear, smell, feel? Do you hear anything?
> Walk around and keep moving. Touch the things you like. Is anything happening?

Now tell your students to find a way out of the picture and to come back to the classroom. Ask them to note down their experiences and to write a text in whatever form they like: a poem, a very short story, a report or ...

3. Your students should now form groups of five and read their texts to each other.

From Picture to Text

Lernstufe: Lower Intermediate
Kontext: variable Themen, kreatives Schreiben
Material: verschiedene Bilder (Postkarten, Zeitschriften-Bilder etc.), DIN-A4-Bögen, Kleber, Schreibgerät
Dauer: 1–2 Stunden

What to do

1. Spread all the pictures out on a table. Ask every student to choose the one they like best. Tell them to paste it on the sheet of paper.
2. Now the students should take a close look at their picture and think of a sentence which they think goes well with it.
3. Ask the students to write their sentences under their picture, but this time not horizontally, but vertically.

© Cornelsen Verlag Scriptor, Berlin • Fundgrube Englisch handlungsorientiert

Two weeks on holidays – in Italy!
Deckchairs have been borrowed. And we
love being the only tourists on the beach. Loving
to hear the waves, smelling the salt it seems to
be paradise. Luckily I'm not
alone.
(This is a poem a pupil wrote about the picture.)

9 The Sound of Music

Making up a Song

Lernstufe: Beginners
Kontext: einfaches Vokabular
Material: Text des Lieds, evtl. Gitarre oder Klavier
Dauer: 10–20 Minuten

What to do

1. Introduce the spiritual "Michael, Row the Boat Ashore" to the students. Sing it a number of times so that everybody gets the feeling of the melody. (Of course, it'd be appreciated if the singing could be accompanied on the guitar or on the piano – either by the teacher or by a student.)
   We suggest singing the following lines:
2. Brother, lend a helping hand.
3. Sister, help to trim the sail.
4. Jordan stream is deep and wide.
5. Jesus is standing on the other side.

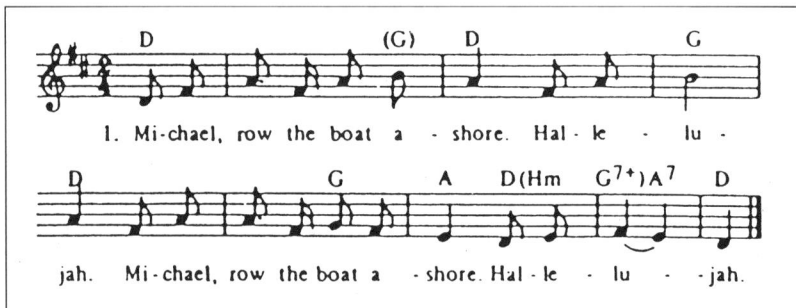

2. Use this melody to make up other lines using very simple (classroom) language. First the teacher sings some lines introducing the words, then the class repeats these lines – according to the following structure:

Teacher: "This is a book. The book is blue. I can see it."
Class: "This is a book. The book is blue. We can see it."
Repeat these lines a couple of times, so that the students know the structure.

3. Now the teacher makes up a couple of lines and sings them (with the class repeating as before), e.g.:

This is a chair. The chair is brown. I can see it.
This is a wall. The wall is white. I can see it.
This is a window. The window is open. I can see it.
This is Sonja, and Sonja is a girl. I can see her.
This is a teacher. The teacher is stupid. I can see her.

Then (very soon) the pupils are asked to make up their own versions: One pupil sings a new set of lines, the rest of the class follows taking up the words sung by the pupil.

This may go on for ten minutes or so. (Use all the nouns and adjectives that have been learnt so far.)

4. You may also ask the class to make up lines that are closer to the original song and activate the students by making them carry out commands:
Teacher/one student: "Simon, come and open the door. Come on, do it."
Class: "Simon, come and open the door. Yes, he's done it."

"Sarah, come and sit on the chair. Can you do it?"
"Sarah, come and sit on the chair. Yes/Well, she's done it."

"Thomas, come and snap your fingers. Can you do it?"
"Thomas, come and snap your fingers. Yes/Well, he's done it."

Further commands: "walk up to the board, give your book to X, throw the chalk/the sponge to X, blow your nose, stamp your feet, turn around, shake hands with X, scratch your head, hide the bag/pen, stand on a chair, go down on your knees, sit on the table ..."

There Was a Man and His Dog

Lernstufe: Beginners
Kontext: buchstabieren, einfache "There was"-Konstruktion
Material: evtl. Gitarre oder Klavier
Dauer: 10 Minuten

What to do

1. Teach the students how to sing the song. If necessary, repeat the alphabet.
2. Make the students stand in two circles.
3. Part A: When the singing starts, the students stand in pairs holding hands and start moving/marching clockwise in a circle (in the same direction). If you should use a distinction according to gender: The boys walk inside, the girls outside.
4. Part B: When the singing gets to the spelling of BINGO, the students face their partners and start swinging around with him – until the line *And Bingo was his name* has been repeated.
5. Part C: The song ends with the students shouting out the spelling of Bingo: B I N G O. While they are shouting the letters, the pupils in the outward circle move anti-clockwise, holding their hands up, ready to clap a partner's hands, and with each letter (that is called out) they move on to another student in the inside circle and clap his or her hands. The students in the inside circle act in the same way moving clockwise. Thus the "outside" students move five partners anti-clockwise, the inside circle moves five partners clockwise.
6. The partners, having found each other, embrace briefly and the singing and marching as in 3. starts again: *There was a man and his dog ...*
7. After some time change the dog's name; e.g.: *and Betty was her name*. You may also use a pupil's name.

Bemerkung

Dieses Tanzspiel benötigt viel Platz. Tische und Stühle sollten zur Seite geräumt werden. Eine Klavier- oder Gitarrenbegleitung, falls möglich, ist zu empfehlen. Der Tanz basiert auf folgendem Lied:

Teil A: Walking in pairs:
    There was a man and his dog and Bingo was his name.
    There was a man and his dog and Bingo was his name.
Teil B: Swinging with a partner, BINGO being spelt:
    BINGO, BINGO, BINGO, and Bingo was his name.
Teil C: Moving along in the circle, holding up hands and clapping the hands of the pupils in the other circle, shouting:
    B – I – N – G – O
    (With each letter being called, moving one partner further ...)

There Was a Man and His Dog

Zeichnung: Karsten Jänner

Play Me a Picture

Lernstufe: Intermediate
Kontext: charakterisieren, Wortschatz, Meinung äußern, Begründungen geben; topic: people
Material: Porträts aus Zeitschriften, auf Pappe geklebt; Musikkassette, Kassettenrekorder
Dauer: 1 Stunde

What to do

1. Ask the class to sit in groups of 4–5 and hand out a set of 3 portraits to each group.
2. Tell your students to note down ways in which the people in the pictures differ from one another. They should take into consideration aspects such as appearance, age, facial expression, clothes, possible profession, gender, possible interests, etc.
3. Play the music to the class. Tell your students that **each** of them should decide for themselves which portrait they think the music "describes". They must jot down a few reasons for their choice. Should anyone have difficulties finding connections between the music and a portrait, they must explain **why** they think the music isn't suitable, i. e. they should describe the person the music conjures up in their mind's eye.
4. Finally, within their own groups, your students should tell each other which person they have chosen, giving detailed reasons for their choice.
5. Each group decides on one portrait whose connection to the music they found particularly surprising • interesting • amusing • etc. and present this to the class.

Bemerkung

Diese Aufgabe eignet sich ganz besonders für das Themenfeld „Personenbeschreibung", wobei die Tätigkeit der Schüler über eine einfache Personenbeschreibung hinausgeht, und Aspekte wie Charakter, Signale, Wahrnehmung einschließt. Es ist sehr interessant für Schüler, sich ihre eigene Wahrnehmung bewusst zu machen und zu entdecken, wodurch diese bei ihnen entsteht. Das Gleiche gilt für den Moment, wenn sie die Bilder in Verbindung mit der Musik sehen und dabei häufig erleben, dass ihre Meinungen und Begründungen einer Veränderung unterworfen sind.

Besonders inspirierend für diese Aufgabe hat sich Musik von Paganini, Tschaikowsky, Gershwin, Brahms und R. Strauß erwiesen.
Diese Aufgabe eignet sich auch sehr gut für Landschaften, Möbelstücke, Haustypen, Tiere, Pflanzen, verschiedene Gegenstände (z.B. Pfeife, Auto, Musikinstrument etc.), je nachdem, welches Wortschatzgebiet angesprochen werden soll.
Eine interessante Variation ist es auch, statt *eines* Musikstückes mehrere unterschiedliche zu spielen. So besteht die Möglichkeit für eine differenziertere Entscheidung.

Penny Lane, a Liverpool Street

Lernstufe: Intermediate
Kontext: History of Pop Music (Beatles), strange people, a Liverpool Street
Material: Text des Liedes mit Lücken, CD-Version (oder Schallplatte) von *Penny Lane*
Dauer: 1–3 Stunden

Vorbemerkung
Für diese Aktivität wird der Text des Liedes mit Lücken, die von den Schülern ausgefüllt werden sollen, benötigt; es muss also ein Lückentext erstellt werden. (Wir gehen davon aus, dass es keine Schwierigkeiten darstellen dürfte, sich die „lyrics" des Beatles-Songs zu besorgen.) Als Beispiel für die Erstellung der „Lückenfassung" folgende Strophe:

In Penny Lane there is a barber _____ photographs
Of every head he's had the pleasure to know.
And all the _____ that come and go
stop and say hello.
...

Missing words: *showing – people ...*

What to do
1. Before the actual beginning of this unit ask the students to collect all the information and the material about the Beatles (and in particular about Paul McCartney) that they can get. (They should ask their parents,

friends, teachers, neighbours or consult some books on the history of pop music or a dictionary or the web.)
2. At the beginning ask the students which Beatles songs they know. Should students be able to sing some lines of a song (or play it on the piano or on the guitar), of course, encourage them to do so. Then let them report on what they have found out. The most important facts may be written on the blackboard, photos can be placed on the walls.
3. Tell the students that you will present and deal with a (further) Beatles song. But first make sure they understand the meaning of the following words:

Vocabulary
beneath – under
hourglass – a glass container which is narrow in the middle like the figure 8 so that sand can run slowly from the top half to the bottom – and it is a way of measuring time.
mac = short for 'mackintosh' – raincoat
poppy – *Mohnblume* (In Britain red paper poppies are sold on Remembrance Day at the beginning of November to remind people of the men who died in the two World Wars.)
shelter – some kind of hut with a roof at a bus-stop (in which you can wait when it is raining)
trim – the act of cutting off a little (e.g. you can say 'My hair or my beard needs a trim.')

4. The students listen to the song **'Penny Lane'** twice; they fill in the missing words and sing along.
5. Check briefly that the class has understood the song and knows what it is all about. Point out to the students that this song deals with ordinary people; some of them seem to be a bit strange, though. The pupils should try to explain this strange behaviour by answering the following questions:
– Why does the barber keep all these photographs of heads?
– Why does everybody say 'hello' to him?
– Why do the children laugh at the banker?
– Why does he never wear a mac?
– Why has the fireman got an hourglass?
– Why has he got a portrait of the Queen in his pocket?
These answers need not be serious explanations, they should be funny or absurd.

6. In the last stanza of the song the barber, the banker and the fireman meet in the barber's shop. Ask the students to form groups and to imagine a conversation between the three of them. (They should write it down and/or act it out.)
7. Ask them to draw a sketch, paint a picture or design a collage of the people and the atmosphere of Penny Lane.
8. The students are invited to make up three or four lines about another strange character in Penny Lane.
9. Tell the students that this song is about a real street in a Liverpool suburb (where the Beatles came from). Ask them to check the internet and try to find this street on a Liverpool map. Where exactly is the (bus) roundabout the Beatles are singing about? Which other Beatles sights can they find and visit in Liverpool?

Here is a list of useful websites:
www.beatle-city.merseyworld.com/map/pennylane/pennylanemap.htm
www.beatle-city.merseyworld.com/map/mapindex.htm
www.scuzz.com/beatles/withthebeatles.html
www.thebeatles.com/html/pennylane
www.beatle-city.merseyworld.com/lyrics/lyrics/penny-single.htm
www.hinduonnet.com/thehindu/2000/07/01/stories/1301110e.htm

Nachbemerkung
Die hier beschriebenen Arbeitsschritte sind nur Vorschläge und brauchen nicht alle behandelt zu werden. Steps 7 und 8 können weggelassen werden, wenn der Zeitaufwand zu hoch erscheint. Aufgabe 9 ist weiterführender Art und kann in ein kleines „Beatles-Projekt" münden.

There Is Music in the Air

Lernstufe: Advanced
Kontext: kreatives Schreiben, Erzählen
Material: große Bögen, Buntstifte oder Wachskreiden, 4–5 Ausschnitte aus einem Musikstück (z. B. Mahler, 1. Sinfonie; Dvorak, Neue Welt; R. Strauß, Alpensinfonie)
Dauer: 2 Stunden

What to do

1. Ask the students to form groups of 5–7 and to sit in circles. Give each of them a sheet of paper and a coloured pencil.
2. Tell them that they are going to hear a piece of music. They should draw whatever comes into their heads when they hear it.
3. Play the music, giving the students about 45 seconds. before you fade it out and ask them to pass on their sheet to the person on their left. Repeat the procedure 3–4 times.
4. Now the students should talk in their groups about what they have drawn and should put their pictures in the order which they think makes a good story.
5. They should then tell their story to the rest of the class using their pictures to illustrate it.

or:

The pupils write down their stories and stick them up on the wall for the rest of the class to read at leisure. It may be a good idea to hang their pictures next to their stories.

You're so vain

Lernstufe: Advanced
Kontext: kreatives Schreiben, Hörverstehen
Material: eine Kopie des Songs, entweder auf CD, oder zweimal hintereinander auf einer Kassette; für jede Gruppe ein großer Umschlag mit Bildern: Wolken, eine Jacht, eine Tasse Kaffee, Menschen auf einer Fete, Pferde (wenn möglich auf der Rennbahn), ein harmonisches Pärchen und, wenn möglich ein attraktiver Mann, der etwas selbstverliebt wirkt! Man kann die Bilder aus Zeitschriften ausschneiden und auf Pappe kleben, evtl. mit Folie bekleben, damit sie lange halten; vergrößerte und ausgeschnittene Textstreifen (vgl. Aufgabe 3).
Dauer: 2 Stunden

What to do

1. Write these words on the blackboard, telling your pupils that they have been taken from a song. What do they think the song is about? After

somebody has had the first idea, the others can go on spinning a yarn. Once the pupils get the hang of it, they usually enjoy this exercise very much!

underworld spy	hat dipped	one eye	wife of a close friend
	apricot		
mirror	eclipse of the sun	gavotte	vain

You walked into the party Like you were walking onto a yacht
Your hat strategically dipped below one eye, Your scarf, it was apricot.
You had one eye in the mirror as you watched yourself gavotte
And all the girls dreamed that they'd be your partner, they'd be your partner
And you're so vain, you probably think this song is about you
You're so vain I'll bet you think this song is about you, don't you, don't you?
You had me several years ago, when I was still quite naive
Well, you said that we made such a pretty pair and that you would never leave
But you gave away the things you loved and one of them was me
I had some dreams. They were clouds in my coffee, clouds in my coffee.
You're so vain ...
Well I hear you went up to Saratoga and your horse naturally won
Then you flew your new jet up to Nova Scotia to see the total eclipse of the sun
Well you're where you should be all the time and when you're not you're with some underworld spy
or the wife of a close friend, the wife of a close friend
You're so vain ...

2. Have your pupils get into groups of about four. Hand out the envelopes and ask the groups to create a story, using the pictures *and* the words on the board. They may work on the basis of a story they heard in the first exercise, but don't have to, if they prefer to think up something new. They should present their stories to the class, holding up their pictures at the appropriate moment.
3. Hand out the jumbled strips of text to pairs of students. Play the song once, during which time they should try to put the strips into the right order. Play the song a second time to enable them to check the answer – and probably to sing along as well!

Dance me to the End of Love

Lernstufe: Advanced
Kontext: Hörverstehen, Wortschatzarbeit, Meinung äußern;
Topics: love, feelings, relationship
Material: Pappstreifen mit Textteilen, CD-Version des Lieds „Dance me to the End of Love"
Dauer: 2 Stunden

What to do

1. There are many ways to say that you love somebody. One way, for example, is by telling someone what you would like them to do to/with you. Ask your students to use this way to make clear to somebody that they love them. All their ideas should be presented in class.
2. Tell the students to work in groups of 3–5. Give each group the cards below. You should enlarge then before you print them. These are very poetic sentences taken from a song. Ask them to try to express the sentiments on the cards in their own way. The ideas might sound a bit strange but nevertheless they can all be accepted. Tell them that imagination and fantasy are necessary.
3. Now the students should listen to the song.
4. Divide the class into 5 groups. Each group gets one verse of the song. The task is to present their verse without words. It's entirely up to them to decide how they want to do this. Give them about 15–25 minutes for preparation.

Dance me to the End of Love

5. The students then should give their presentation while the song is played verse by verse.

Bemerkung
You find the original song on the CD "Various Positions" of Leonhard Cohen. There is also an excellent version sung by Madeleine Peyroux on the CD "Careless Love".

Cards:

Dance me to your beauty with a burning violin
Let me feel you moving like they do in Babylon
We're both of us beneath our love, we're both of us above
Raise a tent of shelter now, though every thread is torn
Touch me with your naked hand, touch me with your glove

Dance me to the End of Love
Dance me to your beauty with a
   burning violin
Dance me through the panic till I'm
   gathered safely in
Lift me like an olive branch and be my
   homeward dove
Dance me to the end of love

Let me see your beauty when the
   witnesses are gone
Let me feel you moving like they do in
   Babylon
Show me slowly what I only know the
   limits of
Dance me to the end of love

Dance me to the wedding now, dance
   Me on and on
Dance me very tenderly and dance me
   Very long
We're both of us beneath our love,
   We're both of us above
Dance me to the end of love

Dance me to the children who are
   Asking to be born
Dance me through the curtains that
   Our kisses have outworn
Raise a tent of shelter now, though
   Every thread is torn
Dance me to the end of love

Dance me to your beauty with a
   burning violin
Dance me through the panic till
   I'm
   gathered safely in
Touch me with your naked hand,
   Touch me with your glove
Dance me to the end of love

10 Write it down

The Starters

Lernstufe: beliebig
Kontext: Sinnstränge bilden, gedächtniswirksame Wortschatzarbeit, kreatives Schreiben; topics: beliebig
Material: Tafel, Kreide
Dauer: beliebig

What to do

1. You (or a student) write a word, a phrase or a short text on the board. Ask your students to give you all the words that occur to them when they read this. Give them plenty of time to do this – usually their ideas need a while to start developing. When you have completed this phase, ask your students to arrange the words in certain categories e.g.: parts of speech, conceptual similarities, headings. They could also explain the development of a certain chain of thought e.g.

from (wedding)   to   (feet)

Here are some different examples to illustrate our point.

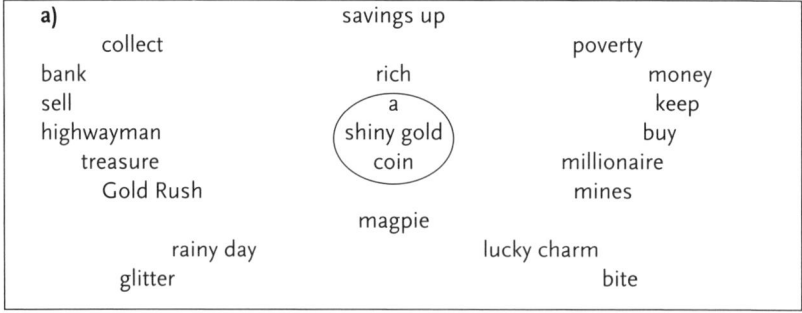

a)
```
           savings up
collect                           poverty
bank              rich                     money
sell               a                       keep
highwayman    (shiny gold)                 buy
  treasure        coin             millionaire
  Gold Rush                           mines
                 magpie
        rainy day          lucky charm
        glitter                       bite
```

© Cornelsen Verlag Scriptor, Berlin • Fundgrube Englisch handlungsorientiert

The Starters

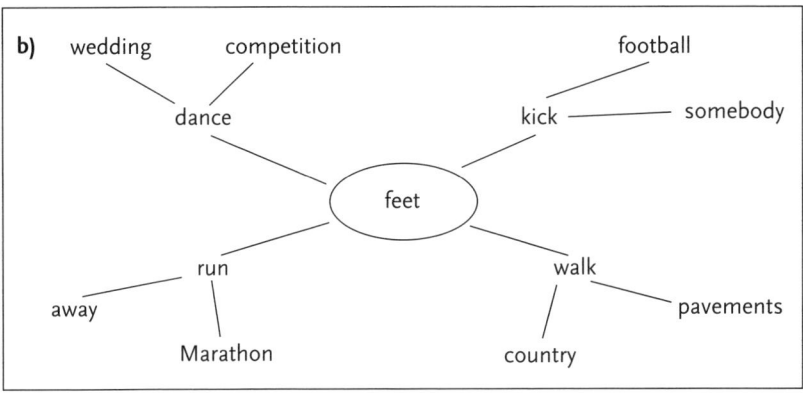

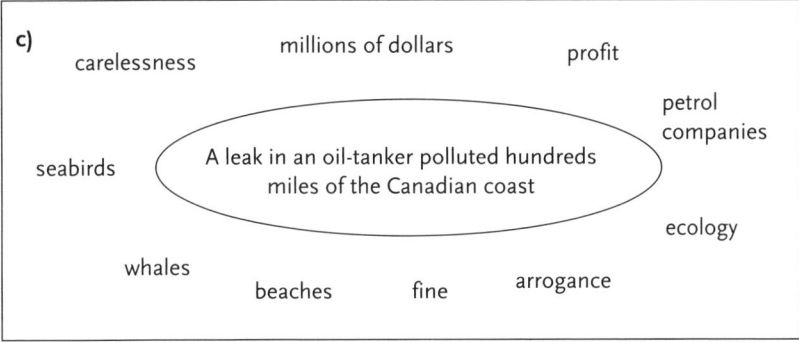

© Cornelsen Verlag Scriptor, Berlin • Fundgrube Englisch handlungsorientiert

You can, of course, develop these ideas further along the same lines as in b).

Bemerkung
Neben den Clustern gibt es weitere assoziative Verfahren, um die Erfahrungen, Kenntnisse und Fantasien von Schülern abzurufen. Die gefundenen Wörter bilden den Ausgangspunkt, eigene Texte zu verfassen. Die Anregungen dazu – ein Wort, ein Satzteil, ein Textteil – können frei gewählt werden oder das Thema des Lehrbuchs, einer Lektüre, eines literarischen Textes, eines Films etc. aufgreifen. Mit der Produktion der eigenen Texte nähern sich die Schüler den zu lesenden und/oder hörenden Texten an.
Die „Starters" können gleichzeitig auch nur als Impulse zum kreativen Schreiben verwendet werden, ohne dass Lese- oder Höraufgaben folgen.

Poetry Corner

Lernstufe: Lower Intermediate
Kontext: kreatives Schreiben, Wortschatzerweiterung, Annäherung an literarische Texte
Material: Tafel, Kreide
Dauer: beliebig

Unsere Schüler lernen besser, wenn sie produktiver tätig sein und ihre Erfahrungen und ihre Fantasie einbringen können. Dabei erweitern sie ihren Wortschatz, denken nach, bestimmen ihr Handeln und beanspruchen beide Hälften des Gehirns.
Das kann durch das Verfassen verschiedener Textsorten geschehen, wozu auch das Verfassen von Gedichten gehört.
In der *„Poetry Corner"* finden Sie Anregungen, die in Ihrer Klasse das „lyrische Feuer" entfachen werden und die gleichzeitig auch die Angst verringern, sich von bekannten Autoren geschriebenen Gedichten zuzuwenden.
In vielen Aufgaben in diesem Buch werden Ihnen Ideen gegeben, wie die von Schülern geschriebenen Texte veröffentlicht werden können. Wir möchten einige an dieser Stelle kurz zusammenfassen: im Klassenraum aushängen • in einer anderen Klasse ausstellen • im Schulflur dekorieren • ein *poem book* oder ein *story book* zusammenstellen • zu Collagen montieren • einen Kalender gestalten • in einer *golden box of poetry* sammeln • in einem Portfolio, als wäre es eine Kunstmappe, sammeln.

Continue along the lines ...

Before your students read the original text of a poem, delete the greater part of each of the lines and ask the students to complete them as they would like.

Example:
There was _____.
Who _____.
She had _____.
She didn't _____.
Without _____.
Then _____.
And _____.

This is the original text of a very well-known English nursery rhyme:

> There was an old woman
> Who lived in a shoe
> She had so many children,
> She didn't know what to do.
> So she gave them some broth
> Without any bread,
> Then whipped them all soundly
> And sent them to bed.

Two-word poems

The rule is very simple. The students may only write two words in each line – the poem may be as long or as short as they wish. Here is an example of what one of our students wrote in the context of "Sea, Lakes and Oceans".

> **Wonderful sea or not?**
>
> wonderful sea
> wonderful silence
> warm water
> warm wind
> white seagulls
> white sand
> sugary sand
> when suddenly
> strong storm
> wild swell
> wild waves
> screaming surfers
> SOS shouts
> shivering survivors
> stupid watchers
>
> wonderful sea?
> LEIF.

Cinquain

Cinquain is pronounced sin-kane. The basis is the French word cinq for 5. It consists of 5 lines, each with a different number of syllables. The pattern is as follows:

_____ 2 syllables	title
_____ 4 syllables	description of title
_____ 6 syllables	action
_____ 8 syllables	feeling
_____ 2 syllables	another word for the title

Ocean
White, blue and green
Waves crashing on shingle
Their sound gives me a lot of strength
Endless   (A pupil's text)

One below the other

For this type of poem almost any fairly simple sentence can be used. Write the sentence vertically and ask your students to integrate each word into a separate line beside the original sentence.

Today	Today it is hot
there	There is no rain
are	The bus-drivers are unfriendly
many	Many passengers are, too.
people	Most people don't like hot buses
at	They'd rather be at the seaside
the	Where the water is cool
bus-stop	Next bus-stop I get off!

Chinese Lantern

The lantern contains five lines.

Line	Syllables	Shape	Examples	
1	1	–	my	our
2	2	– –	mother	garden
3	3	– – –	warm and kind	full of birds
4	4	– – – –	helps and loves me	flowers in bloom
5	1	–	Mum!	sun

We owe some ideas to Arnold B. Cheyney. *The Writing Corner.* Scott, Faresman and Company, Ill./USA

I Am a J

Lernstufe: Lower Intermediate
Kontext: kreatives Schreiben, Wortschatz, Charakterisierung; topic: talking about yourself
Material: Overheadfolie, Overheadprojektor
Dauer: 1 Stunde

What to do

1. Ask your students to think for a moment or two about the letters of the alphabet and to choose the letter which appeals to them most. They may use one of the following criteria to choose their letter – however this is not a must: The letter they feel has got something to do with them • they like most • the month of their birth begins with it • the name of their town begins with it • which immediately brings lots of things to mind etc.
2. Show your students the text on the transparency and tell them that they are going to write something similar with **their** letter.

```
I am a "J"
Born in June
Terribly jealous
I hate jeans and judo
I like juniper berries
And James Dean.
The smell of jam in July
Makes me jump for joy
But I get quite jittery
When January comes around
I am a "J"
                            Laraine MacDevitt
```

© Cornelsen Verlag Scriptor, Berlin • Fundgrube Englisch handlungsorientiert

3. Read the text with them, talk to them about it and give them some time until the idea sinks in.
4. The students write their texts.
5. Finally the students present their texts either on transparencies or in a class book of texts. (A class book is a collection of the students' texts. The students each write their own texts whichever way they wish, handwritten or typewritten, and illustrate them. Then all the texts are duplicated and bound together to make a book.)

Bemerkung
Anstelle der in Nr. 5 beschriebenen Art der Veröffentlichung von Schülertexten als Buch sind noch andere Varianten denkbar. Ideen dazu finden Sie auf Seite 189.

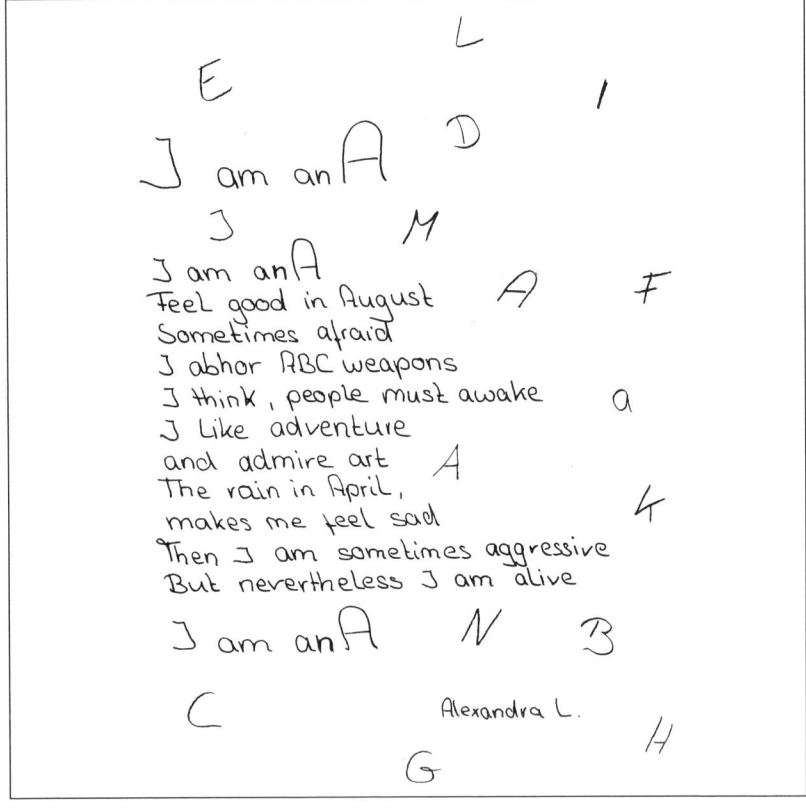

Full Stop and Comma

Lernstufe: Lower Intermediate
Kontext: Textverständnis, Textstruktur, entdeckendes Lernen; topic: nursery rhyme
Material: Textkopie, Stifte, evtl. Overheadfolie mit Originaltext, Overheadprojektor
Dauer: 1 Stunde

What to do

1. Tell your students that a printer wanted to print a rhyme but his machine was broken and did not put in any gaps, full stops, commas or capital letters. Hand out the printer's "mistake". Ask them to take a look at the text and put in strokes where they think one word ends and another begins.

> Pussycatpussycatwherehaveyoubeen
> I'vebeentolondontovisitthequeen
> pussycatpussycatwhatdidyouthere
> Ifrightenedalittlemouseunderachair

> Pussy cat, pussy cat,
>   Where have you been?
>
> I've been to London
>   to visit the queen.
>
> Pussy cat, pussy cat,
>   What did you there?
>
> I frightened a little mouse
>   under a chair.

© Cornelsen Verlag Scriptor, Berlin • Fundgrube Englisch handlungsorientiert

2. Now tell your students to mumble the text until they get a feeling for the lines by listening for the rhymes at the end of each line.
3. Show them the transparency of the original text keeping the last line covered. When the students have compared their text with the original they should now rewrite the text correctly.
4. Tell them to try to find a suitable last line for the poem. They may now illustrate their text.
5. Put up the original rhyme on the wall and get your students to hang their poems all around it.

Collage

Lernstufe: Lower Intermediate
Kontext: kreatives Schreiben, Erzählen, Einstieg in Themen
Material: Zeitschriften, Scheren, Kleber, große Papierbögen
Dauer: 2 Stunden

What to do

1. Tell the pupils the theme of the unit you are going to treat, e.g. Christmas/Man and Media/Weather etc. They may work alone, in pairs or in groups.
2. Ask them to make a collage, which expresses their associations with the topic.
3. When they have finished, ask them to write a short story or dialogue connected with their collage. Pin up their masterpieces with their stories underneath, and invite the students to circulate and compare ideas.

Note

This technique above is suitable for the first approach to a new topic. It enables pupils to call upon their own life experience and knowledge. The same technique can also be applied after reading or listening to a narrative text to give a portrait of the main characters or to summarize the plot.

A Mere Scrap of Poetry

Lernstufe: Lower Intermediate
Kontext: kreatives Schreiben, Gedicht
Material: Wortsammlung auf Karten, pro Schüler ein Umschlag
Dauer: 1 Stunde

What to do

1. Tell your students they are going to write a poem, but they will be restricted to the words which they will find in the envelope you are going to give them.
2. Hand out the envelopes. Tell the students to choose the words that they find most interesting, and to arrange them in an order which they think would make a good poem. It doesn't have to rhyme, but they should try to make it interesting and well-structured. They must use at least half of the words. This is an example one of our students wrote.

> ALL THE YEARS I'VE LOOKED FOR
> THE SECRET OF LIFE
> SEARCHED FOR IT IN PARIS; IN THE COUNTRY
> – AND ALL THE DIFFERENT PLACES
> AFTER ALL
> I FOUND THE ANSWER IN ME; RISING
> LIKE THE SUN IN MY MIND'S EYE:
> LIFE IS ONLY
>   PERFECT WHEN
>   YOU FIND LOVE

3. When your students have finished, ask them to copy their poem onto a sheet of paper. They should pay attention to the way they present it. They could illustrate it with the pictures • underlay it with one picture • use a particular type of lettering • "frame" it in an unusual way. The main thing is that they give their text a particular "flavour".
4. It is advisable to get your students to share their poems with others. There are several ways they could do this: they could publish them in a magazine, in the school year book or as an anthology • they could design a calendar and use their poems instead of pictures • they could frame them and hang them up in their own classroom or in the school corridor • they could arrange a poetry reading for classes in the same grade.

Country	body	PLACE
finish	Silver	LOOK
NOTHING	**start**	YOU
EYE	perfect	love
white	SUN	life
secret	**BABY**	LITTLE
Paris	Find	WOMAN
play	years	CAN`T
GOLDEN	**KILLED**	**ME**

One, Two, Buckle My Shoe

Lernstufe: Upper Intermediate
Kontext: Reime, Textrhythmus, Reimwörter; topic: nursery rhymes
Material: Lückenreim auf Overheadfolie, Overheadprojektor, Reim als Kopien
Dauer: 2 Stunden

What to do

1. Copy the following text fragment onto the board:

   One, two
   buckle my shoe
   three, four
   knock _____

   and invite your students to try to complete the fourth line.
   Collect all the ideas, and by reading them aloud try to attract your students' attention to the importance of rhyme **and** rhythm.
   Ask them to beat the rhythm of the first two lines on the table and to reconsider their suggestions. Do they match the rhythm?
2. Show your students the transparency (see page 192) of the nursery rhyme with gaps and ask them to complete it. They may work in pairs. They will need quite a lot of time for this (see example of students' work, page 193).
3. The students should read out their version. They may rap them, or clap their hands while reading, sing them or step them out rhythmically or accompany them with body movements.
4. Hand out the original nursery rhyme. Which one do they like better, their own ones or the original?

ONE, TWO	ONE, TWO
BUCKLE MY SHOE	BUCKLE MY SHOE
THREE, FOUR	THREE, FOUR
KNOCK _____	KNOCK AT THE DOOR
FIVE, SIX	FIVE, SIX
PICK _____	PICK UP THE STICKS
SEVEN, EIGHT	SEVEN, EIGHT
_____ THE GATE	OPEN THE GATE
NINE, TEN	NINE, TEN
_____	MY BLACK HEN
ELEVEN, TWELVE	ELEVEN, TWELVE
_____	DIG AND DELVE
THIRTEEN, FOURTEEN	THIRTEEN, FOURTEEN
_____	MAIDS ARE COURTING
FIFTEEN, SIXTEEN	FIFTEEN, SIXTEEN
_____	MAIDS IN THE KITCHEN
SEVENTEEN, EIGHTEEN	SEVENTEEN, EIGHTEEN
_____	MAIDS IN WAITING
NINETEEN, TWENTY	NINETEEN, TWENTY
_____	MY PLATE'S EMPTY

© Cornelsen Verlag Scriptor, Berlin • Fundgrube Englisch handlungsorientiert

One, two
Buckle my shoe
Three, four
I close the door
Five, six
We make a remix
Seven, eight
We have a date
Nine, ten
Let's do it again
Eleven, twelve
I do it myself
Thirteen, fourteen
Today is Halloween
Fifteen, sixteen
You know what I mean
Seventeen, eighteen
You must be waiting
Nineteen, twenty
My glass is empty

ger.: Britta, Catrin, Alexandria

Living on an Island

Lernstufe: Upper Intermediate
Kontext: kreatives Schreiben; topic: living in some place
Material: Tafel und Kreide, Overheadfolie, Overheadprojektor
Dauer: 2 Stunden

What to do

1. Draw an associogramme like this on the board and collect all your students' ideas about it.

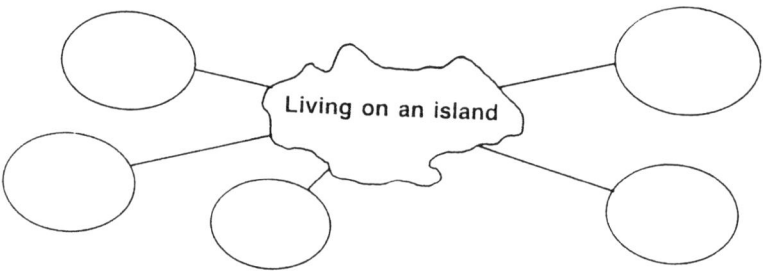

2. Show your students the transparency and ask them to expand on their associogramme with help of the questions.

Imagine you are living on an island.

- Why are you there?
- What is life like on this island?
- What sounds and noises can you hear around you?
- What can you smell?
- Where are you? What can you see from there?
- How do you feel?
- Who else lives there?
- Would you like to live on an island forever?

© Cornelsen Verlag Scriptor, Berlin • Fundgrube Englisch handlungsorientiert

3. Ask your students to put the words they have found under the most suitable heading:

scenery	feelings	smells	sounds and noises

reasons for living on an island	living conditions	people	places and things of interest

If any words are left over they can invent a heading of their own.
4. The students should write a text "Living on an Island" using the above categories and questions as guidelines (see page 194).

Bemerkung

An Stelle der Insel kann natürlich jeder andere Ort gewählt werden: Großstadt, Wüste, Gebirge, Alaska, Leuchtturm, Wohnungen etc. Es ist eine interessante Aufgabe, wenn die Schüler ihre eigenen Texte mit dem des Liedes „Living on the island" von Chris de Burgh vergleichen.

Hilaire Belloc
"A Conversation with a Cat"

Lernstufe: Advanced
Kontext: Literatur, Essays, kreatives Schreiben, darstellendes Spiel; topic: cats
Material: Bogen mit Fragmenten eines Textes, Essay: „A Conversation with a Cat", Wortkarten, Songs aus Andrew Lloyd Webbers Musical „Cats", Texte von T. S. Eliot: „Macavity", „Mr Mistoffelees", „The Old Gumbie Cat"; mehrere Kassettenrekorder
Dauer: ca. 7 Stunden

Hilaire Belloc (1870–1953)
Hilaire Belloc was born in France, but became a British citizen in 1902. His mother was English, his father was a French lawyer. From 1906 to 1910 he was a Member of Parliament as a Catholic Liberal, but soon gave up politics, disillusioned by the party system. In World War I he worked as a driver in the French army. He was a poet, essayist, biographer, historian, novelist and travel-writer. He wrote 150 books altogether. It is for his light, comic verse that he is best-known, in particular for "The Bad Child's Book of Beasts" (1896) and "Cautionary Verses" (1941).

T. S. Eliot (1888–1965)
T. S. Eliot was born in America, but moved to England in 1914 and was naturalized in 1927. He published his first book of poems in 1917, but it was "The Waste Land" which brought him fame in 1922. He also wrote plays, was a literary critic and publisher, and was successful with a collection of poems for children "Old Possum's Book of Practical Cats" (1939), the basis of the successful musical "Cats". T. S. Eliot was awarded the Nobel prize for Literature in 1948 and received 23 honorary doctorates before he died at the age of 76.

What to do

1. Hand out the fragments of the text (see page 198) but be careful not to let your students know that it has got anything to do with cats. Ask them to work in pairs and to write a text integrating all these parts of a

conversation. They must use the last box as a conclusion. Ask the students to sign their texts.
2. When they have finished the students should swap texts until each of them has read them all. Then every student should write the names of the "authors" who in their opinion have written the best text, on a slip of paper. Collect these and announce the names of the winners.
3. Hand out Hilaire Belloc's essay "A Conversation with a Cat". Get your students to find out who the main characters are and how the author sees them. What do they find strange or surprising about the content of the essay?
4. Give your students a word card (see page 199) each and ask them to find out everything they can about their subject and to present it to the class. Make sure that they are careful to establish a connection between their word and cats. Remind them that cats have often been treated in mythological, historical and literary contexts. If available, dictionaries of quotations, of phrase and allusions, of eponyms and of etymology could be helpful for the students. Leave it up to your students whether they wish to present their subject in form of a talk, a poem, or a mini-play.
5. Divide your class into groups of 4–5. Give each group a cassette with one of the three songs and supply them with the texts. It doesn't matter if two different groups have the same song, as the results of the following task will differ from group to group. Ask them to prepare a presentation of *their CAT* which should be as exciting as possible. Leave it **entirely** up to them how and with which requisites they will do so. Let them go away somewhere where they can listen to the music on the cassette and rehearse without being disturbed.

Bemerkung
Aus Copyright-Gründen können leider die Texte aus dem Musical nicht abgedruckt werden. Sie finden sie in T. S. Eliots "Old Possum's Book of Practical Cats" (Faber and Faber, London, 1962; zweisprachige Ausgabe: Gesammelte Gedichte 1909–1962, Suhrkamp, Frankfurt/M., 1988) oder in einer Textbeilage zu der CD des Musicals, die Sie ohnehin benötigen. Überspielen Sie die Songs auf Kassetten, ein Song pro Kassette.

These are fragments of a conversation
Complete it in a way you think fitting.

> Also, I thank you, for this, that you have reminded me of my youth, and in a sort of shadowy way, a momentary way, have restored it to me.

> Were you yourself suffering from loneliness?

> You will never leave me, we will sit here together through all uncounted time, I holding you in my arms and you dreaming of the fields of Paradise.

> But none will praise you more sincerely.

> No man could be so timid after such an approach as not to make some manner of response.

> Love at its most profound is silent.

> What, then, was your motive? Or am I, indeed, foolish to ask, and not rather to take whatever good comes to me in whatever way from the gods?

> I am more than flattered.

> What! When you have chosen me out of seven London millions upon whom to confer the tender solace of the heart.

> Why have you deigned to single me out for so much favour?

Conclusion:

> She walked slowly away from me without so much as looking back over her shoulder; she had another purpose in her mind.

EGYPT	BLACK CATS
CATWOMAN	NINE LIVES
TOM AND JERRY	PUSS IN BOOTS
ANIMAL OF THE NIGHT	BAD LUCK – GOOD LUCK
GARFIELD	WITCHES
WISDOM	CATWALK
CAT O'NINE TAILS	NOT ENOUGH ROOM TO SWING A CAT

A Conversation with a Cat

T H E other day I went into the bar of a railway station and, taking a glass of beer, I sat down at a little table by myself to meditate upon the necessary but tragic isolation of the human soul. I began my meditation by consoling myself with the truth that something in common runs through all nature, but I went on to consider that this cut no ice, and that the heart needed something more. I might by long research have discovered some third term a little less hackneyed than these two, when fate, or some fostering star, sent me a tawny, silky, long-haired cat.

If it be true that nations have the cats they deserve, then the English people deserve well in cats, for there are none so prosperous or so friendly in the world. But even for an English cat this cat has been exceptionally friendly and fine – especially friendly. It leapt at one graceful bound into my lap, nestled there, put out an engaging right front paw to touch my arm with a pretty timidity by way of introduction, rolled up at me an eye of bright but innocent affection, and then smiled a secret smile of approval.

No man could be so timid after such an approach as not to make some manner of response. So did I. I even took the liberty of stroking Amathea (for by that name did I receive this vision), and though I began this gesture in a respectful fashion, after the best models of polite deportment with strangers, I was soon lending it some warmth, for I was touched to find that I had a friend; yes, even here, at the ends of the tubes in S.W.99. I proceeded (as is right) from caress to speech, and said, "Amathea, most beautiful of the cats, why have you deigned to single me out for so much favour? Did you recognize in me a friend to all that breathes, or were you yourself suffering from loneliness (though I take it you are near your own dear home), or is there pity in the hearts of animals as there is in the hearts of some humans? What, then, was your motive? Or am I, indeed, foolish to ask, and not rather take whatever good comes to me in whatever way from gods?"

To these questions Amathea answered with a loud purring noise, expressing with closed eyes of ecstasy her delight in the encounter.

"I am more than flattered, Amathea," said I, by way of answer; "I am consoled. I did not know that there was in the world anything breathing and moving, let alone so tawny-perfect, who would give companionship for its own sake and seek out, through deep feeling, some one companion out of all living kind. If you do not address me in words I know the reason and I commend it; for in words lie the seeds of all dissension, and love at its most profound is silent. At least, I read that in a book, Amathea; yes, only the other day. But I confess that the book told me nothing of those gestures which are better than words, or of that caress which I continue to bestow upon you with all the gratitude of my poor heart."

To this Amathea made a slight gesture of acknowledgement – not disdainful – wagging her head a little, and then setting it down in deep content.

"Oh, beautiful-haired Amathea, many have praised you before you found me to praise you, and many will praise you, some in your own tongue, when I am no longer held in the bonds of your presence. But none will praise you more sincerely. For there is not a man living who knows better than I that the four charms of a cat lie in its closed eyes, its long and lovely hair, its silence, and even its affected love."

But at the word affected Amathea raised her head, looked up at me tenderly, once more put forth her paw to touch my arm, and then settled down again to a purring beatitude.

"You are secure," said I sadly; "mortality is not before you. There is in your complacency no foreknowledge of death nor even separation. And for that reason, Cat, I welcome you the more. For if there has been given to your kind this repose in common living, why, then, we men also may find it by following your example and not considering too much what may be to come and not remembering too much what has been and will never return. Also, I thank you, for this, Amathea, my sweet Euplokamos" (for I was becoming a little familiar through an acquaintance of a full five minutes and from the absence of all recalcitrance), "that you have reminded me of my youth, and in a sort of shadowy way, have restored it to me. For there is an age, a blessed youthful age (O my Cat) even with the miserable race of men, when all things are consonant with the life of the body, when sleep is regular and long and deep, when enmities are either unknown or a subject of rejoicing and when the whole of being is lapped in hope as you are now lapped on my lap, Amathea. Yes, we also, we of the doomed race, know peace. But whereas you possess it from blind kittenhood to that last dark day so mercifully short with you, we grasp it only for a very little while. But I would not sadden you by the mortal plaint. That would be treason indeed, and a vile return for your goodness. What! When you have chosen me out of seven London millions upon whom to confer the tender solace of the heart, when you have proclaimed yourself so suddenly to be my dear, shall I introduce you to the sufferings of those of whom you know nothing save that they feed you, house you and pass you by? At least you do not take us for gods, as do the dogs, and the more am I humbly beholden to you for this little service of recognition – and something more." Amathea slowly raised herself upon her four feet, arched her back, yawned, looked up at me with a smile sweeter than ever and then went round and round, preparing for herself a new couch upon my coat, whereon she settled and began once more to purr in settled ecstasy.

> Already had I made sure that a rooted and anchored affection had come to me from out the emptiness and nothingness of the world and was to feed my soul henceforward; already had I changed the mood of long years and felt a conversation towards the life of things, an appreciation, a cousinship with the created light – and all that though one new link of loving kindness – when whatever it is that dashes the cup of bliss from the lips of mortal man (Tupper) up and dashed it good and hard. It was the Ancient Enemy who put the fatal sentence into my heart, for we are the playthings of the greater powers, and surely some of them are evil.
> "You will never leave me, Amathea," I said; "I will respect your sleep and we will sit here together through all uncounted time, I holding you in my arms and you dreaming of the fields of Paradise. Nor shall anything part us, Amathea; you are my cat and I am your human. Now and onwards into the fullness of peace."
> Then it was that Amanthea lifted herself once more, and with delicate, discrete, unweighted movement of perfect limbs leapt lightly to the floor as lovely as a wave. She walked slowly away from me without so much as looking back over her shoulder; she had another purpose in her mind; and as she so gracefully and so majestically neared the door which she was seeking, a short, unpleasant man standing at the bar said "Puss, Puss, Puss!" and stooped to scratch her gently behind the ear. With what a wealth of singular affection, pure and profound, did she not gaze up at him, and then rub herself against his leg in token and external expression of a sacramental friendship that should never die.

Rewriting Schoolbook Texts

Lernstufe: Upper Intermediate
Kontext: Anwendung und Wiederholung des in einem Schuljahr gelernten Stoffs
Material: Lehrbuch
Dauer: etwa 2 Wochen

What to do

1. The students are informed about the project. After having used the textbook for almost a whole year, they should be able to evaluate this teaching material (the reader). They should know the book's advantages and disadvantages, the positive and negative sides of the various units. (If necessary, you can discuss which unit – in the past school year – the

class liked best and why they liked it and which text (and why) was really disliked or even hated.) Now suggest to your students that they should rewrite (some) texts of the reader. This can be done in different ways, and ideas and suggestions as to how this ought to be done should be discussed with the students. Visual elements such as collages, pictures etc. can be changed or added, too.

Some examples:

The students can improve what they think are bad texts. • They can transform a narrative text into a dramatic form or into a diary entry. • They can draw up a completely new text on the topic given in the unit. • They can compile new/different information on a given topic. • They can ridicule or satirize a text. • They can add strange/absurd/nonsensical elements to the text, alter its geographical or historical setting, so that e.g. the Battle of Hastings is turned into a science fiction story. • They can change the gender/age roles of the text. (e.g. the children tell the adults what to do ...)

2. The class is split up in groups of three to five students. Each group is to take over one unit, i. e. the students have to rewrite a text of this unit and, if they wish, to re-arrange the information/material given there. The groups work independently and the work-progress is checked by the teacher who provides help regarding the use of correct English etc.
3. The students discuss their products (new texts) in class. The texts are corrected, collected and put together as some kind of brochure, so that all the students get a "revised" version of their textbook.

Bemerkung

Dieses Projekt dient einer Globalwiederholung der Lehrbucharbeit innerhalb eines Jahres und sollte gegen Ende des Schuljahrs durchgeführt werden.

11 The Joy of Grammar

Pep it up a bit!

Lernstufe: Lower Intermediate
Kontext: Satzstellung, Schreiben; topic: dreams
Material: Satzstreifen auf Pappe geklebt
Dauer: 1–2 Stunden

What to do

1. Give your students a set of strips (1 set for 2 students). The words on the strips are jumbled up. Ask the students to form correct sentences and to write them down.
2. Then the students rearrange the sentences until they get a meaningful text.
3. Invite 2 or 3 of your students to read the text aloud to get the feel of it. Point out that it is a fairly straightforward text, without any embellishments. They should consider various ways of making their text more interesting, e.g. by the use of adjectives, connectives, time-markers, adverbs of frequency and so on.

   Finally, your students rewrite the text, making it more interesting.

Note: We owe this idea to H.-E. Piepho.

| watch | land | planes | and | I | take off |

| all | planes | about | I | know |

| go | I | to | Tegel Airport | often |

| that | like | I |

| read | about | a lot of | I | books | flying |

| no | I | money | have |

| a bit | feel | sad | I | as well |

| like | flying | I |

| no chance to | I | fly | have |

© Cornelsen Verlag Scriptor, Berlin • Fundgrube Englisch handlungsorientiert

What will be, will be!

Lernstufe: Lower Intermediate
Kontext: Predicting, "will" future; topic: talking about the future
Material: Tafel, Kreide, einzelne Texte, Klebestreifen, Pappen, Scheren, Kleber, Buntstifte
Dauer: 4 Stunden

What to do

1. Write the words "fortune-teller" on the board and collect all the associations your students have with it. Then ask the students which categories these words could be put into. The most common categories are: money, sport, school, work, environment, love, holidays/weather.
2. Divide your class into 7 groups of 4, subdivide each group into pairs. Give each a letter from A to G, making sure they know which letter they have. Stick the 7 texts, which represent a fortune-teller's predictions, on the classroom- and corridor-walls outside. Take care that none of them is close enough to be read without having to get up and walk over to it. Tell your pairs that one of them must be a messenger and one must be a scribe. The scribe must stay at the table, while the messenger goes to the text which has their letter, memorizes as much of the text as possible, goes back to the scribe and dictates what she can remember.
They continue like this until the whole text has been written down. The messenger may help the scribe with the spelling. If you have more than 28 students, it is advisable to write an extra text yourself.)
3. When everyone has finished, the pupils with the same text get together and think up questions they would like to ask a fortune-teller. Ask for a volunteer to be Mrs or Mr Know-it-all. Get the rest of the class to ask their questions. Mrs or Mr Know-it-all will try to predict their future.
4. The students should write a poem, using the device "parallel writing". The title of the poem is "In the Year 2050" and deals with 3 characters – the optimist, who talks about his predictions for the future, the pessimist and the hopeful person, whose predictions are filled out by your students, following the optimist's pattern (see page 208). Hang up one copy of the original text and arrange the pessimists and hopefuls around it.
5. Should you be working on this subject in February, it would be a nice idea to let your students make their own Valentines. They can cut out cards, decorate them or illustrate them and write little texts, telling their Valentine what they will always or won't ever do.
What they then do with their Valentines is up to them!

Bemerkung

Wir haben bei Nr. 2 zwei Streifen mit dem Buchstaben G versehen, damit Sie ein der Jahreszeit passendes Horoskop einsetzen können. „In the Year 2050" haben wir als Idee von Häussermann/Piepho übernommen.

What will be, will be! 207

A
People won't have any work to do because machines will do everything. There will be robots in the factories and in every home. Many people in Europe will be very hungry. They will not have many children because they won't be able to feed them.

B
You will have a very good school report with good marks in English! You will be the best in your class in Sport – your teacher will give you a medal and your parents will be very pleased!

C
Your team will win every game this season. You will be German champions and win a big silver cup. In the year 20xx You will become Olympic Champion in your sport and this will bring you a lot of money.

D
Berlin will get bigger and bigger. Soon, there won't be any cars or buses – only electric airplanes. Children will have to fly to school in machines. People will only eat pills – there won't be any food.

E
The most attractive boy/girl in the school will fall in love with you. She/he will kiss you when the moon is full and will never want to leave you! You will both do everything together and you will think you have never been happier.

F
You will win a money-prize and be the richest person in your street. You will buy a large house and a car for each member of your family. You will spend your holidays in Las Vegas at the Casino.

G1
Next summer it will be hot and sunny. The sky will be blue all the time. You will go to the swimming-pool with your friends every day and you will get very brown very quickly!

G2
It will be wet and rainy in the holidays. There won't be any snow or ice, so you won't have the chance to go skiing or skating. You will have to stay in and play Monopoly or Magic!

© Cornelsen Verlag Scriptor, Berlin • Fundgrube Englisch handlungsorientiert

In the year 2050

The optimist

Our city will be beautiful
and the people will have more than enough to eat.
Our trees will be green again
and our rivers will be clean again.
My family will be healthy.
My child will be happy
and I will feel well in the world!

The pessimist

Our city will be rich but _____

_____ people _____

_____ trees _____

_____ rivers _____

_____ family _____

_____ child _____

_____ I _____

The hopeful

Our city will _____

_____ clouds _____

_____ rivers _____

_____ people _____

_____ children _____

_____ dreams _____

© Cornelsen Verlag Scriptor, Berlin • Fundgrube Englisch handlungsorientiert

The Girl Was Waiting

Lernstufe: Lower Intermediate
Kontext: Satzstruktur
Material: Tafel oder OH-Projektor
Dauer: 10–30 Minuten

What to do

1. Put a simple sentence on the blackboard/OH-projector.
   Examples:
   "The girl was waiting. • The man was watching the bus. • The teacher was standing there."
2. Ask the students (in turns) to expand the sentence (to make it bigger/longer). Let each student write down his expansion on the blackboard/OH-projector.
   Make sure that the sentence as it is being expanded remains grammatically and semantically correct and that, despite its length, its legibility is maintained.
   Example: "The girl was waiting. • The pretty girl was waiting. • The pretty, young girl was waiting. • The pretty, young girl was waiting at the station • The pretty, young girl was impatiently waiting at the station."
   Finally:
   "At five o'clock in the morning, having walked for ten miles, the pretty, young German girl, who was carrying some bars of chocolate in her black handbag, was impatiently and nervously waiting at the station for an elderly gentleman from Italy who was her former lover."
3. The sentence is read out. The class should discuss whether it is grammatically correct and logical.
4. If you want to extend or continue this activity, use this sentence as a starting-point for a narration and ask questions:
   "Why had she walked for ten miles? Why did she meet her 'former' lover? Why was her lover an 'elderly' gentleman? Why was she waiting there at five in the morning? Did her former lover actually turn up? (If yes, what did he say? What were they doing?) What about the bars of chocolate in her handbag? (Were they real?) Was the station in Germany? Why was she nervous and impatient?"

You may even ask the students to write a (short) story culminating in the given sentence. Or, when making up their story, they may use the sentence as a starting-point.

Variation:
Pair the class or form groups of three or four students and tell them to make the sentence on the blackboard as big/long as possible. If you wish, you may tell them that this is a competetive game and the team that constructs the longest sentence is the winner. The students read out their sentences (or put them on the board/OH-projector). The class should discuss whether the sentences are grammatically correct and logical.

What Have You Been Doing?

Lernstufe: Lower Intermediate
Kontext: Beschreiben gegenwärtiger Handlungen, present perfect progressive
Material: 1 Blume, 1 Blockflöte, Kaugummi o.Ä.
Dauer: 1/2–1 Stunde

What to do

1. Ask one student what time it is. (Let's say, 11 o'clock.) Then make one or two students each carry out the following activities:
   sit on the table • look out of the window • walk up and down in the rear of the classroom • read a book • write some words or sentences on the blackboard • stand there and wait (with a rose in his/her hand) • play the recorder (quietly!!) • chew a chewing-gum • stand next to the door • move his/her arms up and down • shake hands with each other • count from one ...
   It is important that most of the class (at least half the class) are involved in these activities.
2. Now ask each of them what they are doing. ("I am sitting on the table. We are shaking hands etc.") Ask some other members of the class what their classmates are doing – in order to practise the third person

singular and plural, too. ("He is looking out of the window. She is reading a book. They are standing next to the door.")
3. Ask somebody what time it is. (about 11:10)
4. Introducing the form of the present perfect progressive, ask the pupils what they have been doing since 11/for the past ten minutes. (If this tense is new for the students, you must carefully repeat the forms so that the pupils are able to understand and comprehend the structure.) The students should answer: "I have been writing. I have been standing here and have been waiting for my girlfriend. I have been playing the recorder."
You should, again, ask some other pupils what their friends have been doing: "She has been walking up and down. They have been chewing chewing-gum."
5. Ask further questions using the present perfect progressive, e.g. "What have you been doing? (sitting here, answering questions) What have I been doing? (asking stupid questions)" etc. Ask some questions using the negative form, too. "Has John been sleeping? No, he hasn't."
6. Make the class write down what each (or ten) pupil(s) have been doing and/or have not been doing. If this tense has already been introduced and this lesson is mere repetition, introduce/repeat "for" and "since" and make the students use these prepositions when writing down their sentences. The students should write some sentences that are untrue – in so far as the classmate mentioned has not been doing what is written about her.
7. The pupils read out their sentences (using present perfect progressive). Their classmates have to find out which information is wrong.

Bemerkung
Situativ wird das *present perfect progressive* eingeführt und geübt. Diese Aktivität basiert auf einer Idee von: Klaus H. Köhring/J. Tudor Morris: *Instant English,* Quelle & Meyer (Heidelberg) 1977, S. 160 f.

Questions and Answers

Lernstufe: Beginners
Kontext: einfacher Wortschatz, Frage-Struktur
Material: kurze Sätze (Fragen und Antworten), aufgeschrieben und ausgeschnitten
Dauer: 10–15 Minuten (evtl. 1 Stunde)

What to do

1. Explain to the class what's going to happen. They will be given a slip of paper on which either a question or an answer is written. The students will have to find their matching partners: the questions must find the answers and vice versa. For each question there is only one correct answer.
2. Let the students stand in a circle and hand out the slips. They must not show their slip to other students.
3. Now make your students find their partners by walking about, speaking out or whispering their question or answer.
4. Once all the partners have met, the students should read out their questions and answers to make sure the two sentences really match.
5. You may repeat this activity once or twice.
6. If you want to continue this activity, let the pairs of students who have found each other role-play a dialogue or a situation in which the question and answer (on the slips of paper) could be spoken. The pupils may also write down this dialogue and then act it out.

Bemerkung

Für diese Aktivität, bei der sich jeweils eine „Frage" und die dazu passende „Antwort" finden müssen, wird Platz benötigt. Tische und Stühle evtl. zur Seite räumen. Achtung: Es kann etwas laut werden!

15 questions and 15 answers (for 30 students)

Have you got a brother?	No, I haven't.
Do you like dancing?	Yes, I do.
What's the time?	It's ten to two.
How many pupils are in this class?	Twenty-six.
Can you speak French?	No, I can't.
How far is it to the town?	About four miles.
Does your mother often watch TV?	No, she doesn't.
Are you from Liverpool?	No, I'm not.
Did you see him?	No, I didn't.
Did she meet you last night?	Yes, she did.
When did Columbus discover America?	In 1492.
Were you at home when he called you?	No, I wasn't.
Were your parents at home?	Yes, they were.
How was the film?	Great.
Where did they play football?	In the garden.

12 Intercultural Learning

Normality

Lernstufe: Lower Intermediate
Kontext: Reflexion über die eigene Kultur, interkulturelles Lernen
Material: Fragebogen
Dauer: 1–2 Stunden

What to do

1. Hand out the worksheet. If your class has no experience in filling in questionnaires, just ask the students to mark yes or no whether the given behaviour or custom is normal for them. If you feel that your class may have more differentiated views on their everyday life and behaviour, ask them to mark each statement as follows:
   1: strongly agree   2: agree
   3: neither agree nor disagree 4: disagree
   5: strongly disagree
2. Take a vote on the various statements and make the class discuss the issues raised here. Hopefully this will lead to controversial and interesting discussions on behaviour and habits at home and at school, on courtesy and etiquette. Of course, it will become very difficult to state whether something is "normal" or not.

Nachbemerkung:
Dieser Fragebogen ist für Schüler konzipiert, die nicht älter als 12, 13 Jahre sind. Interkulturelles Bewusstsein setzt Nachdenken über die eigene Kultur, über eigene Sitten und Verhaltensweisen heraus. Es wird deutlich, dass auch im intrakulturellen Bereich große Unterschiede existieren.

Diese Aktivität basiert auf einer Idee von Simon Gill, entnommen aus dem vom British Council herausgegeben Magazin *Thresholds*, Spring/Summer 2004, S. 18.

Normality

It's normal ...

1. to shake hands when you meet somebody.
2. to take off your shoes when you enter a house or a flat.
3. to say 'goodbye' when you get out of a lift.
4. to wear a uniform when you go to school.
5. to give presents to your friends on your birthday.
6. to eat spaghetti with a fork and a spoon.
7. to drink your coke from the bottle in a restaurant or cafe.
8. to thank your teacher after the last lesson before the holidays.
9. to wait for your mother or father to serve you when you eat dinner.
10. to kiss your friend on his/her cheeks when you say 'good-bye'.
11. to help your mother wash up the dishes.
12. to watch TV until 11 pm.
13. to thank the cook (mother/father) after a meal.
14. to wear good clothes on Sundays.
15. to play with friends in the living-room.
16. to eat cheese after the main course at the end of a meal.
17. to clean your teeth after you get up (before breakfast).
18. to buy a fancy dress that you can wear for the carnival party at school.
19. to top a sandwich with both cheese and meat.
20. to search for hidden eggs at Easter.
21. to address your friend's father with his first (Christian) name.
22. to allow a dog to live in your house or flat.
23. not to say anything before you start your meal.
24. to get up when your teacher enters the room.
25. to shake hands after a football match.

© Cornelsen Verlag Scriptor, Berlin • Fundgrube Englisch handlungsorientiert

Birthday

Lernstufe: Intermediate
Kontext: (internationale) Geburtstagsfeiern und -bräuche, interkulturelles Lernen
Material: Texte, Material aus dem Internet
Dauer: 2 Stunden oder mehr

What to do

1. Give the class some time to jot down notes or write a proper text on how they spent their last birthday or on some other birthday party to which they were invited and which they enjoyed.
2. Form groups of four to six students and let them share their birthday experiences. (Each pupil should report or read out their text and they should exchange their views on the various birthday celebrations ...) If you feel that the students need more time to practise their oral English in small groups, rearrange the groups after some time so that they have the chance of another round of exchanging 'reports'. Eventually each group is to put down their major experiences and the birthday customs and rituals that have been reported on a poster (that will be fixed onto the classroom wall). Give the students time to read the posters.
3. Discuss and evaluate the various ways of celebrating birthday (parties). Make sure the pupils understand that there are specific family traditions and intracultural diversity.
4. Pair the students and hand out the list of birthday habits/rituals. Each pair has to evaluate the various habits and rituals. Discuss them in class.
5. Organize a webquest on "birthday celebrations around the world" – using the websites on birthday customs (as given below). Again, let the students find and report about traditions, habits and rituals that they believe to be recommendable or interesting or rather exotic. (And the rest of the class have to guess the country ...)
6. Let the class celebrate an 'international' or 'multicultural' birthday party for a fictitious person or for a classmate. For this party a number of unusual and unconventional rituals, games, food and drinks must be organized.

Family Birthday Traditions

The Barlow Family: We organize a treasure hunt in the local park and through some side streets. It ends in a Chinese restaurant where we all eat noodles.

The North Family: We go bowling. Afterwards all the kids who are invited sleep in the living room on mattresses or airbeds.

A Hobbit (in 'Lord of the Rings') invites all his friends and gives presents to each of them.

The Byram Family: Each year we have a birthday book in which family and friends write down their wishes for the birthday person or draw a picture or put a photo.

The Hodge Family: Our daughter has a 'birthday tablecloth' and each year her hand and foot prints are printed on it – with the year written and a special decoration to symbolize the year.

The Boardman Family: The whole family goes out for dinner at a place picked by the birthday person. Dessert is ordered and served first, then the main course and last the appetizers. We call it 'dinner backwards'.

The Burt Family: The birthday person is served by the family and has breakfast in bed. There she/he gets her/his presents, too, and can unwrap them – with all the family standing around her/him.

The Lim Family: The birthday child gets a crown on his/her head, sitting on a chair in the middle of family and friends. They hold up the chair with the child and sing 'Happy Birthday'.

The Scott Family: We rehearse a play or a performance with all the children who have been invited. When the parents come to pick them, they can watch this performance.

The Grundy Family: If the birthday is in winter, we switch off the light and, instead, light the living-room and the kitchen with dozens of candles, then we call the birthday person. He or she finds the presents in the living-room and opens them. Then we have dinner in the kitchen – with candles on the birthday cake and all around us.

Birthday International – Webliographie

Birthday traditions

http://www.birthdayexpress.com/bexpress/planning/BirthdayCelebrations.asp

Background information on the history of birthday celebrations, traditions around the world, cake recipes and ideas for party themes. (This site is meant for young kids and is very commercial.)

http://www.ftd.com/350/content/news_views/global_birthday_traditions.epl

A brief overview on birthday traditions and celebrations all over the world.

http://k-6educators.about.com/gi/dynamic/offsite.htm?site=
http://www.kidsparties.com/traditions.htm

A child-friendly web page on international birthday traditions, family traditions and a listing of partying places in the USA so that the kids can choose from Alabama to Wyoming where to celebrate their next birthday party.

http://www.ldssplash.com/traditions/birthday_traditions/birthday_traditions.htm

Overview on birthday traditions and items.

http://groups.msn.com/Traditions/newtraditions.msnw?action=get_message&mview=0&ID_Message=7265&LastModified=4675418204337936501

Interactive discussion board on various birthday traditions around the world.

http://wellnessways.aces.uiuc.edu/pdf/ho_BirthdayCelebrations.pdf

Complete handout (pdf-file) on birthday traditions around the world.

Others

http://www.shabbir.com/romance/bday.html

How to say "Happy Birthday" in 161 different languages.

http://www.danish-deli-food.com/English/cookbook/recepdetail.asp?recid=579

Recipe for a traditional Danish birthday cake.

http://birthday.lifetips.com/

"Life tips" for how to plan a birthday party; with many ideas and background information.

Visitors from Funnia

Lernstufe: Intermediate
Kontext: interkulturelles Lernen, sprechen, schreiben
Material: Arbeitsbogen (Seite 220 f.)
Dauer: 1 Stunde und mehr

What to do

1. Inform the students about the country of "Funnia". Speculate where it is situated, what kind of people live there, whether it is developed or not. Create an imagined "country". If you wish, set the students the task to write a short article about/an introduction to "Funnia".
2. Tell them that a group of Funnian exchange students recently visited your town/city/area/school. (Of course, English was used as *lingua franca* as means of communication.) Explain to the students that while the Funnians had been staying here, some (cultural or cross-cultural) misunderstandings occurred. Apparently something went wrong because "we didn't understand their behaviour and they didn't know about our habits and customs".
Hand out the worksheet and discuss the various incidents. The possible explanations given on the worksheet only provide hints; of course, they should be evaluated, but the students should find further and different explanations themselves.
3. Ask the students to make up further critical incidents and to add possible explanations. This can be done orally or in written form, individually or in pairs/small groups.
Reflect on cross-cultural (mis-)understandings.

Should you like to continue this activity:

4. Inform the class that after having returned to their home country, the Funnians wrote a report about the strange behaviour of the inhabitants of the country they visited. Of course, the students are asked to write this report. (This could be set as homework.)

Bemerkung

Mit Hilfe eines Arbeitsbogens soll für interkulturelles Lernen sensibilisiert werden. Die Einzelstunde kann zu einem Mini-Projekt „*Interculturalism*" verlängert werden.

Some critical incidents that occurred during the Funnians' visit

1. When Ms Winter, a geography teacher, patted the head of Earnest, a Funnian boy, Earnest got terribly upset. At first, he pushed Ms Winter away – rather violently. Then he shouted at her, but apparently he was so agitated that his English got all mixed up so that nobody could understand him. Finally he ran away and hid behind some bushes. And only after some of his friends had talked to him for a long time, was he ready again to communicate with his hosts.

   Possible explanations:
   a) In Funnia you are not allowed to touch somebody's head, because the head is the holy part of the body.
   b) In Funnia patting somebody's head means that you are superior and that you despise this person.
   c) In Funnia patting somebody's head means: I want to adopt you.

2. Anita invited some of the Funnians to attend a party at her place. At exactly 9.43 p.m. they all emptied their glasses on the floor and walked out on her – without saying anything. Of course, Anita thought this was very rude.

   Possible meanings:
   a) For Funnians this behaviour is a very warm-hearted way of expressing their gratitude for the hospitality and their deep wish to be invited again soon.
   b) Anita had insulted them, because she hadn't refilled their glasses.
   c) 9.43 is the exact time when parties in Funnia are over. Emptying the glasses is a way of saying goodbye, and if they had stayed any longer than 9.43, in Funnia that would have been rather impolite.

3. When Joya, a Funnian girl, was invited by the Schelp family, after some time she started sucking her thumb in a rather obvious manner. As she continued this thumb-sucking for more than an hour, the Schelps asked if there was anything the matter with her thumb. They didn't get any reply, but soon after Joya said she wanted to leave (still sucking her thumb)

   Possible explanations:
   a) She urgently had to use the toilet. It would have been very impolite to mention this need to the host family. In Funnia sucking your thumb means "Please, show me the bathroom!"
   b) She was still hungry, and in order to "control" her hunger, she sucked her thumb.
   c) She saw the two young children of the Schelp family sucking their thumbs and thought that was some normal, "decent" behaviour.

4. Mr Wiemeyer, the Headmaster, wanted to talk to some Funnians to learn more about their country and their educational system. He invited them to his office and offered them lemonade and cakes, but he was really shocked when the Funnians started howling (as if they were dogs) whenever he mentioned the word FUNNIA. After a short time he gave up the conversation and told the Funnians to leave. As you can imagine, he was rather angry.

Possible explanations:
a) In Funnia it is forbidden by law to mention the name of the country in public. The Funnians' howling was a way of preventing other people from hearing that Mr Wiemeyer was breaking the law.
b) The Funnians are not allowed to accept compliments. Whenever they or their country are complimented, they should howl. And the headmaster was talking in a very flattering way about them.
c) Cakes in Funnia are only eaten by dogs. By way of howling the Funnians made it clear that when being offered cakes, they felt insulted and treated like dogs.

5. When going on the train to a famous sight, the Funnians kissed the ticket inspector's hand and each of them gave him a yellow sweet. The ticket inspector was so surprised and embarrassed that he even forgot to ask for the tickets.

Possible reasons for this kind of behaviour:
a) In Funnia you don't pay for public transport. As a sign of appreciation you kiss the hands of civil servants or public employees and provide them with sweets.
b) The Funnians intended to distract and confuse the ticket inspector so that he would not ask for the tickets. They didn't have any.
c) It was the first time the Funnians had been on a train. They were so happy and thought the ticket inspector had invited them. Therefore they just wanted to be grateful.

© Cornelsen Verlag Scriptor, Berlin • Fundgrube Englisch handlungsorientiert

Balan and Bungan: A Borneo Tale

Lernstufe: Intermediate
Kontext: fremdes Land, fremde Sitten, Mythologie, exotische Erzählung
Material: Text der Erzählung, Zusatztext zu „Dayaks"
Dauer: 2–4 Stunden

Vorbemerkungen

Sagen oder Fabeln aus fremden Ländern eignen sich gut dafür, jüngere Schüler in eine ferne Welt zu führen und sie mit völlig anderen (exotischen) Erzählinhalten vertraut zu machen. Dies ist eine Möglichkeit, sie für Fremdes und Fremde zu sensibilisieren. Der Mensch als „story-telling animal" erzählt seine Geschichte und Geschichten immer wieder anders – je nach soziogeographischer und kulturhistorischer Situierung. Hier wird ein Erzählbeispiel aus Borneo vorgestellt – eine Sage von den Kenyah, einem kleineren Stamm aus Sarawak, dem nördlichen Teil der Insel, der zu Malaysia gehört. Die Kenyah bewohnen vor allem das Gebiet der Oberläufe der Flüsse Baleh und Rajang. (Übrigens: Es wird häufig übersehen, dass Malaysia nicht nur die Halbinsel Malaya umfasst, sondern auch zwei Regionen – Sarawak und Sabah – auf der Insel Borneo.)

Der für die Schüler vermutlich etwas schwierig zu fassende Fremdheitsgrad der Sage muss auf die völlig anderen Lebensumstände, aus denen diese Erzählung stammt, zurückgeführt werden. Animistische Auffassungen sind evident. Es ist zu hoffen, dass die Auseinandersetzung mit einer solchen Sage bei der Lerngruppe ethnologisches Interesse hervorruft.

Der Text stammt aus einer Sammlung, die das Borneo Literature Bureau in den sechziger Jahren des letzten Jahrhunderts zusammengestellt hat.

What to do

1. Ask the students to find out where Borneo is (and where on Borneo you can find Sarawak and the Rajang River). A map of South East Asia or Malaysia will help to locate the setting of the tale.
2. The following text provides some background information that is necessary to comprehend the story. Either you tell your students about the 'Dayaks' and the 'long houses' or you use the text (in which the pupils have to fill in the gaps with the right words). We recommend explaining the following words before reading:

   Vocabulary
   blowpipe – Blasrohr (You can imitate/show the pupils how you blow darts through an imaginary pipe …)
   stilt – Stelzen (Draw a house on stilts on the blackboard or show your students how to walk on stilts.)
   speedboat – a very fast boat

Balan and Bungan: A Borneo Tale

> **Read the text and fill in the missing words:**
>
> Dayak is the general term for the 200 different _____ living on North Borneo. The largest tribes are the Ibans (or Sea Dayaks) in Sarawak, and the Kadazan in Sabah who make up about 25% of the population there.
> Many tribes live in longhouses, they are farmers, plant _____, vegetables or rubber, and keep pigs and chicken; but some of them still go hunting, using blowpipes.
> Longhouses are long wooden houses on stilts. They are like a _____ where the whole population lives under one roof, with separate rooms for each family and one long common veranda called ruai. Longhouses are usually on the rivers so that the people can get water and also have some way of transport-boats. The headman (tuai rumah) and his family live in the _____ of the longhouse, and the rest of the families live to the right and to the left. A longhouse is a way of life, not just a building. The people live closely together.
> Today longhouses can be quite _____ with satellite TV, electricity, even speedboats etc. And many young people today have found work down the coast in the towns. But the old tales are still told among the Dayaks.
>
> *Words to fill in: middle   rice   modern   tribes   village*

© Cornelsen Verlag Scriptor, Berlin • Fundgrube Englisch handlungsorientiert

Sollte Bildmaterial von den Dayaks, ihren Tätigkeiten und den Langhäusern durch Internet und Bildbände (aus Bibliotheken) besorgt werden können, diente dies als notwendige visuelle Konkretisierung. Weiteres Wissenswertes zu den Dayaks findet sich auf der folgenden Website: http://www.sarawaktourism.com/main.html (general information about Sarawak: culture, ethnic groups, environment, events etc.)

3. Let the pupils read the text up to line 19 *(not to use a needle for seven days)*. Let the pupils speculate about what is going to happen. Let them also think of some more advice that might have been given to Bungan after the wedding. (Examples: Don't use a knife – it can be dangerous, too. Don't swim in the river. Why not? The crocodiles will eat you ... This additional need not be serious, it may be funny or ironic or nonsensical ...)

4. Let the pupils read on to line 51 *(waiting for her)*. Divide the class into groups. The groups make up, write down and eventually role-play the conversation between Balan and Bungan. (This is a preparation for the dramatisation of this tale, as suggested below – No. 8.)

An additional task (e.g. homework): Imagine the following situation: The king of the dead has overheard this conversation between Balan and Bungan. What is he going to do? What is going to happen? Think about and write down the continuation of the plot and a possible (unhappy, sad or tragic) ending.
5. The students read the text right up to the end. While or after it is being read, the action can be mimed or role-played. Discuss the story and the ending briefly, pointing out the mythological aspects (e.g. fighting/overcoming death – because of an untimely death of a relative or friend, fear of death, what is happening after death?). Find out if the pupils know of other mythological characters who embarked on a journey to the 'underworld' (e.g. Orpheus or Ulysses).
6. Let the students read the tale again and make up a list of all the aspects of Kenyah life that appear in the text. ('What do we find out about the life of the Kenyah when reading this tale?')
Possible answers: They plant rice and produce rice wine. Boars and other wild animals are hunted with darts and blowpipe, and apparently they are very good at using the blowpipe. The men also have a sword – presumably a 'parang' (= a long jungle knife) – and fight with it. (The Kenyah have been known to be excellent at working with metal.) Chickens are kept behind the longhouse, and the women are responsible for the chicken and the rice.

The wedding ritual takes place in the presence of the older members of the longhouse. At parties they sing and dance on the ruai. The girls/women dance, their fingers decorated with hornbill feathers. Journeys take place on boats/canoes on the rivers.
7. Today most children and adolescents in the longhouses attend school. Let your pupils conduct a 'fake' interview with a Kenyah boy or girl. They should ask about the present-day life of the Kenyah, about school, whether they know the tale about Balan and Bungan. Of course, the fictitious answers might not be right. But, still, this is a good activity to train the ability to change one's cultural perspective and to identify with young people of a rather different culture.

You may also ask your students if they know of any other narrative that has a cultural background and setting that is very different and strange for us. Of course, they should reproduce these stories. This might give pupils from other ethnic origins the chance to narrate tales common in their tradition.

8. **Possible project:** Let the students write a dramatic version of this tale (in groups) and produce and eventually perform a play. Ask the arts teacher to help prepare the costumes and the stage setting.
For this dramatisation the narrative could be divided into the following scenes:
1: The wedding. 2: The god of the dead is envious. 3: Admonitions after the wedding, 4: Bungan is mending Balan's shirt, she hurts herself and dies. 5: Balan dreams, prepares his blowpipe, blows his darts up in the sky and climbs up on the ladder. 6: He meets the souls of the dead people. 7: Disguised as a cock he meets up with Bungan. 8: Bungan tells Lenjot Iot that she would like to have a party. 9: The party: Bungan escapes. 10: Fight between Balan and Lenjot Iot. 11: They happily return to the village.

Nachbemerkung
Bei und nach dieser Unterrichtseinheit bieten sich Vergleiche zu Märchentopoi und zu Vorstellungen vom Totenreich an – und zu Versuchen, Verstorbene, insbesondere verstorbene Geliebte wieder zurückzuholen, wie es etwa auch im Orpheus-Mythos berichtet wird. (Auch Odysseus besucht ja die Unterwelt.) Die aus Pfeilen gestaltete Himmelsleiter kann mit dem englischen Märchen „Jack and the Beanstalk" verglichen werden. Dort steigt Jack an einer riesigen Bohnenpflanze gen Himmel und trifft auf einen bösen Riesen (ogre). Der Topos, dass eine Warnung nicht ernst genommen wird, erscheint in vielen Märchen: Rotkäppchen (Little Red Ridinghood) z. B. soll nicht den Weg verlassen und nicht mit Fremden reden. In „Dornröschen" („Sleeping Beauty") piekst sich die Prinzessin beim Spinnen und fällt in einen todesähnlichen Schlaf.

Hornbills

The Marriage of Balan and Bungan

There was once a famous longhouse on the banks of a large river called Aloh Moh. The chief of the longhouse was a young man called Balan Nyareng. He was a great fighter and a good and honest man. The harvest time was over and people were getting things ready for Balan's wedding. He
5 was to be married to a beautiful girl called Bungan. Some of the men were making rice wine and others went out hunting in the forest for wild boars. Hundreds of sacks of rice were prepared. Messages were sent out to the surrounding longhouses to invite as many people as possible to the wedding.
10 But these preparations were watched from the Land of the Dead. The King of the dead people, Lenjot Iot, also wanted Bungan to be his bride.
At last the wedding day came. Early in the morning everybody came to the ruai. The old men of the longhouse sat in front with Balan's and Bungan's parents. The young couple were dressed in their finest clothes. They sat on
15 two gongs in front of the elders and made their marriage promises. The wedding feast went on all day and night with dancing and singing. The next morning it ended and as always after weddings everybody went to give advice to the bride. The women told her not to use a needle for seven days.
20 But during the day Bungan wanted to mend her husband's shirt. In spite of what people had said she took a needle and thread and started to sew. Before long she pricked her hand and the blood started to pour out. She ran to her husband but he could not stop the blood. Then the villagers were called, but they could do nothing. Before that evening was over she died.
25 Balan was very sad.
The next day Bungan was buried. That night Balan had a dream. He dreamt that he saw his wife in the house of Lenjot Iot, the King of the Dead. She begged him to come and take her back.
When Balan woke up he started to make darts for his blowpipe. He worked
30 for seven days and seven nights and made millions of darts. On the eighth day, when everybody was sleeping, Balan went out into the bright moonlight carrying his blowpipe and darts. After walking some way from the longhouse he started to blow his darts up into the sky.
The first dart struck the top of the sky and the second one struck the first
35 one, and so on, until he had made a long ladder of darts hanging down from the top of the sky to the ground. It took him five hours to climb the ladder to the top of the sky. There he cut a hole and jumped through into the Land of the Dead. He came to a village where the souls of dead people from his own longhouse lived. They told him that a boat with fifty men and a
40 beautiful girl had passed up the river two days before. Balan was sure it must have been Bungan and he also paddled up the river. He passed some rice fields and at last he saw the longhouse of the King of the Dead.

© Cornelsen Verlag Scriptor, Berlin • Fundgrube Englisch handlungsorientiert

About a hundred yards from the longhouse he changed himself into a cock. He went round to the back of the house and there to his surprise and
45 happiness he saw his bride. Bungan was drying rice and chasing the chickens away from it. Still looking like a cock Balan tried to eat the rice. Bungan was angry with the cock and caught it. Then she heard the cock speak to her and tell her that he was her husband. He told her to get the longhouse people to have a dance that evening and that she should go to
50 bathe in the nearby waterfall. He promised that he would be there waiting for her.
So, when evening came Bungan told Lenjot lot that she wanted a dance that evening. He thought it was a good idea and told everybody to come to the ruai. Bungan was the first to dance and everybody came to see her dance
55 with hornbill feathers on her fingers. She was famous for the way she danced. Then the other people started to dance and everybody was happy. When she saw this, Bungan went off to the waterfall.
Later Lenjot lot saw that she had gone and he could not find her in the longhouse. One of the women told him that she had gone to the waterfall.
60 He did not think that she would bathe so late at night, so he took his sword and went to see what she was doing. As soon as Balan saw him coming he drew his sword, too, and a terrible fight began. They knew it was to be a fight to the death. Balan fought as he had never fought before and at last Lenjot lot became tired. Balan struck him a great blow with his sword and Lenjot
65 lot was dead immediately. Then Balan and Bungan ran quickly to their boat. After six days they reached the hole in the sky. Thankfully they climbed down the long ladder to the ground.
All this time the people in Balan's longhouse had been very sad because they thought that both were dead. When they saw them walking up to the
70 longhouse, they were very glad. Soon everybody came and heard the good news of their safe return. That night a great feast was prepared and Balan told the people of his adventures.

(Kenyah Stories, Borneo Literature Bureau 1967, S.1–7; abridged and simplified)

Annotations:
ruai – veranda or meeting-place in a longhouse
to mend – nähen
thread – Faden
to prick – (here) to make a very small hole in the skin so that it bleeds
dart – Don't you know the game of 'darts'? (Pfeil)
blowpipe – Blasrohr
ladder – Leiter
hornbill – a common bird in South East Asia
feather – what birds have on their body (Feder)

The Simpsons discover Tokyo

Lernstufe: Intermediate
Kontext: Hörverstehen, Stereotypen, Eigen- und Fremdverstehen
Material: DVD-player, TV-Gerät, DVD: *Die Simpsons. In 80 Donuts um die Welt*, Laufzeit: ca. 88 Minuten, FSK: freigegeben ab 6 Jahren [beinhaltet 4 Folgen: *Die japanische Horror-Spielshow* („30 Minutes over Tokyo"), *Das ist alles nur Lisas Schuld* (Brasilien), *Die Sippe auf Safari* (Afrika) und *Die Queen ist nicht erfreut* (England)]. Verfügbare Sprachen: Englisch, Französisch, Deutsch, Italienisch, Spanisch. Verfügbare Untertitel: u. a. Englisch, Deutsch u.v.a. (insgesamt 12 Sprachen)
Dauer: 3 Stunden und mehr. Dauer der Simpson-Folge *30 Minutes over Tokyo*: 20 min.

Vorbemerkungen

Gegenstand dieser Unterrichtssequenz ist die Folge *30 Minutes over Tokyo* der amerikanischen TV-Serie „Die Simpsons", in der die Familie Simpson nach Tokio/Japan fliegt. Anhand dieser Folge sollen die Schüler die „stereotype" Darstellung japanischer Kultur und Lebensweise in der Sitcom erkennen, analysieren und diskutieren.

Empfohlen wird eine stoffliche Vorentlastung zum Thema „Japan" zu folgenden Bereichen: Geographie, Politik, Kultur, Geschichte, Essen, Erziehung bzw. Schulsystem, Arbeits- und Lebensbedingungen, Technologie usw.

Background information

The Simpsons is a very famous and successful American animated sitcom by Matt Groening. It is known all around the globe. The show makes fun of and satirises many aspects of the human condition, but primarily parodies the "Middle American" lifestyle embodied in the Simpson family, as well as American culture, society, and even television itself.

The Simpson Family

Homer, father of Bart, Lisa, and Maggie, husband of Marge, works as a safety inspector at the Springfield Nuclear Power Plant. He is not that smart, which is highly visible in each episode, and that draws him into outrageous schemes and adventures. He is addicted to food (especially doughnuts) and alcohol, namely Duff beer.

Marge, mother of Bart, Lisa, and Maggie and Homer's wife, is of French origin, was once intelligent and sophisticated, but has become the stereotype of a housewife and mother.
Bart, the oldest child at the age of 10, is a troublemaker and classroom terror who thinks of himself as a rebel.
Lisa, the 8-year-old girl has an enormous intellect as well as an extraordinary articulation, but over the years has also developed interest in alternative lifestyles. She is a vegetarian, Buddhist and loves jazz music and dreams of a better future.
Maggie is a baby who is shown to be comically smart and self-reliant.

More information on the Simpsons can be found on the following websites:
General information: www.thesimpsons.com; http://en.wikipedia.org/wiki/The_simpsons; http://www.snpp.com/
Information on "30 minutes over Tokyo": http://www.snpp.com/episodes/AABF20; http://iteslj.org/Lessons/Meilleur-Simpsons.html; http://en.wikipedia.org/wiki/30_Minutes_Over_Tokyo

Some notes for the teacher
Rashômon – film made by Japanese director Akira Kurosawa (1951: Academy Award – best foreign film)
haiku – form of Japanese poetry (three unrhymed lines of five, seven, and five syllables; themes: nature/seasons)
Jim Belushi – famous American actor
toga – cloth worn by Roman citizens in ancient times
sliding paper doors – typical Japanese doors
imperial gardens – die kaiserlichen Gärten
Woody Allen – famous American actor and director
Meiji Shrine – holy place of worship for Meiji Tenno (1867–1912), Japanese emperor, who is famous for the abolition of feudalism and the advancement of (Western) technology and science
"Hello Kitty" – a purple cartoon kitten which has become a famous brand all over the world
the cartoon "Battling Seizure Robots" – This scene is based on a real event in Japan. There really was a Japanese cartoon that caused seizures when watching it.
Nantucket – an island that belongs to the state of Massachusetts
sumo – traditional Japanese wrestling

glandular – of a gland (Lymphdrüse)
kabuki play – traditional Japanese drama (male actors play male and female parts)
origami – Japanese art of paper folding
yen – unit of Japanese currency
crane – symbolises good luck in Japan
piñata – is a container made of colourful paper and filled with candy and/or toys that hangs from the ceiling. Children try to break the piñata to get what is inside.
hernia – Leistenbruch
wasabi – Japanese horseradish (Meerettich)

What to do

1. Tell your students that the lesson will deal with stereotypes. Let them try to define the term, ask for some examples and make sure everybody understands what stereotypes are.
   Definition: Stereotypes are impressions or generalisations that people have about different cultures or groups. There are usually good and bad stereotypes about any culture. Although they may be based in truth, they generally don't reflect the reality of a diverse group of people. E.g. French always drink wine./Italians only eat spaghetti.
   (source: http://iteslj.org/Lessons/Meilleur-Simpsons.html)
   Divide the class into groups of 3–5 students. Each group has to think about stereotypes of a specific country and its people, e.g. France/French, UK/British, Italy/Italian, China/Chinese, USA/Americans. Ask the students to talk about these stereotypes in the class and to discuss them.
2. As a next step refer to Japan, the country to be visited by the Simpsons. Therefore hand out worksheet A "Let's visit Japan". Let the students speculate why people would/would not like to go to Japan, make them name places they want to see and things they would like to do there. Now focus on stereotypes about Japan. Let the students work in groups to fill in the box on worksheet A "Let's visit Japan". After 5 minutes the ideas should be shared in an in-class discussion.
3. Inform the students that they will now watch an episode of "The Simpsons", a popular TV sitcom from the USA. Most of your students

will be familiar with the Simpson family and they will also know some episodes. Make them talk about the sitcom, the characters and episodes they know for some minutes. Afterwards ask them to write down the names of the Simpson family members on the blackboard and let them characterise the individual members in an in-class discussion. You can also make students draw a sketch for each single character on the blackboard.

4. The students watch the episode "30 Minutes over Tokyo" (season 10, episode 23). Start the viewing at chapter 4 (at 5 minutes) because this is when the Simpsons go to Japan. Tell them, that they will watch the episode twice. The first time they have to get used to language and pronunciation. (Especially Homer Simpson is hard to understand.) They are also asked to focus on the following aspects: What is happening in Japan? Do the Simpsons like it there? What is happening in the game show?

5. Hand out worksheet B "The Simpsons in Japan". Let your students read out the questions. Now, tell each group which questions they especially should focus on. Let them watch the episode again. As before, start at 5 minutes and let the students watch it to the end. (Repeat, if necessary. You may need to stop the DVD, if students have problems to understand the scenes.) Afterwards discuss the answers in class and make the students fill in the worksheet.

6. The students are now asked to answer the following questions and discuss them in class.
   a) Which Japanese stereotypes did you notice? (At least the five most striking ones should be found out.)
   b) What do you think about this episode? Do you think all stereotypes are true? Why or why not?
   (Depending on how much time you want to spend on the session and how old your students are let them watch the episode again – but without sound. Tell them to focus again on stereotypes and to write down the ones they have missed earlier.)

7. To end the unit on the Simpsons suggest 4 (according to the number of groups/students) different tasks to the whole class. Each group has to decide for one option. Hand out the role-cards.

The Simpsons discover Tokyo
Role-cards

Role-card 1: Have a 5 minute group discussion about the different Simpson characters! Who learns what about Japan and Japanese culture? Who is really interested in Japanese culture?
After your discussion: Each student has to choose one character and write a short report (10–15 sentences) about the holidays in Japan from his/her character's point of view. Note: According to the character you choose – use as many stereotypes as necessary! Some of your reports will be read out in class. The other students have to guess which member of the Simpson family wrote the report.

Role-card 2: Make up a new scene for the episode and act it out in front of the class! Use one or more stereotypes about Japan or Japanese! You are not allowed to use a stereotype which already appeared in one of the original scenes! At least one character of the Simpson family should be involved. Other characters may be made up. Each pupil belonging to the group has to be involved (acting and talking).
(After the scene is performed, the rest of the class have to guess which member of the Simpson family featured in the scene and which stereotype/s was/were used.)

Role-card 3: Imagine the Simpsons did not fly back to their home town Springfield, but to Germany! Make up a scene that is set in Germany and act it out in front of the class!
First of all try to collect stereotypes about Germany/Germans. Make a list! Use stereotypes in your scene! You have to choose a town where the Simpsons go to as well as activities they carry out and places/sights they visit. At least two members of the Simpson family should be involved. Others can be invented. All students of the group have to take part in the presentation (acting and talking).
(The rest of the class have to guess which member/s of the Simpson family wrote the report and which stereotypes were used.)

Role-card 4: Have a short group discussion about the Japanese game show. Write down at least 3 characteristics of this show. Talk about a German game show you all know!
Your task is to role-play a German game show. But you also have to include elements of Japanese game shows. Each member of the group has to be involved (acting and talking).
(The rest of the class have to guess which German game show you have imitated and which elements of Japanese game shows have been used.)

© Cornelsen Verlag Scriptor, Berlin • Fundgrube Englisch handlungsorientiert

The Simpsons discover Tokyo

Worksheet A

Let's visit Japan

1. Why do you think people want to go to Japan? Write down three different reasons!

_____

_____

_____

2. Which places would you like to see in Japan?

_____

_____

_____

_____

3. What would you like to do in Japan?

_____

_____

_____

_____

4. Which Japanese city would you like to visit? Write down three reasons!

City: _____

_____

_____

_____

Stereotypes about Japan

Do you know any stereotypes about Japan? The categories will help you! Try to find one example for each category and write it in the list below!

Customs/culture:

_____

_____

_____

Sport:

_____

_____

_____

Food:

_____

_____

_____

Technology:

_____

_____

Work:

_____

_____

© Cornelsen Verlag Scriptor, Berlin • Fundgrube Englisch handlungsorientiert

Worksheet B

The Simpsons in Japan

The Simpsons fly to Japan for a short visit. Please answer the following questions.

1. Which city have they arrived in? How do you know?

2. What kind of places does Lisa want to visit?

4. Where do the Simpsons go to eat? Where does Lisa want to go to eat?

5. Why is Homer sent to prison? What is the prison like? What do Homer and Bart learn while in prison?

6. Why do they go to the American embassy?

7. Where do the Simpsons work to earn money?

8. What prize do they want to win on the game show?

9. Why aren't they killed in the vulcano?

Barnga – A Simulation on Cultural Communication

Lernstufe: Advanced
Kontext: Simulation, Kartenspiel, interkulturelles Lernen
Material: je Gruppe ein Kartenspiel mit den Karten 2–10 in allen vier Farben und die 4 Asse (d.h. es werden 3 Romméspiele für 6 Gruppen benötigt), Spielregeln
Dauer: 1–2 Stunden

Bemerkungen

"Barnga" is an intercultural simulation: The pupils experience a situation in which they come across the fact that, despite many similarities, people of different cultures view things differently or play by different rules.

People often don't realise that there are distinctions between their culture or group and another group or culture until in interactions these differences cause communication problems. The idea of "Barnga" is to make students experience these subtle cultural differences.

While apparently playing a simple card game, the pupils realize that people behave differently – according to different rules. That is due to the fact that each group has been given slightly different rules to play the game. Therefore it is important that these differences in playing the game must be kept hidden from the players. The students suddenly face difficulties once they join another group that keeps to modified rules. This problem has not been expected by the participants. Of course, the card game rules stand for different and diverging cultural standards and habits. And moving from one group to another means facing a new culture, and the students should understand and solve the differences as if they are faced with "intercultural" interactions.

The problems are increased by the fact that during the simulation the participants are not allowed to talk. They are therefore required to mime, gesture or draw pictures to get their message across, as if they had no common language.

It is difficult to predict how the students will cope with this situation. They may play harmoniously with each other or get involved in – hopefully peaceful – quarrellings. This unpredictability is one of the aspects that makes playing "Barnga" so exciting – both for the students and for the teacher.

"Barnga" was originally developed to prepare 'international' managers for cultural misunderstandings and clashes.

It is essential that the teacher knows the rules well. Thus they should be read carefully, before the simulation starts.

What to do

1. Divide the class into groups of four to six players. Each group sits at a table, separated from one another. (Place the tables as far away from each other as possible so that there is no interference from other groups.) A deck of *Rummy* cards (hearts, diamonds, clubs, and spades from 2 to 10, and aces from all suits) is given to each group. That means for six groups six sets of cards are required. Tell the students that they are going to play a card game similar to *Skat* or *Rummy*.
2. Before the beginning of the simulation some words should be explained:
   – the colours of a card game: diamonds (*Karo*), clubs (*Kreuz*), spades (*Pik*), hearts (*Herz*)
   – suit (*Kartenfarbe*)
   – trump (*Trumpf*)
   – trick (*Stich*)

   The pupils must be familiar with these expressions so that they follow the instructions. Make sure that they also know the 'paper-rock-scissors' scheme *(Stein-Schere-Papier)*. This is applied in case there is a tie *(Unentschieden)* after a round.
3. Before finally playing "Barnga", each group must be given a – different – sheet containing rules (one copy for each participant). Tell the students to read the instructions very carefully and intensively and make sure that they understand them.

   The rules are modified for each table/group. (The students don't know about this and **don't tell them!**):

   Here are the modifications:
   Table 1: ace is the highest, no trump
   Table 2: ace is the lowest, no trump
   Table 3: ace is the highest, clubs are trump

Table 4: ace is the highest, spades are trump
Table 5: ace is the lowest, hearts are trump
Table 6: ace is the lowest, diamonds are trump

When each single player has comprehended the rules, the students return the rule sheets. They should be told again that they must not speak at all during the tournament. This is *the* most important rule for a successful effect of the simulation. The students may mime, gesture or draw pictures, but must not talk or write down words. **(During the game intervene sharply if this rule is broken.)**

4. (The rules of this game are very close to the card game *Skat*, though "Barnga" is not as complex. In general, the first player is playing any card and the others have to follow with the same suit. If they cannot serve the suit, they can play any card or a trump (if the rules allow this). In order to win the game, the players must outbid the first card with a higher number of the same suit or with a trump. All this information is explained on the various rule sheets.)

    Let the pupils practise the game first for some minutes before the actual beginning of the tournament. Then start the game officially. After about five or six minutes stop the game. For each of the tables make out who has won or lost by adding up the tricks won. Then the winners move clockwise to the next table; the players who have lost will move counter-clockwise. (But at this stage the pupils are not aware of the fact that each table observes a different set of rules.)

    Let the groups play the game a number of rounds – stopping it after every five or six minutes – until everyone has moved to another table. It is important that each player has experienced different rules (or ways of behaviour).

    Observe the reactions of the participants. Do they express confusion, misunderstanding, frustration, ignorance? You should talk about these feelings when you evaluate this simulation.

5. It is recommendable to let the students take some notes of what they experienced before a general discussion starts.

    Ask the students to formulate their first impressions on a piece of paper, how they found out about the difficulties/differences and how they coped with them.

Possible questions:
- What were your expectations at the beginning of the simulation?
- What did you experience when you were playing the game?
- When and how did you find out that something was wrong?
- How did you deal with this problem?
- How did you feel about the fact that you were not allowed to speak?
- Could you imagine any 'real life' situation where similar difficulties might arise?
- In which way is this game an activity for 'intercultural learning'?
- Have you yourself come across similar encounters/problems etc.?

In the course of the evaluation, the intercultural aspect should be more and more emphasized. The students should be made aware of the fact that the card game with its different rules corresponds to cultural varieties, and the frustrations and misunderstandings that have come up in the game are supposed to equal experiences in intercultural clashes.

Further information on Barnga can be found under:
http://plato.acadiau.ca/courses/educ/reid/games/Game_descriptions/Bafa_Bafa_Draft1.html
Sivasailam Thisagarajan. *Barnga. A Simulation Game on Cultural Clashes.* Sietar International Publications, 2005.

Barnga – Rules

- **Players:** 4–6 people per table
- **Cards:** Only 40 cards are used: Ace, 2, 3, 4, 5, 6, 7, 8, 9, 10 of each suit. Aces are the highest.
- You will have about **5 minutes** to study the rules and practice playing before the tournament begins. The rules will then be taken away and **no verbal communication** will be allowed. From then on, you may gesture or draw pictures **(but NO words!).**
- **Dealer:** The oldest person on the table shuffles the cards and deals them one at a time. Each player receives five cards.
- **Start:** The player to the left of the dealer starts by leading *any* card. The others must follow the given colour/suit, in clockwise order. If a player does not have that colour/suit, a card of any suit must be played. Once everyone has played a card, this constitutes a trick. The trick is won by the person with the *highest* card of the *original* suit. The winner of the trick collects all the cards and puts them face down in a pile. The winner of the trick then leads the next one which is played as before.
- **End/Win:** The game ends when all cards have been played. The player who has won the most tricks wins the game. And you may start again, shuffling the cards and dealing them etc.
- **Game winner:** The player who takes the most tricks in the *game*. If a game is not complete when the round ends, the player who has won the most tricks up to then is the winner.
- **Round winner:** The player who wins the most games in the *round*. Several games will be played during a round.
- Each round will last about 5 minutes.
- **Players move** then according to the following rules at the end of each round:

The player who has WON the most games during the round will move clockwise to the next table!! The player who has LOST the most games during the round will move counter-clockwise. Everyone else stays at the home table.

Ties are resolved by paper-rock-scissors.

Barnga – Rules

- **Players:** 4–6 people per table
- **Cards:** Only 40 cards are used: Ace, 2, 3, 4, 5, 6, 7, 8, 9, 10 of each suit. Aces are the lowest.
- You will have about **5 minutes** to study the rules and practice playing before the tournament begins. The rules will then be taken away and **no verbal communication** will be allowed. From then on, you may gesture or draw pictures **(but NO words!)**.
- **Dealer:** The oldest person on the table shuffles the cards and deals them one at a time. Each player receives five cards.
- **Start:** The player to the left of the dealer starts by leading *any* card. The others must follow the given colour/suit, in clockwise order. If a player does not have that colour/suit, a card of any suit must be played. Once everyone has played a card, this constitutes a trick. The trick is won by the person with the *highest* card of the *original* suit. The winner of the trick collects all the cards and puts them face down in a pile. The winner of the trick then leads the next one which is played as before.
- **End/Win:** The game ends when all cards have been played. The player who has won the most tricks wins the game. And you may start again, shuffling the cards and dealing them etc.
- **Game winner:** The player who takes the most tricks in the GAME. If a game is not complete when the round ends, the player who has won the most tricks up to then is the winner.
- **Round winner:** The player who wins the most games in the ROUND. Several games will be played during a round.
- Each round will last about 5 minutes.
- **Players move** then according to the following rules at the end of each *round*:

The player who has WON the most games during the round will move clockwise to the next table!! The player who has LOST the most games during the round will move counter-clockwise. Everyone else stays at the home table.

Ties are resolved by paper-rock-scissors.

Barnga – Rules

- **Players:** 4–6 people per table
- **Cards:** Only 40 cards are used: Ace, 2, 3, 4, 5, 6, 7, 8, 9, 10 of each suit. Aces are the highest. Clubs are trump.
- You will have about **5 minutes** to study the rules and practice playing before the tournament begins. The rules will then be taken away and **no verbal communication** will be allowed. From then on, you may gesture or draw pictures **(but NO words!)**.
- **Dealer:** The oldest person on the table shuffles the cards and deals them one at a time. Each player receives five cards.
- **Start:** The player to the left of the dealer starts by leading *any* card. The others must follow the given colour/suit, in clockwise order. If a player does not have that colour/suit, a card of any suit must be played. Once everyone has played a card, this constitutes a trick. The trick is won by the person with the *highest* card of the *original* suit or with a trump. The winner of the trick collects all the cards and puts them face down in a pile. The winner of the trick then leads the next one which is played as before.
- If you do not have a card of the first (original) suit, you may play a club. This is called *trumping*. You win the trick even if the trump you played is a low card. However, if more than 2 players play a trump, then the highest trump wins the trick.
- **End/Win:** The game ends when all cards have been played. The player who has won the most tricks wins the game. And you may start again, shuffling the cards and dealing them etc.
- **Game winner:** The player who takes the most tricks in the *game*. If a game is not complete when the round ends, the player who has won the most tricks up to then is the winner.
- **Round winner:** The player who wins the most games in the *round*. Several games will be played during a round.
- Each round will last about 5 minutes.
- **Players move** then according to the following rules at the end of each *round*:

The player who has WON the most games during the round will move clockwise to the next table!! The player who has LOST the most games during the round will move counter-clockwise. Everyone else stays at the home table.

Ties are resolved by paper-rock-scissors.

Barnga – Rules

- **Players:** 4–6 people per table
- **Cards:** Only 40 cards are used: Ace, 2, 3, 4, 5, 6, 7, 8, 9, 10 of each suit. Aces are the highest. Spades are trump.
- You will have about **5 minutes** to study the rules and practice playing before the tournament begins. The rules will then be taken away and **no verbal communication** will be allowed. From then on, you may gesture or draw pictures **(but NO words!)**.
- **Dealer:** The youngest person on the table shuffles the cards and deals them one at a time. Each player receives five cards.
- **Start:** The player to the left of the dealer starts by leading *any* card. The others must follow the given colour/suit, in clockwise order. If a player does not have that colour/suit, a card of any suit must be played. Once everyone has played a card, this constitutes a trick. The trick is won by the person with the *highest* card of the *original* suit or with a trump. The winner of the trick collects all the cards and puts them face down in a pile. The winner of the trick then leads the next one which is played as before.
- If you do not have a card of the first (original) suit, you may play a spades. This is called *trumping*. You win the trick even if the trump you played is a low card. However, if more than 2 players play a trump, then the highest trump wins the trick.
- **End/Win:** The game ends when all cards have been played. The player who has won the most tricks wins the game. And you may start again, shuffling the cards and dealing them etc.
- **Game winner:** The player who takes the most tricks in the GAME. If a game is not complete when the round ends, the player who has won the most tricks up to then is the winner.
- **Round winner:** The player who wins the most games in the ROUND. Several games will be played during a round.
- Each round will last about 5 minutes.
- **Players move** then according to the following rules at the end of each *round*:

The player who has WON the most games during the round will move clockwise to the next table!! The player who has LOST the most games during the round will move counter-clockwise. Everyone else stays at the home table.

Ties are resolved by paper-rock-scissors.

© Cornelsen Verlag Scriptor, Berlin • Fundgrube Englisch handlungsorientiert

Barnga – Rules

- **Players:** 4–6 people per table
- **Cards:** Only 40 cards are used: Ace, 2, 3, 4, 5, 6, 7, 8, 9, 10 of each suit. Aces are the lowest. Hearts are trump.
- You will have about **5 minutes** to study the rules and practice playing before the tournament begins. The rules will then be taken away and **no verbal communication** will be allowed. From then on, you may gesture or draw pictures **(but NO words!)**.
- **Dealer:** The youngest person on the table shuffles the cards and deals them one at a time. Each player receives five cards.
- **Start:** The player to the left of the dealer starts by leading *any* card. The others must follow the given colour/suit, in clockwise order. If a player does not have that colour/suit, a card of any suit must be played. Once everyone has played a card, this constitutes a trick. The trick is won by the person with the *highest* card of the *original* suit or with a trump. The winner of the trick collects all the cards and puts them face down in a pile. The winner of the trick then leads the next one which is played as before.
- If you do not have a card of the first (original) suit, you may play a hearts. This is called *trumping*. You win the trick even if the trump you played is a low card. However, if more than 2 players play a trump, then the highest trump wins the trick.
- **End/Win:** The game ends when all cards have been played. The player who has won the most tricks wins the game. And you may start again, shuffling the cards and dealing them etc.
- **Game winner:** The player who takes the most tricks in the GAME. If a game is not complete when the round ends, the player who has won the most tricks up to then is the winner.
- **Round winner:** The player who wins the most games in the ROUND. Several games will be played during a round.
- Each round will last about 5 minutes.
- **Players move** then according to the following rules at the end of each *round*.

The player who has WON the most games during the round will move clockwise to the next table!! The player who has LOST the most games during the round will move counter-clockwise. Everyone else stays at the home table.

Ties are resolved by paper-rock-scissors.

Barnga – Rules

- **Players:** 4–6 people per table
- **Cards:** Only 40 cards are used: Ace, 2, 3, 4, 5, 6, 7, 8, 9, 10 of each suit. Aces are the lowest. Diamonds are trump.
- You will have about **5 minutes** to study the rules and practice playing before the tournament begins. The rules will then be taken away and **no verbal communication** will be allowed. From then on, you may gesture or draw pictures **(but NO words!)**.
- **Dealer:** The youngest person on the table shuffles the cards and deals them one at a time. Each player receives five cards.
- **Start:** The player to the left of the dealer starts by leading *any* card. The others must follow the given colour/suit, in clockwise order. If a player does not have that colour/suit, a card of any suit must be played. Once everyone has played a card, this constitutes a trick. The trick is won by the person with the *highest* card of the *original* suit or with a trump. The winner of the trick collects all the cards and puts them face down in a pile. The winner of the trick then leads the next one which is played as before.
- If you do not have a card of the first (original) suit, you may play a diamond. This is called *trumping*. You win the trick even if the trump you played is a low card. However, if more than 2 players play a trump, then the highest trump wins the trick.
- **End/Win:** The game ends when all cards have been played. The player who has won the most tricks wins the game. And you may start again, shuffling the cards and dealing them etc.
- **Game winner:** The player who takes the most tricks in the *game*. If a game is not complete when the round ends, the player who has won the most tricks up to then is the winner.
- **Round winner:** The player who wins the most games in the *round*. Several games will be played during a round.
- Each round will last about 5 minutes.
- **Players move** then according to the following rules at the end of each *round*.

The player who has WON the most games during the round will move clockwise to the next table!! The player who has LOST the most games during the round will move counter-clockwise. Everyone else stays at the home table.

Ties are resolved by paper-rock-scissors.

Means of Communication among the Naeporue

Lernstufe: Advanced
Kontext: Textverständnis und -analyse, kreatives Schreiben, talking about cultures, freies Sprechen, Eigen- und Fremdreflexion
Material: je eine Kopie des Arbeitstextes, Folien für Mind-Map-Präsentation, Folienstifte
Dauer: 5–6 Stunden

Some background information
Whereas in Germany we use the term 'Ethnologie' to refer to research into customs, habits and institutions of tribes and peoples, in the US this is called cultural anthropology. The term ethnography, on the other hand, refers to the actual act of describing and portraying ethnic groups of people. Cultural anthropology accompanied the colonial age: the unknown territories and the people there, invaded and conquered by the Western colonial powers, had to be explained, analysed and categorised. In the 20th century, the emphasis of anthropology on 'uncivilised' 'tribes', on people that had not developed a written culture and tradition, gave way to a more general observation and analysis of the behaviour and the culture of people in any kind of environment. Thus even city life in Europe and the US has become a quite normal topic for cultural anthropology.

This unit deals with an example of anthropological research and methods – directed at our own culture and habits. It is based on and imitates a 'classic' anthropological parody, Horace Miner's 'Body Rituals among the Nacirema' (= America), which first appeared in the journal *American Anthropologist* in 1956. For further information on 'Nacirema' consult the internet (Nacirema) or *Englisch betrifft uns,* 4/2005, S.13–17.

What to do
1. Before the actual beginning of the unit the students need some information on areas such as culture, anthropology and ethnographic research. In order to obtain this information they may consult encyclopaedias or browse the internet. (This could be done as homework.)

2. Ask the students to work together in groups of 3–4 to exchange the information they found on culture, ethnology and anthropology. They should use the technique of mind-mapping, put their results on a. transparency and present and explain them in a mini-report in front of the class.
3. Hand out the text and ask for a close reading. The students should make a list of the most important facts about the newly discovered tribe.
(In the course of further activities dealing with the text, the teacher should take great care to find out if and – if so – when individual students have grasped the hidden meaning of the text. They must under no circumstances reveal what they have found out, but rather side with the teacher leading their classmates up the garden path. If the true message of the text is revealed too early, the success of this unit will be significantly reduced.)
4. Ask the students about their first impressions of the text. From which perspective is this report written? What is their reaction to this culture? Which of the described objects/things and aspects of life are especially interesting/disturbing/remarkable? What can we learn/transfer from the Naeporue culture?
5. Hopefully the students have not yet found out that the tribe described in the text corresponds to our very own culture (Western civilisation). The following activities, however, might lead them towards a 'better', i.e. real understanding. Ask the students to work in pairs or in small groups; they can choose between various tasks. (Make sure that all the tasks are covered.)
a) Imagine, describe and draw what a potpal looks like. Explain what it is good for and whether we could use it in our culture.
b) What does an elibom look like? Describe and draw it. Can we use it in our culture?
c) How do you imagine a poth? Describe and draw it. Describe the way that it needs to be treated to be of best use to the Naeporue. Could our culture profit from such a unique item?
d) Imagine you have the chance to make use of the 'window to the world'. What could you do with it? What could be the advantages to have something like that in our culture?
e) Imagine you are a Naeporue trying to meet another lonely person. Describe what the place looks like. What would the Naeporue talk about? Who could you possibly meet there? What about the effects of

the liquid? Why would members of the tribe decide to isolate themselves from the other members in the first place? (Act out a conversation or a scene portraying the meeting.)
The results of the pair/group work must be presented and explained to the class.

6. Eventually tell the students who still have not grasped the secret meaning of this culture that Naeporue is European (read backwards). Make them reflect upon the fact that and why they needed such a long time to really understand the text. What has caused this 'delayed' reaction and realisation? In which way did the ethnographic perspective make us believe that this was a presentation of some kind of 'peculiar' culture?
Have the class discuss the solutions. After this initial and more general discussion and exchange of opinions ask the students to analyse and decode the various aspects of the culture described in the text.

7. Creative Writing: Ask the students to write about aspects and gadgets from their culture in an ethnological and scientific way. They can think of items that they might use daily, e.g. radio, MP3-player, bicycle, dishwasher, (electric) toothbrush, email etc.

Means of Communication among the Naeporue

In our modern times people yearn for sensations, for something that colours their lives and makes them experience something we might call 'diversity' or entertainment. Although mankind believes that it has already discovered every wonder that resides on earth, we sometimes discover
5 evidence that evolution has never stopped.
Professor James West – who holds the chair of anthropology at the University of Nottingham – has gained a reliable reputation with his publications in the field of anthropological studies. In his latest essay he discusses a newly discovered tribe that he has been observing for over 10
10 years now. Although West and his team have spent rather a long period of time among the people of the tribe, they have not completely grasped all the details and complexities of the 'Naeporue' culture.
In his publication about the Naeporue, West says that there is "... one remarkable characteristic about these people that needs to be further scrutinised."
15 This characteristic is the fact that the Naeporue are obsessed by communication and they make use of extraordinary means to communicate

with each other. One Naeporue group invited the professor and his team
into their dwelling. A younger member of that family showed them a magical
item that caught their attention. Linked with an unknown energy source the
20 'potpal', as it is called, can be used for many diverse and extraordinary
activities. Most of the Naeporues have at least one of these items.
Apparently, it has become necessary to organise and structure the tribe's
everyday life with it and it is for this reason that the potpal has become an
indispensable tool, as the family pointed out to the professor. In order to
25 protect the sacred secrets of a family, every owner of this item needs to
prove his identity to the potpal with ritual finger movements that are unique
for each individual – the 'nigol'. Once the item is inspired with the 'breath
of life', strange symbols appear on a luminescent surface. So far the
professor's team has been able to determine that the symbols apparently
30 have various meanings. One of the symbols that the professor has examined
in some detail was described by him as appearing in "... a shade of blue and
[to be] shaped in the form of what we could describe as something close to
the letter 'W', if we dared to apply our very limited reservoir of symbols ..."
Apparently it is used to combine elements of the many Naeporue dialects
35 in a mysterious manner. At the end of this ceremony the professor describes
seeing something that he calls "... the ritual manifestation of symbolic
figures that serves the purpose of passing on knowledge from one Naeporue
to other members of the tribe ..."
Another symbol links one potpal to many others. Once enchanted and after
40 having invoked nigol, the Naeporue can visit places they have never visited
before, obtain food, hear about exciting tales or scandals in their settlements,
and most importantly contact other members of their tribe.
The 'window to the world', as the Naeporue call it, is not the only means of
communication. Another magical item that is very common among the
45 people is the 'elibom'. Some people do not only have one elibom, but
several – one for each occasion. The most important function of the elibom
is to deliver brief messages, either spoken or written. Once a Naeporue has
cast a certain magic spell the voice of almost any member of the tribe can
be conjured up. The device does not only bring joy to the people, as the
50 professor and his team found out. Especially younger members of the tribe
cast too many spells which causes anger among the adult members of the
tribe.
These various means of communication do not only make it easier for the
people to keep in contact with each other, but it also affects family structures
55 among the Naeporue. Whereas the families usually consist of one male and
female adult and several younger members, the anthropologists found
evidence that some people spend their time alone instead of agreeing to
live within the boundaries of these family structures. This self-inflicted

loneliness brings along strange rituals among the isolated Naeporue. Some
60 people reject these mystic items, ceremonies and magic which seem to be
too stressful for them. They choose instead to go to places where they try to
meet like-minded people. In order to bear the pain of being alone they
infuse themselves with substances that affect their brains. These substances
make it harder to express their thoughts clearly, but apparently they have a
65 soothing effect on their feelings and increase their potential to interact.
Excessive infusions, however, often lead to aggressive behaviour.
The last discovery the professor describes as "striking" is that of the 'power
of the horse' or 'poth', as it was named by one of the anthropologists. The
poth, though completely unknown to our culture, is very controversial
70 among members of the tribe. As it seems, people enjoy the comfort that a
poth can offer, but they are also very frustrated when it needs to be attended
to by specialised members of the tribe or when the expensive nutrients on
which it feeds need to be provided.
Within Naeporue culture the poth is considered to be the most precious
75 possession you can acquire. Thus it is handled with extreme care and
caution. Especially the male members of the tribe have strange rituals to
worship their poth. From time to time they wash it with a special lotion, dry
it carefully and add a protective layer to prevent its hide from being
scratched. When a male bonds with his poth he is overwhelmed by
80 indescribable feelings of joy and pleasure that arise from its delightful
purring. Most of the poths frequently move people from one place to
another using all its magical powers. One of its powers is that a well-trained
poth is able to reach any destination, if a Naeporue can lead it along the
correct route. That is why the poth is also considered a means of
85 communication, because it enables the Naeporue people to see and visit
other members of their tribe who live in distant locations.
The lifespan of a poth is not endless, though. Many poths are injured when
treated inappropriately, for example when they meet other poths and feel
the need to fight the 'battle of acceleration'.
90 It is hard to imagine how this remarkable people could have existed for
centuries alongside our very own culture without having been discovered.
The Naeporue are what we might call a culturally highly advanced tribe, they
have nevertheless succeeded in preserving their traditions, magical
ceremonies and mystical items. Mankind needs just the unrestricted belief
95 they have in their culture in order to enable us to completely understand the
mysteries of the world – an understanding, which is sometimes hidden
underneath a veil of ignorance.

For the teacher: Some words and expression might not be known to the students

- diversity – Vielschichtigkeit
- dwelling – house
- hide – (hier) skin
- inappropriate (Adj.) – unsachgemäß
- indispensable – you cannot live without it
- luminescent – full of light
- nutrients – ingredients
- purring – e. g. sound produced by cat
- reliable – verlässlich
- remarkable – fascinating
- reputation – Ruf
- scriptures – writings
- self-inflicted – sich selbst zugefügt
- to be conjured up – to be made audible by magic
- to be imprinted – to be put onto sth.
- to be obsessed by – besessen sein von
- to cast – to say
- to grasp – to understand
- to inflict – to force sth on so
- to infuse – to fill so with sth
- to predict – to see the future
- to reside – to live
- to scrutinise – to examine
- to soothe – to calm down
- to worship – to idolise, to admire
- to yearn for – to long for (sich sehnen nach)
- veil – Schleier

For the teacher: solutions for terms used in the text

- Naeporue – European
- potpal – laptop
- nigol – login/password
- breath of life – electricity
- luminescent surface – screen/monitor
- symbol resembling a 'W' – Microsoft Word
- window to the world – Internet
- elibom – mobile, cell phone
- to cast a magic spell – to dial the number, to use the phone
- anger among parents – young people addicted to sending out text messages, debts because of mobile phone bills etc.
- isolated people – singlehood; looking for partners e. g. in pubs
- infused substances – alcohol
- poth – "power of the horse" = car
- injured poths – cars damaged in accidents
- battle of acceleration – road rage

© Cornelsen Verlag Scriptor, Berlin • Fundgrube Englisch handlungsorientiert

13 Working with Film

Es empfiehlt sich, allen Schülerinnen und Schülern bereits sehr bald zu Beginn einer Unterrichtseinheit zum Thema Film einen Bogen mit der einschlägigen Terminologie an die Hand zu geben und mit ihnen wichtige Dimensionen – graphics, camera range, camera movement, montage/editing/ punctuation, manipulation of time, sound, lighting, narrative style (s. „A Taste of Terminology", S. 262 ff.) – durchzugehen, damit sie davon Gebrauch machen können, wenn ihnen dies sinnvoll erscheint. Inhaltlich isolierte Wortschatzarbeit im engeren Sinne wäre unangebracht. Nur in Verbindung mit einer Auseinandersetzung mit einer Filmpassage und ihrer Wirkung macht die Beschäftigung mit filmerzählerischen Mitteln und ihrer Begrifflichkeit Sinn. Bei den folgenden Vorschlägen wäre spätestens bei den Aufgaben zu „Storyboarding" und allen darauffolgenden das Bereitstellen von Begriffen in Form eines Glossars sinnvoll.

Cinema Experiences

Lernstufe: Intermediate/Advanced
Kontext: beginning of a unit on film
Dauer: 1 1/2 Stunden

Bemerkung
Die Schülerinnen und Schüler haben bereits intensive Filmerfahrungen, wenn sie in der Schule mit Film konfrontiert werden. Diese Erfahrungen sollten am Beginn einer Unterrichtseinheit zum Thema Film im Mittelpunkt stehen.

What to do
1. Prepare copies of the questionnaire and distribute them to the students for individual work (possibly homework). Take a copy yourself.

2. Put up enlarged copies of the individual questions in an appropriate distance from each other along the classroom walls and ask the students to fasten their answer sheets below the respective questions. Add your own answers.
3. Leave sufficient time for everyone to study their classmates' answers.
4. Ask the students to choose one answer only that they would like to discuss with its author and have author and interested student(s) get together for that discussion. Should a larger number of students show interest in the same answer, stage a class discussion.
5. Leave the answers for a week or so, then collect them to serve as a first chapter in a class portfolio accompanying the work on film.

Name (optional) _____

Task: *Select two of the following questions (groups of questions) that correspond best to your personal film experience and answer them in detail. Write each answer on a separate sheet (one side only). Attach your answers beneath the respective questions on the classroom wall.*

1. When did you last go to the cinema? Did you go on your own? What film did you see? Why that particular one? What was your response?
2. Have you ever left the cinema before the end of the film? Why?
3. In what way does watching a film in a cinema feel different from watching a film at home (via TV/DVD/VHS)?
4. What film or film scene has stayed on your mind for a long time/is still on your mind?
5. Did you ever/do you often cry during films? Try to explain what made/makes you cry.
6. Which film(s) would you like to see again and again? Try to explain the attraction.
7. What is your favourite type of film (genre)? What do you like about it?

© Cornelsen Verlag Scriptor, Berlin • Fundgrube Englisch handlungsorientiert

Thinking about film

Lernstufe: Intermediate/Advanced
Kontext: media literacy
Dauer: 1 1/2 Stunden

Thinking about film

Bemerkung
Im Folgenden werden Fragen für Gruppendiskussionen vorgeschlagen, die ein Nachdenken über das anregen, was Film ist bzw. sein kann. Sie eignen sich sowohl für den Beginn einer Filmeinheit als auch zu deren Abschluss.

What to do

1. Present the group tasks below on a transparency.
2. Ask the students to get together in groups according to the task they would like to tackle. Alternative: Have the students get together in five groups and ask a member of each group to draw lots to decide on their group's task.
3. Give them 20 mins. to work before presenting their results to the class.

An alternative, esp. for younger students: Give each a card/sheet with the following sentence to complete:

Watching a film in the cinema is like ...

Collect the answers on a pinboard for all to review and talk about.

Thinking about film

Group A:
How would you describe *film* to someone who has never watched one? (You could explore this question by way of a role play with some of you playing the experts, the others pretending they have never heard of such a thing.)

Group B:
The role of a film spectator has been described as "voyeuristic". Find out what that term means. Do you consider the term appropriate or not?

Group C:
Films often give the illusion of reality. Why? How do they achieve this illusion? Try to think of examples.

Group D:
Alfred Hitchcock is supposed to have said: "Ours is not to reason why, ours is to scare the shit out of people." How do films manage to scare their audiences? Describe your own experience and try to explain what scared you.

Group E:
Why are films which deal with very distant issues, the lives and fate of others (e.g. Titanic, E.T.) popular all over the world?

Storyboarding

Lernstufe: Intermediate/Advanced
Kontext: visuelles Erzählen
Material: Folie mit dem Beispiel eines Storyboards für die Einführung; je nach Klassengröße zwei bis drei Kopien mit je einer der drei Gruppenaufgaben sowie ausreichend Leerfolien und Folienstifte (löslich) für die Gruppenarbeit.
Dauer: 1 1/2 Stunden

Bemerkung
Filme erzählen Geschichten. Ihre besondere Erzählweise kann durch die Analyse von Filmen erforscht werden, aber auch – wie hier vorgeschlagen – durch eigene Versuche, Wortgeschichten in Bildgeschichten zu übersetzen.

What to do

1. Tell the class that they will be asked to produce storyboards. Explain that a storyboard is a visual script telling the story to be filmed in a series of rough sketches in preparation of the shooting of a film.

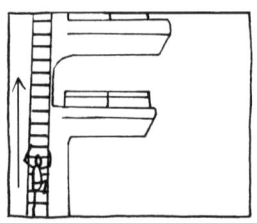 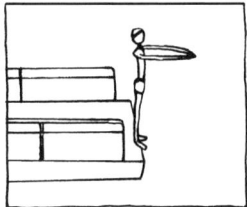 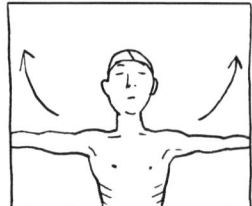
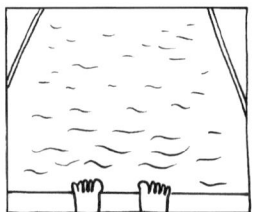 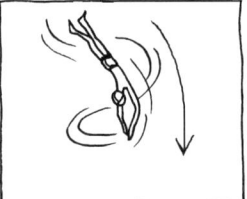 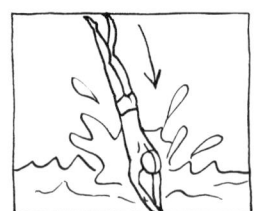

© Cornelsen Verlag Scriptor, Berlin • Fundgrube Englisch handlungsorientiert

Storyboarding

2. Ask the class to get together in groups of four or five. Give each group one task sheet (see below). Make sure that each task is assigned to at least one group and that the groups do not contact each other. Hand out empty transparencies and pens. Give the groups about half an hour to work on their task.
3. Ask group(s) A to tell their story and show their storyboard sequences.
4. Have group(s) B present their storyboards without any comment. Ask the others to tell the story on the storyboard.
5. Have group(s) C do the same.
6. Pick one or two storyboard examples and invite the class to explore the producers' and the viewers' contributions to making sense of the picture sequences.

Task sheets

Task A:
Imagine a film sequence in which a man gets out of a car, walks into a building, goes up a staircase, unlocks a door, and goes into a flat. To get from the car to the flat, he has to go through all these actions, but as a filmmaker you do not have to shoot every step he takes.
- As a first exercise, develop a storyboard with the minimum shots necessary to convey the man's movements and his surroundings.
- Develop a second, more extensive storyboard with more shots.
- Make suggestions as to the sound accompanying your second version.
- Embed the sequence in a story: What happened before the man got out of his car, what are the events following his entrance into the flat?
- Prepare to tell/present the story.

Task B:
Draw two storyboards for a short film telling the following limerick, one telling it in a minimum of pictures, the other one telling it more extensively.

> There was a young lady from Riga
> Who smiled as she rode on a tiger?
> They came back from the ride
> With the lady inside
> And the smile on the face of the tiger.

Make suggestions for a soundtrack to accompany the strips.

> **Task C:**
> Draw two storyboards for a short film telling the following limerick, one telling it in very few pictures, the other one telling it more extensively.
>
> There was a rich man in Nantucket
> Who saved all his gold in a bucket.
> His daughter, called Nan,
> Ran off with a man,
> And as for the money: Nantucket.
>
> Make suggestions for a soundtrack to accompany the strips.

© Cornelsen Verlag Scriptor, Berlin • Fundgrube Englisch handlungsorientiert

Film Beginnings

Lernstufe: Intermediate/Advanced (je nach Film)
Kontexte: Auseinandersetzung mit filmischem Erzählen
Material: einige Filme auf DVD or VHS, z. B.
– für fortgeschrittene Lerngruppen *Citizen Kane* (1941), *Psycho* (1960), *Full Metal Jacket* (1967), *The Truman Show* (1998);
– für jüngere Lerngruppen *Ice Age* oder *Jungle Book*.
OH-Folien mit den Aufgaben.
Dauer: 2 Stunden

Bemerkung

Die Eröffnung eines Films ist eine besondere Herausforderung für die Filmproduktion wie für die Filmrezeption. Sie muss dem Publikum den Eintritt in die Filmwelt ermöglichen und seine Vorstellungskraft in besonderem Maße mobilisieren, weil es noch nicht auf innerfilmische Zusammenhänge zurückgreifen kann, sondern auf mediales, narratives und allgemeines Weltwissen angewiesen ist. Wie fangen Filme an? Wie führen sie in das noch vor den Zuschauerinnen und Zuschauern Liegende ein? Auf welche mentalen Zuschaueraktivitäten bauen sie? Welches Spiel treiben sie mit dem Publikum, welches das Publikum mit ihnen? Hier sind vier Vorschläge.

What to do

1. **Predictions and taste**
   - Begin with a conversation about the specific role of film beginnings.
   - Then show the first two minutes of three or four films just once. Ask students who know the films to keep quiet.
   - After each showing, give the class time to jot down their impressions and predictions.
   - Allow some time for an exchange in class.
   - Then play the beginnings once again, but this time two minutes longer.
   - Ask the students to reconsider their first views.
   - Have them discuss the composition of one of the beginnings (majority choice) more thoroughly by playing the beginning again, once without sound and once without vision.
   - Lend the films to students who want to see them completely.

   Transparency explaining the task:

   Studying film beginnings

   You are going to see the first minutes of a few films.
   After each showing take notes paying special attention to the following aspects:

   - What are your immediate reactions to the film opening?
   - Do you find anything remarkable in it?
   - What do expect the film to be about?
   - Would you like to see more of it? Why (not)?
   ---

2. **Creating an opening sequence**
   - Divide the class into groups.
   - Present a short narrative text on transparency (such as "There was a young lady from Riga ...", s. Storyboarding, page 254 ff. or "Ten Jugs of Wine", s. below).
   - Ask the groups to create an unusual opening sequence for a film narrating the story.

> **Ten Jugs of Wine**
> *A Tale from Japan*
>
> Ten old men decided to celebrate the New Year with a big bowl of hot sake wine. Since none of them could provide for all, they agreed to bring one jug of wine each for the large heating bowl. On the way to their wine cellars, each old man thought, "My wine is too valuable to share! I'll bring a jug of water instead. No one will find out. It'll still be fine." – When they gathered with the jugs they brought, all ten old men poured the contents of their jugs ceremoniously into the big bowl. With downcast eyes they drank the hot water, pretending to enjoy its delicious taste.

3. **Reconsidering first impressions**
   - Show the introductory sequence of a film you want to show in full length and ask the class to write down their first impressions and expectations on that basis. Collect the notes for later reference.
   - Proceed with your film unit.
   - At the end of your unit, show the beginning again.
   - Pick two or three of the notes produced by the students after their first viewing (or gather all the notes in a hat and ask the students to pick two or three at random) and read out the first impressions and expectations expressed in the notes. Did the predictions come true?
4. **Investigating how an audience makes sense of a scene**
   Example: Hitchcock's *Psycho* (see excerpt below).
   - Do not reveal the title or the director's name of the film, and ask those who know the film not to join in the discussion.
   - Deconstruct the opening sequences: Instead of beginning with the famous graphics/title sequence, begin your showing with the caption: FRIDAY, DECEMBER THE ELEVENTH. Play on until Marion's line: "You make respectability sound – disrespectful."
   - Ask the class what they expect the film to be about.
   - Then show the film from the very beginning and discuss the change of expectations effected by this addition.

PSYCHO

Pulsing music drives titles across a black screen.
Main title gives way to a gray metropolitan landscape.
The music softens as subtitles continue to slide in, indicating:
PHOENIX, ARIZONA

And as the camera pans across the city:
FRIDAY, DECEMBER THE ELEVENTH

The camera selects and slowly zooms in on one large old building:
TWO FORTY-THREE P.M.

The camera eye focuses on an open window whose slightly raised blind leaves a narrow gap for the camera to slip through. The dim light within reveals a seedily furnished bedroom. An attractive woman in underwear lies on the bed, gazing up at a shirtless man who stands alongside. Some fast-food items are on the table.

SAM: You never did eat your lunch, did you?
MARION: (sitting up) I better get back to the office. These extended lunch hours give my boss excess acid.
SAM: Why don't you call your boss and tell him you're taking the rest of the afternoon off? It's Friday, anyway – and hot.
(Sam sits on the bed. They caress and kiss during their conversation.)
MARION: What do I do with my free afternoon? Walk you to the airport?
SAM: Well, we could laze around here a while longer.
MARION: Checking out time is three p.m. (They sink down on the bed, facing each other, kissing and caressing.) Hotels of this sort aren't interested in you when you come in, but when your time is up – Oh, Sam, I hate having to be with you in a place like this.
SAM: I've heard of married couples who deliberately spend an occasional night in a cheap hotel.
MARION: When you're married you can do a lot of things deliberately.
SAM: You sure talk like a girl who's been married.
MARION: Sam, this is the last time.
SAM: Yeah? For what?
MARION: For this. Meeting you in secret, so – we can be secretive. You come down here on business trips – we steal lunch hours and – I wish you wouldn't even come!
SAM: All right, what do we do instead? Write each other lurid love letters?
MARION: (rises from the bed to get her clothes) I have to go, Sam.

SAM:	I can come down next week.
MARION:	No.
SAM:	Not even just to see you? To have lunch – in public?
MARION:	(*putting on her blouse*) Oh, we can see each other. We can even have dinner. But respectably, in my house, with my mother's picture on the mantel, and my sister helping me broil a big steak for three.
SAM:	(*picks up his shirt and sits in a chair*) And after the steak, do we send sister to the movies? Turn mama's picture to the wall?
MARION:	Sam!
SAM:	(*broadly submissive*) All right. (*Marion turns to face him. He gets up and puts on his shirt.*) Marion, whenever it's possible I want to see you. And under any circumstances – even respectability.
MARION:	You make respectability sound – disrespectful.

© Cornelsen Verlag Scriptor, Berlin • Fundgrube Englisch handlungsorientiert

A Scene of their Choice

Lernstufe: Intermediate/Advanced
Kontext: group work outside and inside class to accompany a unit on film
Material: task sheets, scene selected and provided by the pupils
Dauer: one lesson in the wake of the scene presentations; about three lessons for the presentations themselves.

Bemerkung

Am Anfang einer mehrwöchigen Unterrichtseinheit zum Film könnte eine begleitende Hausarbeit gestellt werden. Dazu erhalten die Schülerinnen und Schüler einen Aufgabenbogen, der im Plenum vorgestellt und durchgesprochen werden muss, damit eventuell auftretende Fragen geklärt werden können. Für die Gruppenzusammensetzung ist es sinnvoll, die Schülerinnen und Schüler zunächst selbst beraten zu lassen, damit sich solche zusammenfinden, die einen ähnlichen Filmgeschmack haben.
Es kann aber auch dirigistisch ausgezählt werden oder das Losverfahren angewendet werden. Alle Verfahren haben ihre Vor- und Nachteile. Die Präsentationen selbst sollten dann gegen Ende der Unterrichtseinheit stattfinden.

> ### A Scene of Your Choice: Task Sheet
>
> **Your task**
>
> - Your task is to prepare a group presentation of a film scene of your choice (no more than 3 mins. long) to the rest of the class. Your presentation must not exceed 15 mins.
> - The presentations will take place on ..., so you need to start to work on this task immediately.
> - The lesson before the presentations begin will be reserved for the final preparations of the group.
>
> **How to go about it**
>
> **Group homework to be done by ...:**
> - Form a group of 4 to 5 pupils to work on this task.
> - Find a film scene your group would like to present. Do not let anybody else know about your choice!
> - Make sure you have a copy of your scene in English.
> - Study the scene carefully (maybe you can find the script on the internet to help you) and analyse its composition, using a glossary of film terms.
>
> **Group work in class just before the presentation:**
> - Discuss ways of presenting your scene (s. below) in 15 mins., including the viewing of the scene.
> - Prepare your presentation without revealing anything about it to the rest of the class.
>
> **Aspects to include in your presentation:**
> - the scene itself
> - reasons for your choice of that scene (How did you come to an agreement? What do you find fascinating about the scene?)
> - an analysis of its composition
> - its place in the film as a whole (this aspect is optional)
>
> © Cornelsen Verlag Scriptor, Berlin • Fundgrube Englisch handlungsorientiert

A Film of their Choice

Lernstufe: Intermediate/Advanced
Kontexte: gemeinsame Auswahl eines Films
Material: Filmsequenzen
Dauer: 1–2 Stunden

Es wird kaum möglich sein, einen Film zu finden, der alle gleichermaßen anspricht. Dennoch ist es möglich, die Schülerinnen und Schüler in die Auswahl einzubeziehen.

What to do

1. If you want to study a film in class and involve the students in its selection, film beginnings or selected scenes can help.
   Bring a choice of three or four or more films that you think worth studying, incl. those suggested by the students.
2. Tell the class to take notes while they are watching the first three minutes or a scene from these films.
3. Ask them which of the films they would like to see more of. Make a hit list.
4. Take the film that is on top of the list and prepare to study it with the class.
5. Give the other films to those who have become interested in them to watch at home.

A Taste of Terminology

Lernstufe: Intermediate/Advanced
Kontexte: Nachvollziehen und Beschreiben technisch-darstellerischer und ästhetischer Verfahren des Films
Material: eine kurze Filmsequenz, z.B. der Beginn von *Psycho* (s.o.) oder *Ice Age* (für Jüngere), Glossar.
Dauer: 1–2 Stunden

Bemerkung

Fast alle Publikationen über Film im Unterricht befassen sich auch mit der sogenannten „language of film" oder „grammar of film". Darunter verstehen sie die technisch-darstellerischen Mittel des Films und ihre ästhetische bzw. kommunikative Wirkung. Eine systematische Einführung in die Filmsprache ist sicher nicht Sache des Englischunterrichts. Dennoch kann es wichtig sein, über Mittel zu verfügen, eine Szene oder eine Einstellung genauer in Bezug auf ihre Bauformen hin zu beschreiben und dafür auch Fachausdrücke zu benutzen.

Eine möglichst knappe Wortliste mit einem Grundfachwortschatz sollte an alle Schülerinnen und Schüler ausgeteilt werden, sodass sie auch für diesen Aspekt von Film Aufmerksamkeit entwickeln. Eine solche Liste sollte während des Unterrichts zu Film ständiger Begleiter sein.

Im Internet befinden sich zahlreiche Handreichungen dafür, die für die jeweilige Klassenstufe und die Gewichtung, die diesem Aspekt zukommen soll, angepasst werden können, z.B. unter den Suchbegriffen

- Movie Terminology Glossary
- Reading a Film Sequence
- film-glossary
- Wolf Liebelt – Dead Poets Society

Im Verlag für Medienliteratur in Hamburg ist 1993 das umfassende Film-Wörterbuch (deutsch/englisch, englisch/deutsch) *Film Talk* von Paula K. Read und Anja Bartsch erschienen.

What to do

1. Give each student a copy of the list of terms below. Explain the terms in bold print, discuss examples.
2. Let them get together in seven groups, each group responsible for one of the aspects in bold print, i.e. group 1 for the title sequence, group 2 for the camera range etc.
3. Play a brief film sequence repeatedly for the students to investigate under the aspect assigned to them, until they feel ready to deliver their findings.
4. Ask them to present them and guide a discussion about the cumulative effects achieved.

Note

Not all of the terms in film glossaries are clear-cut categories: There is no law as to where a close-up ends and a medium shot begins, to name but one example. Accordingly, the aim of this exercise is not precision and accuracy, but a feeling for the potential of audiovisual narration.

TERMS, TERMS, TERMS	
From frame to shot to scene to sequence to film.	
Graphics	start of programme: credits; their style can establish expectations, normally shown near or at beginning of the programme, rest of actor and others at the end. Often superimposed on action or stills.
Camera range	
point of view	position from which the camera is filming
point-of-view shot	shows scene from a character's point of view
establishing shot	long or wide shot showing the general location of the scene, usually at the opening of a scene or sequence, setting the scene
full shot	camera shows person from head to toe
medium shot	camera shows character from a medium distance, from head to knee
close-up	camera is very close to object, e.g. shows reactions/emotions in character's face
detail shot/extreme close-up	e.g. the camera focuses on the mouth, hand of the protagonist
Camera movement	
zooming in or out	camera remains stationary, the zoom lens bringing the object nearer or further away
following pan	camera follows a moving subject from the same base position
surveying pan	camera searches the scene
tilt	camera moves vertically, up or down, but stays fixed
tracking/dollying	camera itself is moving
Montage/editing techniques	
cut	sudden change from one viewpoint or location to another
match cut	two shots or scenes are linked by visual, aural or metaphorical parallelism, so that the cut is hardly noticed
jump cut	abrupt switch from one scene to another
cutting rate/rhythm	amount and arrangement of cuts
parallel action/cross-cut	intermingling the shots of two or more scenes so that they appear to happen simultaneously

© Cornelsen Verlag Scriptor, Berlin • Fundgrube Englisch handlungsorientiert

A Taste of Terminology

fade/dissolve	gradual transition between shots
wipe	optical effect marking a transition by wiping image off the screen
Manipulation of time	
screen time	time represented by events within a film
subjective time	time conveyed as experienced by film character, e. g. when a frightened person's flight from danger is prolonged
compressed time	achieved with cuts and dissolves
simultaneous time	events in different places presented as occurring at the same time by parallel editing, cross-cutting, multiple images or split-screen
slow motion	slower than real life movement
accelerated motion	faster than real life movement
flashback and forward	moving between events in the past and the present/future of the film narration
Sound	
diegetic sound	direct sound, live
studio sound	selective sound (for example heart beat or bomb or watch ticking), non-diegetic
sound bridge	creating continuity through sound by running a sound across a cut to make the action seem uninterrupted
asynchronous sound/non-diegetic sound	recorded separately from the visuals, e. g. voice-over or a commentary spoken off-screen, orchestra music during a love scene
Lighting	
key lighting	main light
underlighting/lowlighting	light form below the subject
sidelighting	to emphasise shadows
backlighting	to create a halo
Narrative style	
subjective treatment	viewer is treated as participant, first-person treatment of camera
objective treatment	viewer is treated as observer, privileged/omniscient point-of-view. Example: camera does not move with the subject.

© Cornelsen Verlag Scriptor, Berlin • Fundgrube Englisch handlungsorientiert

parallel development/ cross-cutting/parallel editing	intercut sequence, e.g. a chase showing the person pursued and the pursuer
'invisible editing'	omniscient style of the realist feature film developed in Hollywood; unobtrusive cuts that support rather than dominate the narrative. The conventions have become so familiar to filmgoers that they hardly notice them.
montage editing	unlike invisible editing, m.e. uses conspicuous techniques, i.e. close-ups, frequent cuts, dissolves, superimposition, jump cuts etc.
talk to camera	allowed for newsreaders, announcers, key public figures. In a feature film break of naturalistic convention.

© Cornelsen Verlag Scriptor, Berlin • Fundgrube Englisch handlungsorientiert

A Film in 45 Minutes

Lernstufe: Intermediate/Advanced
Kontext: Filme kennenlernen/Filmgenres erforschen
Material: Film auf DVD (weniger gut, aber möglich: auf VHS)
Dauer: 1 Stunde

Bemerkung

Ein organisatorisches Problem für die Filmarbeit in der Schule ist die Länge von Spielfilmen, die ja nicht an der Schulstunde, sondern, so Hitchcocks Erklärung, an der „endurance of the human bladder" orientiert ist. Das hier vorgestellte Vorgehen einer Kombination von gespielten und nacherzählten Filmpassagen erleichtert es, nicht nur einen, sondern mehrere Filme in den Unterricht einzubeziehen. Es bietet sich z.B. dann an, wenn ein Filmgenre erforscht werden soll. Nicht zuletzt eignet es sich auch für Filmpräsentationen durch die Schülerinnen und Schüler.

What to do

1. Go through the film chosen and select the sections that you would like to show on screen and those that could be skipped or briefly summarized.

2. Mark the sections you want to show, so that you can find them without delay (counter). Find out how much time they take in all. The remaining time in the lesson can be devoted to your summaries of the interim scenes and to questions and clarifications.
3. Take notes for your summaries so that they are clear and brief. It may be helpful to select a significant shot of the section you want to tell and project it as a still on screen while you sum up the events of that part.

Beispiel eines Vorbereitungsbogens zu „Bend It Like Beckham"

Counter	Scene	Notes for the presentation
0:00:40	Jess' daydream, roughly interrupted by her mother	Szene zeigen
0:03:20	Shopping with sister	mündlich zusammenfassen: ● Jess forced to accompany sister looking for a dress for her engagement party ● meet fashionable girls from the neighbourhood ● Jess' sister and the other girls, bitchy remarks and glances, rivalry ● Jules and her mother buying bra
0:05:55	Football in the park	● J. is only girl amongst boys ● not intimidated by sexist gestures, returns them humorously ● Jules watches her, smiling
0:07:00	Jess in her room etc.	Szene übergehen
0:08:00	Engagement party	Szene zeigen
0:09:30	Football in the park	mündlich zusammenfassen: ● J. plays football with the boys ● three girls on park bench with love and sex interest in the boys – incomprehensible for J.

© Cornelsen Verlag Scriptor, Berlin • Fundgrube Englisch handlungsorientiert

Tackling a full-length film

Lernstufe: Intermediate/Advanced
Kontext: Auseinandersetzung mit einem ganzen Film
Material: Film auf DVD (weniger gut, aber möglich: auf VHS)
Dauer: mehrstündig

Der fragwürdige Schulstundenrhythmus kommt (auch) der Arbeit mit Filmen nicht entgegen, muss sie aber nicht zum Scheitern bringen. Hier nun einige Anregungen zum Umgang mit einem ganzen Film.

Zum Umgang mit dem Zeitrahmen
Wenn Sie den Film in voller Länge ohne Unterbrechung zeigen wollen, brauchen Sie mindestens eine Doppelstunde. Wenn diese einschließlich der Pausen davor und danach nicht reicht, bitten Sie die/den Kollegen/in, die vor oder nach Ihnen Unterricht hat, Ihnen einen Teil der Stunde im Tausch zur Verfügung zu stellen.
Oder zeigen Sie den Film über zwei bis drei Stunden als Fortsetzungsfilm, möglichst mit „cliffhangers", sodass die Fortsetzung mit Spannung erwartet wird.
Oder gliedern Sie ihn in sinnvolle Abschnitte und zeigen Sie ihn im Wechsel mit Phasen der Arbeit zu dem jeweiligen Abschnitt über mehrere Stunden hinweg.

Zum Umgang mit der Sprache
Englischsprachige Filme bringen nicht-didaktisierte Sprache in den Unterricht. Dieser Vorzug stellt zugleich eine Herausforderung dar. Hier einige Vorschläge zum Umgang damit, die je nach Ziel der Filmarbeit genutzt oder modifiziert werden können:
Nutzen Sie die Untertitelung auf DVD. Sie können z.B. sprachlich schwierige Passagen mit englischen Untertiteln zeigen. Oder Sie können Passagen zunächst ohne Untertitel, dann mit englischen Untertiteln, dann mit deutschen Untertiteln zeigen – oder auch in umgekehrter Reihenfolge, je nach Ziel und Lerngruppe. Untertitel helfen, schon in den ersten Jahren des Englischunterrichts Filme und Filmausschnitte einzubeziehen. Beispielsweise lässt sich Disneys *Jungle Book* in sprachlich gestufter Weise zeigen: Die Liedszenen können vorgezogen eingeübt und diese Liedpassagen können dann ohne Untertitel gezeigt werden, andere Passagen können mit

deutschen Untertiteln vorgeführt, andere Passagen für intensive Arbeit zum Hörverstehen genutzt werden usw.

Das Verstehen eines fremdsprachlichen Films kann entlastet werden, wenn die (Haupt-)Personen und die Beziehungen zwischen ihnen vorher kurz vorgestellt werden – natürlich ohne dass der Filmerzählung vorgegriffen wird.

Das Internet stellt eine Quelle für erstaunlich viele Filmskripte dar. Auszüge daraus können vor oder nach dem Betrachten einer Passage gelesen werden. Oder Sie wenden ein *clozing*-Verfahren an, indem sie aus dem Text einer Schlüsselszene zentrale Begriffe entfernen und diese beim (wiederholten) Betrachten einfügen lassen. Hier einige Internet-Adressen:
- Drew's Script-O-Rama
- JoBlo's Movie Scripts
- Awesome Movie Scripts

Nicht immer entspricht das Drehbuch bzw. Skript im Internet präzise der Endfassung des Films, sodass ein Vergleich von Text und Film und ggf. Korrekturen ratsam sind bzw. zur Aufgabe für die Lernenden werden kann.

Zur interaktiven Auseinandersetzung mit Filmen (einige Beispiele):
1. Schalten Sie bei geeigneten Passagen Bild bzw. Ton aus und lassen Sie über das Ungehörte bzw. Ungesehene spekulieren.
2. Rücken Sie das Wiedergabegerät in die Mitte des Klassenraums und lassen Sie die Hälfte der Schülerinnen und Schüler vor dem Gerät, die andere hinter dem Gerät Platz nehmen. Führen Sie eine ausgewählte Passage vor und fordern Sie die Schülerinnen und Schüler hinter dem Gerät auf, Vermutungen über den Bildablauf anzustellen, und diejenigen vor dem Gerät, das Gesehene zu beschreiben.
3. Wenn Sie den ganzen Film bzw. eine längere Passage des Films gesehen haben, regen Sie eine Rekonstruktion des Filmablaufs an. Bitten Sie die Schülerinnen und Schüler, auf je eine DIN-A5-Karteikarte eine Szene/Begebenheit, an die sie sich erinnern, mit einem Stichpunkt zu notieren. Eine/r beginnt und legt eine Karte auf den Boden (z.B. im Flur vor der Klasse oder an einer freien Wandseite). Die anderen legen nach und nach ihre Karten so ab, dass sie in die Reihenfolge kommen, in der sie nach ihrer Erinnerung im Film vorkommen. Karten, die sich auf die gleiche Szene beziehen, werden übereinandergelegt. Wenn alle Karten abgelegt haben, sollte gemeinsam festgestellt werden, wo Lücken oder Unsicherheiten hinsichtlich der Sequenzfolge bestehen, und im Ge-

spräch und im Zweifelsfall mithilfe des Films bzw. Filmskripts Klärung geschaffen werden.
4. Bitten Sie die Schülerinnen und Schüler, eine Szene zu wählen, mit der sie sich intensiver beschäftigen wollen. Klären Sie mit ihnen die Rolle der Szene im Filmganzen. Lassen Sie arbeitsteilig eine detaillierte Rekonstruktion herstellen: Ortsbeschreibung, Dialog/Ton, Kameraführung, Schnitte, Beleuchtung etc. und über Alternativen der Verfilmung nachdenken. Vielleicht stellt sich ein/e Schüler/in für ein „hot chair"-Verfahren zur Verfügung, lässt sich also die Augen verbinden, versetzt sich in die Rolle des für die Szene wichtigen Filmcharakters und stellt sich den Fragen der anderen nach Beweggründen, Gefühlen, Entscheidungen, Gedanken.
5. Sammeln Sie mit den Schülerinnen und Schülern Ideen für weitere Auseinandersetzungsmöglichkeiten mit dem Film für arbeitsteilige Gruppenarbeit:
   – graphische und pantomimische Darstellung der Beziehungen zwischen den Filmgestalten;
   – Weiterentwicklung einer Nebenfigur;
   – Verfassen einer Vor- und Nachgeschichte des Films als screenplay oder in Prosa;
   – Umschreiben des Films in Hinblick auf einen Genrewechsel, z.B. vom traditionellen Western zur Comedy oder zum Psychodrama, oder eines Atmosphärenwechsels, z.B. vom Komischen zum Tragischen;
   – Ersinnen von zusätzlichen Szenen und Figuren;
   – Übersetzung einer Szene in die jeweiligen Muttersprachen der Schülerinnen und Schüler, z.B. für Untertitelung;
   – Nachspielen einer Szene;
   – Befragungen/Interviews/Verhöre, z.B. der Charaktere im Film, aber auch der Regie, der Schauspieler/innen etc.;
   – autobiographisches Schreiben einer der Figuren;
   – Entwickeln von Remake-Ideen etc.

14 Projects

Class Library

Lernstufe: Beginners/Lower Intermediate
Kontext: extensives Lesen (evtl. auch Verfassen einer Erzählung)
Material: 6–10 verschiedene Lektüren; bei großen Lerngruppen sollten jeweils 2 Exemplare vorhanden sein.
Dauer: etwa 3–4 Monate

Bemerkung

Das Projekt benötigt wenig Unterrichtszeit, da die Hauptarbeit im Wesentlichen von den Schülern zu Hause geleistet wird. Die Auswertung findet überwiegend durch Arbeitsbögen statt, die von der Lehrkraft überprüft und korrigiert werden.
Exemplarisch wird das Projekt hier für eine Lerngruppe nach etwa einem Jahr Englischunterricht vorgestellt. Mit unterschiedlichen Inhalten kann die Form des Projekts jedoch auf alle Schulstufen – sogar auf einen Leistungskurs – übertragen werden.
Sollte mit der Lerngruppe noch keine Lektüre behandelt worden sein, ist es sicher hilfreich, als Einstieg zunächst im Klassenverband eine kurze, einfache Lektüre durchzunehmen.

What to do

1. 6–10 Lektüren, die für das Niveau der Lerngruppe geeignet sind, müssen ausgewählt und für die *English Class Library* angeschafft werden. Zwei Schüler werden als *librarians* eingesetzt. Ihre Aufgabe ist es, dafür zu sorgen, dass die ausgewählten Lektürehefte möglichst rasch und problemlos innerhalb der Klasse weitergegeben werden. Nach etwa 3 Monaten sollten sämtliche Lektüren von allen Schülern gelesen sein. Beispiele für Lektüreauswahl nach einem Jahr Englischunterricht; die kursive Zahl in Klammern gibt den Umfang des verwendeten Grundwortschatzes an: *The boy who cried wolf* (*400*, Cornelsen 105046) • *The*

milkmaid and her pail (600, Cornelsen 105054) • *Professor Puffendorf's Secret Potions* (Oxford University Press) • *The Reward* (Klett 57039) • *Winnie the Witch* (Oxford University Press) • *The Magic Stone* (Ladybird/Klett 570720) • *Belling the cat* (600, Cornelsen 105062) • *Aunt Sophy* (Klett 57038)

2. Mit der Ausgabe eines Lektüreheftes erhält jeder Schüler einen Arbeitsbogen (vgl. Beispielbogen Seite 273), der im Anschluss an die Lektüre zu Hause selbstständig bearbeitet werden muss. Mögliche Aufgabenstellungen reichen (je nach Leistungsstand differenziert) von einfachen *Wh*-Fragen über das Lösen von Rätseln, Nacherzählungen bis zu Interpretationen, literarischen Kommentaren sowie kreativen Aufgaben wie z.B. das Verfassen von Briefen, Tagebucheinträgen oder Gedichten. Wenn die Schüler eine Lektüre gelesen und bearbeitet haben und sie an ihre Mitschüler weiterreichen, wird der fertige Arbeitsbogen dem Lehrer zur Korrektur übergeben. Bei jüngeren Lerngruppen bietet es sich an, im Klassenraum eine Übersicht über den Lektürefortgang der einzelnen Schüler anzubringen. Das Projekt kann an dieser Stelle abgeschlossen werden.

3. Als Fortsetzung des Projekts bietet sich die Erarbeitung einer eigenen Erzählung an. In einer Unterrichtsstunde werden an der Tafel noch einmal sämtliche Personen (auch Tiere usw.) aufgelistet, die in den Erzählungen auftauchen. Die Schüler wählen sich jeweils mindestens drei (oder mehr) Figuren aus unterschiedlichen Lektüren aus und entwerfen aus dieser Personenkonstellation eine eigene, kurze Handlung (in Stichpunkten).

4. Bevor die kurze Erzählung (als Hausaufgabe) niedergeschrieben wird, sollen die Schüler noch einmal in einer Art „Geschichtenwerkstatt" die Möglichkeit bekommen, sämtliche Lektüren durchzublättern und daraus geeignetes Sprachmaterial (Wörter, Sätze, Wendungen) für ihre eigene Story zu entnehmen. Sie können also ihre Geschichte aus Zitaten zusammenstellen bzw. ihre eigenen Sätze und Abschnitte immer wieder mit „authentischen" und richtigen Strukturen und Wendungen verknüpfen und bereichern.

5. Die Schüler verfassen ihre Geschichten, die dann korrigiert werden.

6. Die fertigen Produkte können im Unterricht vorgelesen werden. Als motivierende Alternative dazu bietet es sich an, die Erzählungen (vielleicht als fächerübergreifendes Projekt mit dem Kunstunterricht) auch künstlerisch-grafisch zu gestalten. Aus praktischen Gründen sollte der Um-

fang der Geschichten auf eine oder zwei DIN-A4-Seiten (Vorder- und Rückseite) beschränkt bleiben. Alle Erzählungen werden gesammelt, kopiert, geheftet, mit einem Deckblatt versehen und als Broschüre herausgegeben: *The Collected Stories of Class 6 a.* Jeder Schüler erhält eine solche Geschichtensammlung.

The boy who cried wolf

Stepping into English

1. Peter is a shepherd and he is often bored. What could he do?
Make suggestions, talk to him.
a) "Why don't you..

b) " When you are bored, you could

c) " ....

d) " ....

2. One day later an interview with Peter, the shepherd, appeared in the local newspaper.

COUNTRY NEWS

Wolf kills sheep
An Interview with the shepherd

CN: Yesterday the wolf attacked your sheep. How many did he kill?
Shepherd:

CN: Why did you not scare away the wolf ?
Shepherd:

CN: Why didn't the townspeople help you?
Shepherd:

CN: What did the farmer say about all this?
Shepherd:

CN: Are you going to lose your job?
Shepherd:

Extra-terrestrials

Lernstufe: Intermediate
Kontext: Anwendung des bislang Gelernten; schreiben, sprechen
Material: Kostüme und Requisiten
Dauer: etwa 1 Monat

Bemerkung

Dieses Projekt, bei dem der Besuch Außerirdischer auf der Erde thematisiert wird, kann der Einübung interkulturellen Verhaltens dienen. Die Schüler sollen dabei lernen, mit Fremdheitserfahrungen umzugehen. Es wäre günstig, wenn dieses Theater- oder Sketch-Projekt gemeinsam mit dem Kunstunterricht durchgeführt werden könnte. Auch der Deutschunterricht kann vorbereitend mitwirken; dort besteht z.b. die Möglichkeit, Prinzipien oder Bausteine eines Theaterstücks (z.B. Dialoge, Szeneneinteilung, Regieanweisungen usw.) zu besprechen.

What to do

1. In einer einführenden Unterrichtsstunde wird der Klasse die Projektidee mitgeteilt: Sie soll ein Theaterstück verfassen und aufführen, dessen Thema der Besuch Außerirdischer in der Heimatstadt der Schüler ist. Eine Grobplanung entsteht: Entwicklung des Handlungsstranges, Skripterstellung, Verteilen und Einüben der Rollen, Herstellung von Kostümen und eventuell eines Bühnenbildes, Proben, Aufführung.

2. Im Verlauf dieser Stunde wird eine Handlungsstruktur entwickelt. Dabei ist zu beachten, dass im Sinne einer „offenen" Dramenform die einzelnen Szenen nicht durch ein kompliziertes Kausalgefüge verbunden werden, sondern dass sie möglichst selbstständig für sich stehen. Nur dadurch ist gewährleistet, dass die Szenen jeweils von einer Arbeitsgruppe unabhängig gestaltet werden können, ohne dass permanent mit den anderen Gruppen Ab- und Rücksprachen zu treffen sind.
Folgende Vorgehensweise empfiehlt sich: Die Schüler werden mit der Schlagzeile *„Extra-terrestrials are going to visit you"* konfrontiert. Dann werden sechs Szenen als Grundmuster (an der Tafel) entwickelt und festgelegt:
Scene 1) The visit of the extra-terrestrials is announced. How: by letter, e-mail? Make up an unconventionial way of announcing this visit! Where does it happen? In the class-room?

Scene 2) The extra-terrestrials arrive and are made welcome. Where do they arrive: at the station, at the airport, on a field? Think about a welcoming ceremony. The first meeting, the first interaction with these strange beings... Are they very formal? Are there any misunderstandings? Where do the aliens come from?

Scene 3) The extra-terrestrials attend school. They have a different idea about school. Therefore they behave in a very strange, unusual way. The teacher gets angry.

Scene 4) The extra-terrestrials are confronted with something/an object they don't know. And they don't know how to behave towards this object: roller-blades, a bike, a video camera, a camera, ear-phones, a dog, a cat, a cuddly toy?

Scene 5) A love scene. An alien and a human being fall in love with each other. There might be some 'cultural' misunderstanding; e.g. kissing in extra-terrestrial meaning is something awful ... they show love in a completely different manner.

Scene 6) Saying goodbye. How do they leave? From where do they leave? Have they become friends?

Am Ende dieser ins Projekt einführenden Unterrichtsstunde sollte die hier konzipierte oder eine ähnliche Handlungsstruktur entwickelt sein. Als thematischer Grundwortschatz sollten bei den Schülern folgende Begriffe bekannt sein: *alien, extra-terrestrial (ET), creature, intelligent creature, being, human being, planet, interplanetary (travel, voyage), space, spaceship, UFO (unidentified flying object), flying saucer, science fiction, host, hospitality, to invite, invitation.*

3. In der nächsten Unterrichtsstunde beginnt die Skripterstellung: Die Klasse wird in sechs Gruppen eingeteilt. Jede Gruppe übernimmt eine der konzipierten Szenen und erhält folgenden Auftrag:

"First you must draw up and write the script of your scene. Take note: Later on you, the group members, will take over and act the (major) roles in this scene and therefore you should not include more major roles than there are pupils in your group. Other classmates may only take up minor roles or can be extras. You should also make up a list of all the stage props etc. needed for this scene. It is essential that your scene can be performed. It should be "realistic" – despite the fact that extra-terrestrials appear. It is e.g. not possible to have the extra-terrestrials "fly" nor can you include huge flying objects.

When you design your scene you should bear in mind that the aliens hardly know anything about life on earth. Whatever they do, whatever they see, wherever they go, things/people are strange for them. They might not even know what they can eat and what is not edible. In your text you should, if possible, include sequences or passages in which this element of strangeness, of not knowing anything is shown (to the audience). That is why the aliens must make mistakes – in their cultural and social behaviour, neither do the human beings know how to behave towards the ETs or how to interpret their behaviour."

Da jede Gruppe später auch ihre Szene spielen muss, ist garantiert, dass alle Schüler an der Aufführung aktiv, d. h. als Schauspieler beteiligt sind. Die Gruppe ist also von Beginn bis zur Aufführung für „ihre" Szene verantwortlich.

4. Schon in diesem Stadium des Projekts sollten – evtl. im Kunstunterricht – Kostüme und Make-up (vor allem der „aliens") besprochen werden (grüne Gesichter? Antennen? Plastikkleidung, z.B. blaue Müllsäcke?). Auch ein Bühnenbild sollte schon jetzt entworfen, konstruiert und hergestellt werden. Eine Reihe von Szenen spielt im Klassenzimmer, was relativ einfach auf der Bühne dargestellt werden kann; evtl. muss für Szene 2 und 6 mit ein paar Kulissen und Hinweisschildern ein Bahnhof oder Flughafen angedeutet werden; Szene 4 und 5 können z.B. in einer Wohnung oder auf der Straße oder auch in der Schule spielen.

Auch über den Einsatz von Musik und über eine mögliche „Lautkulisse" sowie über Beleuchtungsfragen sollte schon gesprochen werden. Evtl. müssen Musik- und Beleuchtungsverantwortliche bestimmt werden.

5. Die Schüler stellen ihren Skriptentwurf zur jeweiligen Szene der Klasse vor. Die Klasse äußert sich zu dem Entwurf und macht gegebenenfalls Verbesserungsvorschläge. Das Skript wird vom Lehrer sprachlich-idiomatisch korrigiert, und die Gruppen tippen oder schreiben – gut lesbar – die Endfassung auf DIN-A4-Papier, damit die Seiten kopiert werden können. Falls noch nicht geschehen, werden jetzt innerhalb der Gruppen die Rollen verteilt.

6. Das Theaterstück wird zur Aussprache- und Intonationsschulung mehrmals in der Klasse gelesen.

7. Die Schüler lernen ihre Rollen auswendig; in Gruppen inszenieren und proben sie ihre jeweilige Szene. Die Lehrkraft muss die einzelnen Gruppen kontrollieren und beraten, Regieempfehlungen geben und darauf achten, dass laut, deutlich und verständlich gesprochen wird.

8. Vor der Aufführung sind zwei oder drei Proben mit der gesamten Klasse auf der Bühne (bzw. am Aufführungsort) zu empfehlen. Dies ist beson-

ders dann wichtig, wenn in einzelnen Szenen viele Schüler oder gar die gesamte Klasse als Statisten beteiligt sind.
9. Der Besuch der „extra-terrestrials" wird – mit einem schlagkräftigen und werbewirksamen Titel versehen – aufgeführt.

Beispiel eines Szenenausschnitts (Szene 4) The Bike

KATE (running up to Lighty and Righty): Hi, you are from Mars, aren't you? We met at the station yesterday. Don't you remember me? I'm Kate.
LIGHTY: Hi, (very formally) it is a real pleasure to see you. My name is Lighty.
KATE: Lighty? What a strange name! And who are you?
RIGHTY: Oh, I'm awfully sorry. Oh, I'm Righty. (formally) It is a pleasure. (pointing towards Chris and her bike) Oh, what is this???
  ("It" seems to be frightened.)
KATE: Don't be afraid. That's a bike.
LIGHTY: A bike???
RIGHTY (trying to shake hands with Chris): Hello, bike.
CHRIS: No, no, no, (pointing to the bike) that's a bike!
LIGHTY: Oh, I'm terribly hungry. It looks tasty. (tries to eat it)
CHRIS: Leave it alone. That's my new bike. No, no, you can't eat it!
RIGHTY: Well, Lighty, it's strange, isn't it? I don't understand this. You can't eat it. What is it?
LIGHTY: I think we have to be careful. And very polite.
RIGHTY (talking to the bike in a very polite manner): Hello, I'm Righty. May I ask you what you are doing here?
LIGHTY: It doesn't answer. May be it doesn't speak English.
CHRIS: It can't speak!
LIGHTY: ... can't speak? Well ...
KATE: It is a bike. You can ride it.
RIGHTY: Ride it? But where's the computer?
KATE: Chris, come on. Why don't you explain it?
CHRIS: OK. I'll show you how this bike works. Don't be afraid. Come here. Now, get on.
  (She helps Righty onto the bike and gives the bike a push.)
RIGHTY (riding on the bike): Stop, stop. I want to stop. I want to get off. Help, help!
  (Kate grabs the bike and stops it.)
KATE: Come on, get off. That's no problem, really.
CHRIS (showing Righty the brakes): Look, here are brakes. You pull here, and the bike stops. It's very simple.
RIGHTY: I see ...
LIGHTY: Please, let me try. (It takes the bike and rides off.) Oh, it's fun, it's fun.
CHRIS: Stop! Oh, no! Stop! My new bike.

AUSTRALIA

Lernstufe: Upper Intermediate
Kontext: Landeskunde
Material: vergrößerte Landkarte von Australien, Textkarten (s. Material 1), Bilder (aus Kalendern, Bildbänden, alten Lehrbüchern, Zeitschriften, Reiseprospekten etc.), Schnur, Kleber, Pappen, Packpapier, Stecknadeln, Pinwand, Scheren, Tesafilm, reichliche Auswahl an Foto- und Textmaterial, Zugang zum Internet, Wörterbücher, Overheadprojektor, CD-Player
Dauer: 6 Stunden und Präsentationszeit

What to do

Before you begin; Paste a large map of Australia onto a sheet of cardboard and cut it into equal squares. Shuffle them well.

1. **Approaching Australia.**
   Ask your pupils to write down what comes to mind when they think about Australia. Collect their associations on a large sheet of paper and hang it up in the classroom.
2. **Create Australia!**
   – Invite your pupils to draw one of the cards you have made from the map. They should try to locate their part of Australia by looking into an atlas or by putting it beside another piece etc. Together the pupils will reconstruct the map by pinning the pieces onto the pin-board. To get the puzzle going, you might pin one piece onto the board yourself.
   – Ask your pupils (in pairs or groups of 3) to draw one of the cards with the texts about certain areas of Australia (page 280–281). When they have read it, they should try to find "their" place on the map. Using pins and a length of string, they connect the card with its place on the map.
   – Hand out photos of places/animals/people/vegetation in Australia. Ask your pupils to find out where their photo could be placed on the map. They must read all the cards to do this. When they feel they have found a suitable place, they should pin their picture beside the card.
   – Hand out the crossword puzzle (material 2). Encourage your pupils to have another look at the map with its texts and pictures to help solve the puzzle.

3. **Finding topics and forming groups**
   - Ask your pupils to note down three topics that they are particularly interested in concerning Australia.
   - Get them to write these on three slips of paper and stick them on the blackboard with cellotape.
   - Invite them to have a good look at all the suggestions and to reorganize them on the board so that similar ideas are together. Get them to decide on headings to categorize their ideas. (These might be e.g. Wild Life, Getting around, Flying Doctor, Aborigines etc.)
   - In order to form groups, your pupils now should write their names under the topics they would like to work on. The ideal size of a group is three. Should there be several pupils interested in one topic, they can form more than one group.
4. **Working on the topics**
   - Give your pupils time to become familiar with the topic they have chosen by reading the material provided and by researching in the internet. As well as this they should look for material at home and in their local library.
   - Hand out the guidelines for presentation.
5. **Presentation of the results**

Guidelines

The next step will be to work on the aspect you have chosen.
Remember these important points:

a) *You* know lots about your topic – your classmates don't. So try to prepare a presentation which will be easily understood by everyone. You can do this by using transparencies, pictures, CDs, music, posters etc.

b) Rehearse your presentation in your group. Remember to speak loudly and clearly, without reading your text word for word, and to keep eye-contact with your audience. Try to make your presentation as lively and interesting as possible.

c) Wind up your presentation with at least one activity to make sure your classmates have understood everything and that they remember what it was all about.

d) Be ready for presentation on …

Cards

Like other cities, I had a prison colony. It was in Moreton Bay, and was used for the most dangerous convicts that came to us from New South Wales. For 20 years, no other settlers were allowed to live here. But that was a long time ago. Now I'm the 3rd biggest city in Australia. I have a very modern Business Centre with high buildings, directly on the river which has the same name as I do. To the south there are marvellous beaches which deserve their name – Queensland's Gold Coast. It's a surfer's paradise!

I'm the only big city in the centre of Australia and I'm a good place to start tours to the Outback. I've got a Flying Doctor Station and a School of the Air broadcasting centre for children in the Outback. If they live on farms too far away from school, they can have lessons by TV or radio. I'm famous for my camel-racing.

The most famous building in Australia is here at my harbour. Tourists and yachtsmen love to visit me here at Botany Bay, where the history of Australia began over 200 years ago. The first Europeans to settle here were not exactly the finest of people! But I've forgotten all that and so did everybody else, when thousands of people came here to be the first to celebrate the Millenium on New Year's Eve in 1999 in the "Manhattan of the Pacific".

I'm in a national park, almost in the centre of Australia.
Actually I'm only the tip of a mountain – the rest of it is under the sand. The Aborigines call me Uluru – they say that I belong to them and that I am a sacred place. People come from all over to climb me (348 m) or just to enjoy looking at my amazing red colour. 35 miles away I can see the Olgas – this means "many heads" in aborigine language. They are mountains that look like red heads.

I got my name from the man who discovered Australia. Now I'm better known for the area "where the reef meets the rainforest". On the way to Port Douglas you might meet a 'salty' – that's a crocodile that lives in salt water, or a flying-fox, a sort of bat that lives in the tree-tops in the rainforest.
The rainforest here has got the largest number of different species of fauna in Australia. Tourists can take trips on the Daintree River or admire aborigine cliff-paintings.

AUSTRALIA

Some people call me the 8th wonder of the world.
I'm over 2000 km long and I'm made of coral – tiny little shells that pile up to make a wall. I am a nature reserve – but I'm in danger of being eaten up by starfish! One part of me is open to tourists – but not more than 120 at a time. I'm on the north-eastern coast, near a group of islands which were discovered by Captain Cook. He was surprised that the sea was so calm – later he saw that it was because of me.

I was founded in 1856. The first telegraphic connections with Adelaide and the first railway joining me with the eastern coast helped me become a wealthy city. I've got the best climate in Australia, so a lot of people have moved here to live. They enjoy all the sailing and surfing. From Fremantle, to the south, wheat, wool and meat are exported to countries all over the world. There are two natural wonders not far away Wave Rock and the Pinnacles.

I'm a very hot area in the north-west part of the country.
The inhabitants of Marble Bar have got to live with an average temperature of 33,8 °C in the shade – in December!
With Gibson, Victoria and Simpson, I encircle the heart of the continent – that's why we are ocre-coloured and red. Nothing has changed much here since prehistoric times.

I'm an unusual part of the continent – a small island belonging to a larger one! Unlike the rest of Australia, I've got a really wild, rocky coast. Inland, the lakes are calm, surrounded by mountains and forests. I used to have a different name – Van Diemen's Land – and everyone was afraid to come here because I had a terrible prison colony. It was built beside a port, so that the ships could bring the convicts directly to the prison, which looks a bit like a castle – but it certainly wasn't one!
I've got an attractive harbour town (beginning with H) in the south.

I'm a national park – in the north of the country. I got my name from a white bird which is a bit like a parrot. I'm between the Mary River and the S. Alligator River, to the west of the Arnhem Land Reservation, which belongs to the Aborigines. They act as tourist guides. I am a real paradise, with lakes surrounded by sheer cliffs.
There is one famous lake with a funny name, and a waterfall which attracts lots of tourists, who come to take photos. There are crocodiles here, too, but they are freshwater ones, so they are harmless – or that's what the guidebooks say!

Some more ideas for projects

Project: The Sea
Some possible topics might be:
- Physical and geological aspects
  salt content, currents, Gulf Stream etc.
- Submarine life
  different types of fish, dolphins and whales, endangered environment threads etc.
- Seascapes
  Mediterranean, Atlantic, Poles etc.
- Exploitation
  source of food, tourism, sports, alternative energy, means of traffic etc.
- History
  colonisation, battles, conquest, pirates etc.
- Literature
  stories, poems etc.
- Music and Art

Project: Woods and Forests
Some possible topics might be:
- Geographical aspects
  National Parks, wooded countries etc.
- Different types
  coniferous, deciduous etc.
- Environmental dangers
  acid rain, bark beetle etc.
- Animals
  foxes, insects, ants etc.
- Source of food
  fruits, mushrooms etc.
- Exploitation
  saw-mills, tourism, heating material, hunting, deforestation, housing etc.
- History
  Shipbuilding, battles, Robin Hood etc.
- Literature
- Music and Art

How to do project work – Guidelines for Students

1. Introducing the topic
   - Talk about the topic, collect associations and ideas.
   - Agree on the aspect you want to work on.
   - Form groups.

2. Organizing work
   - Decide on tasks for everybody in the group.
   - Decide on material you need and who is going to get it.
   - Agree on how you want to organize your group work.
   - Agree on length of time you want to spend on your work.

3. Doing the project
   - Decide on the activities which are necessary to complete your product: e. g. writing texts, drawing pictures, diagrams etc, carrying out interviews, possibly making recordings, arranging texts and visuals.
   - Agree on and prepare your presentation.

4. Presenting
   - Keep it well structured so everybody can easily follow – writing words on the board or on a transparency might help.
   - Support your talk by using visuals (pictures, transparencies, posters, Power Point etc.).
   - Keep your audience interested, be creative.
   - Keep eye-contact, be friendly and smile.
   - Encourage your audience to ask questions.
   - Have a quiz, riddle, puzzle or just questions ready to make sure everybody has been listening.
   - Prepare a handout for everybody to take away.

© Cornelsen Verlag Scriptor, Berlin • Fundgrube Englisch handlungsorientiert

Students as Storytellers

Lernstufe: Beginners/Advanced
Kontext: storytelling
Material: Die sechs Aesopschen Fabeln in der für den Anfangsunterricht bearbeiteten Fassung (Stepping into English. Erste Lektüre für den Englischunterricht. 6 Hefte und eine Lehrerhandreichung. Berlin: Cornelsen), ggf. Kopien der Bilder und Magnetstreifen, OH-Projektor
Dauer: 3–4 Stunden

What to do

1. Tell your advanced students that you are currently involved in a storytelling unit in your beginners' class and that you need their help because you want to give the children the chance to listen to and talk about a story in small groups. Inform them that you would like to tell the children six of Aesop's fables the following week: "The City Mouse and the Country Mouse", "The Lion and the Mouse", "The Rabbit and the Turtle", "The Boy who Cried Wolf", "The Milkmaid and her Pail" and "Belling the Cat".
2. Tell the students to get together in groups of six. Give each group the texts, asking them to take a different text each. Tell them to practise reading the fables to one another.
3. Get the students to discuss how they would tell their stories, concentrating on emphasis, pitch, tone of voice, etc.
4. Each student rehearses *telling* his or her story on their own. Once they feel competent, they get together again in their group and tell each other their stories, giving each other advice.
5. When they are satisfied with their work, the groups make a CD with all six texts on it and copy it, one CD for each junior pupil.
6. Before appearing in front of their audiences, the storytellers decide how to organize the session, i.e. will they need a costume? Or pictures? How will they start the session? Perhaps with a gong, or by darkening the room etc. Where will they sit or stand? On cushions? On a soap-box? How will they stand out from their audience?
7. Prepare the younger class for the story-telling lesson. Tell them that a group of older students will tell them different stories.
8. Your students give their performance. When it is over, each child from the junior classes gets a CD.
9. In the following lessons tell both classes to exchange their experiences and their opinions about the activity.

Bemerkung

In Gesamtschulen und Gymnasien ergibt es sich häufig, dass sich Englischlernende von der 5. bzw. 7. Klasse bis zum Abitur unter einem Dach befinden und die Lehrkräfte in weit auseinanderliegenden Klassenstufen unterrichten. Ältere Schüler können also in den Unterricht mit den jüngeren aktiv als Geschichtenerzähler einbezogen werden.

Bildnachweis

Dorina Tessmann: 159, 167, 254
Bernd Streiter: 51, 66, 163 f.
Barbara Druschky: 26 oben, 29, 84, 155
Daniel Decke-Cornill: 26, 108
Edward Lear, Originalzeichnung: 71, 73
Autoren und Verlag: 82, 91, 161, 163 f.
Karsten Jänner: 171

Textnachweis

S. 77: © Oxford University Press, Köln (Walter de la Mare, The Fly)
S. 96: by William Carlos Williams, from Collected Poems 1939–1962, Volume II. © 1962 by William Carlos Williams. Reprinted by permission of New Directions Publishing Corp.
S. 122 f. und 124 ff.: © A. P. Watt, London (Somerset W. Maugham, The Outstation)
S. 128 ff.: Ray Bradbury: The Illustrated Man. Doubleday and Co. Inc./Bantam Books, New York
S. 200 f.: © Peters, Fraser & Dunlap Group Ltd., London (Hilaire Belloc, A Conversation with a Cat)

Register

A
Aesop 284
Asien 107, 117, 221, 228
Außerirdische/Sciencefiction 274
Australien 278
Autos 50, 83, 157, 173

B
Ballade 78
Belloc, Hilaire 196
Bilder (Arbeit mit Bildern) 15, 16, 17, 30, 36, 83, 156, 157, 158, 165, 166, 172, 176, 278, 283
Biographie 11, 17, 57, 86, 156, 158
Blake, William 99
Bradbury, Ray 127
Brettspiele 36
Browning, Robert 86

C
Carroll, Lewis 78
Charakterisierung 15, 17, 61, 95, 158, 172, 185
Collage 159, 175, 182, 188
Creative Writing s. Kreatives Schreiben

D
Debattieren 40, 59, 232
Dialoge 11, 13, 15, 23, 49, 57, 64, 154, 158, 274

E
Einkaufen 42
Eisenbahn 44
Eliot, T. S. 196
Empire 117
Erzählen 25, 100, 105, 157, 158, 159, 160, 165, 166, 175, 188, 216, 221, 245, 254, 256, 271, 283
Ethnologie 245

F
Fabel 86, 222, 271, 283
Fernsehen 38, 57, 228
Film 56, 59, 101, 251 ff.
Filmsprache 262, 264 ff.
Flugzeug 117, 154
Fragebogen 214, 251
Fragepronomen 15
Fußball 267

G
Geburtstagsbräuche 216
Gedichte 26, 70 ff., 182, 189, 191, 229
Gericht 59, 61
Geschlechterverhältnis 107, 150
Gesellschaftsspiele 30, 31, 36, 235
Grammatik 204 ff.

H
Hardy, Thomas 94
Henry, O. 112

Herstellung von Spielen 30, 35, 36
Hitchcock, Alfred 253, 259, 266
Hörspiel 50
Human Interest Story 57, 112, 117, 127

I
Ideogramme 29
Interaktives Spiel 11, 13, 31, 38
Interkulturelles Lernen 214 ff.
Interview 15, 16, 57, 64, 224

J
Japan 228

K
Kindheit/Adoleszenz 107, 150
Kooperation Oberstufe/Anfänger 64, 283
Kreatives Schreiben 16, 23, 29, 71, 75, 78, 83, 89, 100, 154, 156, 157, 158, 159, 160, 161, 165, 166, 175, 176, 180, 182, 185, 188, 189, 194, 196, 245
Kurzgeschichte 112, 117, 127
Kuscheltier (Arbeiten mit Kuscheltier) 13

L
Lear, Edward 71
Lehrbuch 35
Lektüre 121, 271
Liebe 44, 71, 83, 112, 141, 178

M
Märchen 59, 75, 141
Mare, Walter de la 77
Marlowe, Christopher 83

Maugham, Somerset W. 117
McCullers, Carson 150
Memory (Spiel) 30
Metapher 25
Musik 83, 168 ff.
Mythologie 221

N
Namjoshi, Suniti 107
Nonsense 71, 78
Nursery Rhymes 70, 182, 191

O
Owen, Wilfred 94

P
Parodie 44, 57, 88, 200
Present Perfect Progressive 210
Problemlösung 59, 161, 219

R
Reflexion über Sprache 26, 78, 98, 112, 245
Regenbogen 75
Reise(n) 23, 86, 154, 161, 194, 219, 228
Rollenspiel 11, 40, 42, 57, 71, 75, 120, 154, 156, 158, 196, 212, 223, 235
Roman 150

S
Satzstruktur 204
Schule 50, 64
Shelley, Percy Bysshe 89
Simpsons 228
Sitcom 228
Sketch 40, 44, 50, 114, 274

Spiritual 168
Sport (Sprachunterricht in Verbindung mit sportlichen Aktivitäten) 22
Stereotype 228
Storyboarding 254

T
Taboo (Spiel) 31, 35
Tanz 169
Texas 112
Tiere 13, 71, 76, 107, 141, 169, 196

U
Übersetzen (literarisches) 98, 114
USA 228

V
Verkehrsunfall 50
Videoeinsatz 13, 40, 78, 117

W
Warming-up-Activities 11, 20
Werwolf 53
Widersprechen 40
Wilde, Oscar 141
"will"-future 205
Williams, William Carlos 95
Wortschatzarbeit 11, 22, 23, 25, 26, 29, 30, 35, 38, 151, 156, 158, 185

Z
Zeichensetzung 187